WORDS FOR THE HEART

WORDS FOR THE HEART

A Treasury of Emotions from Classical India

Maria Heim

PRINCETON UNIVERSITY PRESS
PRINCETON AND OXFORD

Published by Princeton University Press
41 William Street, Princeton, New Jersey 08540
99 Banbury Road, Oxford OX2 6JX

press.princeton.edu

Library of Congress Cataloging-in-Publication Data

Names: Heim, Maria, 1969– author.
Title: Words for the heart : a treasury of emotions from classical India / Maria Heim.
Other titles: Treasury of emotions from classical India
Description: Princeton : Princeton University Press, 2022. | Includes bibliographical references and index.
Identifiers: LCCN 2021055682 (print) | LCCN 2021055683 (ebook) | ISBN 9780691222912 (hardback) | ISBN 9780691222929 (ebook)
Subjects: LCSH: Buddhism—Psychology. | Emotions—Religious aspects—Buddhism. | Emotions—Social aspects—India—History. | Emotions—Terminology.
Classification: LCC BQ4570.P76 H45 2022 (print) | LCC BQ4570.P76 (ebook) | DDC 294.3/42—dc23/eng/20220222
LC record available at https://lccn.loc.gov/2021055682
LC ebook record available at https://lccn.loc.gov/2021055683

British Library Cataloging-in-Publication Data is available

Editorial: Fred Appel and James Collier
Production Editorial: Sara Lerner
Text Design: Carmina Alvarez
Jacket Design: Heather Hansen
Production: Erin Suydam
Publicity: Alyssa Sanford and Kathryn Stevens
Copyeditor: Jennifer Harris

Jacket Credit: Shutterstock

This book has been composed in Charis SIL

Printed on acid-free paper. ∞

Printed in the United States of America

1 3 5 7 9 10 8 6 4 2

FOR ZACK

King Suddhodana did say that love for one's children pierces the skin, sinews, and soft tissues, and then pierces the bone. It comes to rest there, pressing into the marrow.

DAY AFTER DAY,

FROM THE BEGINNING OF TIME,

GOOD POETS DRAW FROM THE TREASURY

OF WORDS,

AND STILL ITS LOCK

REMAINS UNBROKEN.

Gauḍavaho 87 of *Vakpati*, translated by David Shulman
(*More Than Real: A History of the Imagination in South India*,
Harvard University Press, 2012, p. 97)

Contents

Entries

A

D

E

G

H

I

J

K

L

M

Acknowledgments

I am full of *kritajna* for the many teachers over the decades who have shared with me what they know, including Edwin Gerow, Charles Hallisey, Masatoshi Nagatomi, Stephanie Jamison, Muni Jambuvijayaji, Nagin J. Shah, Narayan Kansara, John Cort, Paul Dundas, and W. S. Karunatillake. I have benefited enormously from many *kalyanamitras* with whom I have discussed emotions, including Charles Hallisey, Chakravarthi Ram-Prasad, Roy Tzohar, Vanessa Sasson, and the late Anne Monius. Fellow traveler Curie Virág helpfully read a draft of the introduction. Paul Dundas, that inexhaustible treasury of knowledge about Indian texts, graciously read a draft of the whole work, and made the final product better.

I am deeply indebted to Chakravarthi Ram-Prasad. I had his support at multiple stages of the project, reading drafts and offering sympathetic insights and suggestions. Our many discussions yielded the development of ecological phenomenology as an approach to experience that has enriched this work in countless ways.

Thanks to my colleagues in the Pioneer Valley who cheered this on, including Jay Garfield, Andy Rotman, and Susanne Mrozik. Jay Garfield's enthusiasm, wise counsel, and gifting me a copy of Murray Bail's *Eucalyptus*—because something in my book put him in mind of it—flattered me terribly and gave me much-needed confidence to see this book through. Andy Rotman's patient and sound advice made this a better book.

Many thanks to my student assistant, Teodosii Ruskov, who read a draft and made many thoughtful suggestions. Thanks to Amherst College for providing institutional and collegial support for my research. I am also grateful to Fred Appel at Princeton University Press for seeing the possibilities in this quirky and idiosyncratic book and for steadfastly standing by it. Thank you to Pat Hanley for providing the index.

And of course, *prema*, *priti*, and *sneha*, and much more to Steve, Soren, and Zack, as ever.

List of Abbreviations

AKB *Abhidharmakośabhāṣyam*, volumes I, III, IV, trans. from the Sanskrit by L. de La Vallée Poussin, trans. from the French by L. Pruden. Berkeley, CA: Asian Humanities Press, 1988, 1989, 1990.

BAM *Bright as an Autumn Moon: Fifty Poems from the Sanskrit*, trans. A. Schelling. Honolulu, HI: Mānoa Press, 2013.

BCA *Bodhicaryāvatāra of Śāntideva*, trans. K. Crosby and A. Skilton. Oxford: Oxford University Press, 1995.

BGC *The Bhagavad Gita with the Commentary of Sri Sankaracharya*, trans. A. M. Shastry, Madras: Samata Books, 1979.

BK *The Birth of Kumāra*, trans. D. Smith. New York: New York University Press, Clay Sanskrit Library, 2005.

BP *The Bodhisattva Path to Unsurpassed Enlightenment*, trans. A. Engle. Boulder, CO: Snow Lion, 2016.

BR *The Bhaktirasāmṛtasindhu of Rūpa Goswāmin*, trans. D. Haberman. Delhi: Motilal Banarsidass, 2003.

BRH *The Bloomsbury Research Handbook of Emotions in Classical Indian Philosophy*, ed. M. Heim, C. Ram-Prasad, and R. Tzohar. London: Bloomsbury, 2021.

BRRR *Bouquet of Rasa & River of Rasa by Bhānudatta*, trans. S. Pollock. New York: New York University Press, Clay Sanskrit Library, 2009.

BW *In the Buddha's Words*, trans. Bhikkhu Bodhi. Somerville, MA: Wisdom Publications, 2005.

CDB *The Connected Discourses of the Buddha*, trans. Bhikkhu Bodhi. Somerville, MA: Wisdom Publications, 2000.

CS *Agniveśa's Caraka Saṃhitā, Text with English Translation and Critical Exposition Based on Cakrapaṇī Datta's Āyurveda Dīpikā*, volume I, trans. R. K. Sharma and V. B. Dash, Varanasi: Chowkhamba Sanskrit Series, 2012.

CSL Clay Sanskrit Library, New York University Press.

DL *The* Dhvanyāloka *of Ānandavardhana with the* Locana *of Abhinavagupta*, trans. D. Ingalls, J. Masson, and M. V. Patwardhan. Cambridge, MA: Harvard University Press, 1990.

EU *The Early Upaniṣads: Annotated Text and Translation*, trans. P. Olivelle. Oxford: Oxford University Press, 1998.

EX Rhys Davids, *The Expositor*, trans. P. M. Tin and C.A.F. Rhys Davids. Oxford: Pali Text Society, 1999 (1920).

FA *"Friendly Advice" by Nārāyaṇa and "King Vikrama's Adventures,"* trans. J. Törzsök. New York: New York University Press, Clay Sanskrit Library, 2007.

HB C. Ram-Prasad, *Human Being, Bodily Being*. Oxford: Oxford University Press, 2018.

HN *Handsome Nanda*, trans. L. Covill. New York: New York University Press, Clay Sanskrit Library, 2007.

IP *Indian Psychology, Vol. II: Emotion and Will*, by J. Sinha. Delhi: Motilal Banarsidass, 2008.

KS *The Kamasutra*, trans. W. Doniger and S. Kakar. Oxford: Oxford University Press, 2002.

LD *The Long Discourses of the Buddha*, trans. M. Walshe. Somerville, MA: Wisdom Publications, 1995.

MCLI Murty Classical Library of India, Harvard University Press.

MLD *The Middle Length Discourses of the Buddha*, trans. Bhikkhu Ñāṇamoli and Bhikkhu Bodhi. Somerville, MA: Wisdom Publications, 2001.

NDB *The Numerical Discourses of the Buddha*, trans. Bhikkhu Bodhi. Somerville, MA: Wisdom Publications, 2012.

PP *The Path of Purification*, trans. Bhikkhu Ñāṇamoli. Onalaska, WA: BPS Pariyatti, 1991.

PV U. Singh, *Political Violence in Ancient India*. Cambridge, MA: Harvard University Press, 2017.

RLA *Rāma's Last Act by Bhavabhūti*, trans. S. Pollock. New York: New York University Press, Clay Sanskrit Library, 2007.

RR Sheldon Pollock, *The Rasa Reader*. New York: Columbia University Press, 2016.

SPCM *"Self-Surrender," "Peace," "Compassion," and "The Mission of the Goose,"* trans. Y. Bronner and D. Shulman. New York: New York University Press, Clay Sanskrit Library, 2009.

ŚR *Śāntarasa and Abhinavagupta's Philosophy of Aesthetics*, trans. J. L. Masson and M. V. Patwardhan. Poona: Bhandarkar Oriental Research Institute, 1969.

YŚ *The Yogaśāstra of Hemacandra*, trans. O. Quarnström. Cambridge, MA: Harvard University Press, 2002.

YSU *Yoga: Discipline of Freedom*, trans. B. Stoler Miller. New York: Bantam Books, 1998.

WORDS FOR THE HEART

INTRODUCTION

In Sanskrit, a "treasury" or *kosha* is a storehouse of gems, but it can also mean a collection of words, poems, and short literary pieces. This treasury contains 177 terms, jewels in fact, from classical India for what English speakers refer to as emotions, affects, dispositions, and feelings. These jewels are drawn from literary, philosophical, religious, aesthetic, medical, social, and political texts in three classical languages—Sanskrit, Pali, and Prakrit. This collection offers the English-speaking world a wealth of experiences, evoked and discussed in over two millennia of some of the most extraordinary reflection about human experience available in world history.

The idea of a storehouse of words has an ancient history in India. In the fifth century, Amarasimha, himself considered a gem at the court of the emperor Chandragupta II, composed the *Treasury of Amara*, a thesaurus giving synonyms for words used in nearly every sphere of life. The study of language had been well under way at least a millennium before Amara, and he cites precursors to his lexicon that have been lost to us. Amara's *Treasury* was valued by poets (what aspiring poet doesn't need a thesaurus ready to hand?), and it went on to attract numerous erudite commentaries over the centuries adding to and expanding its lists and meanings. It also traveled far beyond the shores of India—eastward in a seventh-century translation in Chinese, southward as it was rendered into Pali in Sri Lanka, northward in a Tibetan version in the medieval period, and westward to Europe in an Italian translation in the late eighteenth century.

This *Treasury* continues this long-standing Indian love of collecting words and their meanings, but unlike Amara, I focus exclusively on emotion-type words. In this sense, the *Treasury* should be seen as a modern enterprise too, at a time when lists and lexica of emotions have great currency. Some scholars have aimed in a reductive fashion to arrive at a list of the most basic and universal emotions. Descartes came up with a list of six primitive passions: wonder, love, hatred, desire, joy, and sadness. More recently, social psychologist Paul Ekman has arrived at a different set of six basic emotions: happiness, anger, disgust, fear, sadness, and surprise, and argued that their universality is clear from how they are tractable in the expressions of the human face. Other scholars have aimed not for reduction and brevity but for prolixity and inclusivity, as Tiffany Watt Smith does in her collection of 156 feelings from many languages. She argues that we need *more* terms for emotions from many cultures, as they help us identify and discover finer shades of experience possible for human beings.[1] This is an impulse with which I am inclined to agree, and I offer this collection as a further contribution to this very project.

The concept of "emotion" is of course of relatively recent vintage. What may feel like a natural or universal category to modern English speakers in fact has a history. In early modern Europe, emotion was at first rather vague, describing bodily movement or the commotion of a crowd of people. Before the nineteenth century, English speakers would more likely have referred to affections, appetites, passions, humors, and sentiments for much of what we speak of as emo-

[1] Tiffany Watt Smith, *The Book of Human Emotions: An Encyclopedia of Feeling from Anger to Wanderlust*, London: Wellcome Collection, 2015.

tion today. This began to change in the 1830s, when the term was fashioned into a theoretical category in the moral philosophy lectures of Edinburgh professor Thomas Brown, and it attracted systematic scientific study in the early work of both Charles Bell and Charles Darwin (culminating in the latter's 1872 *The Expression of the Emotions in Man and Animals*). By the time William James asked in his influential 1884 essay, "What Is an Emotion?" emotion was well on its way to becoming a central term in psychology.[2] Today, it seems hard to imagine life without it.

But, of course, such a specific history has no obvious analogue in India before the modern period and no single word in Indian languages gets at the range of ideas and phenomena that the English word emotion has now come to suggest. Conversely, the classical languages of India offer up categories that have no clear correlates in modern English. And not only do meta categories like "emotion" differ, but also more granular terms for affect and feeling. We have words for particular experiences in Indian languages that are not named in English, and vice versa. Still, the English term "emotion" can get us in the door and help us locate the kinds of phenomena we are interested in, which include feelings, affects, bodily states, moods, dispositions, temperaments, and sentiments widely conceived. The *Treasury* does not attempt to police these categories or identify strict criteria for them, which would seem to be a task about English-language usage rather than ideas in Indian texts. While English

[2] William James, "What Is an Emotion?" (*Mind* 9, no. 34 [1884]: 188–205). See Jan Plamper, *The History of Emotions: An Introduction*, translated by Keith Tribe, Oxford: Oxford University Press, 2012; Thomas Dixon, *From Passions to Emotions: The Creation of a Secular Psychological Category*, Cambridge: Cambridge University Press, 2003; and Ute Frevert, *Emotional Lexicons: Continuity and Change in the Vocabulary of Feeling 1700–2000*, Oxford: Oxford University Press, 2014, for reliable and thorough treatments of the history of emotion in the modern West.

is my medium for exploring these ideas, my word-based approach is meant to resist the all-too-prevalent assumption that modern English words name, in some easy way, universal categories.[3]

That languages and cultures differ in their words for emotion, feeling, and sentiment has vexed philosophers, anthropologists, and scientists for the past two centuries. Is it that the terrain of human experience is demarcated and described variously across different languages, but remains, basically, *the same terrain*? Or is it that the language used for experience itself shapes what humans can experience, so that culture inflects or even determines what is possible for people to feel? Or does the answer lie somewhere in between—perhaps there is a basic human endowment or range of possibilities shared by all of us, but culture and language do shape what can be described and thus felt, at least to some extent.

I don't have the answers to these questions, but for me, the overlap between classical Indian languages and modern English on ideas about emotions has the delightful possibility of bridging our time to theirs. Many experiences described on the pages that follow will be instantly recognizable to modern readers. But I am equally moved by experiences that seem quite different, where we get names and descriptions of feelings unfamiliar to the modern reader.

[3] I share Barbara Cassin's critical eye on that strand of Anglophone analytic philosophy where English presents itself, despite its own historical particularity, as the language of "common sense and shared experience," a language of philosophy that somehow conveys, unproblematically, a universal logic true in all times and all places. I offer my wordbook, as she does her "untranslatables," in part to counter this assumption with rich and complex vocabularies otherwise situated and often with their own universalist pretensions (see the *Dictionary of Untranslatables: A Philosophical Lexicon*, ed. Barbara Cassin, translated from the original French by S. Rendall et al., Princeton, NJ: Princeton University Press, 2004: xviii).

These are opportunities to expand our understanding of what it is to be human, as they suggest new possibilities for us not only to think about, but also, perhaps, to feel.

The History of Emotion

Within Western ways of telling the story (and to date we *only* have Western ways of telling the story), the category of emotion begins with the Greeks, though of course they did not use the term "emotion" either. Plato and Aristotle spoke of *pathē*, and argued that pathos is to be distinguished from reason and the spirit. Saint Augustine modified this tripartite model slightly to discern a faculty psychology of reason, passion, and the will, setting the stage for a long battle in Western thought between reason and the passions, one carried forward in the modern period by Descartes and Kant. It is from this legacy that theorists and modern people have often assumed that emotions are, by their very nature, irrational. Yet others have argued that, going back to Greek thinkers like the Stoics, emotions are a certain kind of cognitive judgment, albeit one that delivers an affective impact. Still others emphasize the *feeling* quality of emotions.

Further, Descartes initiated a sharp metaphysical divide between body and mind that has had enduring implications for subsequent theorists of emotions who have wondered whether emotions should be considered "mental" or "physical." Determining the ontological nature of emotions according to these divisions of the human person occupies philosophers to this day.

In addition, the rise of anthropology has had scholars studying languages and cultures worldwide, leading to the idea that emotions are culturally constructed and vary significantly from one culture to the next. In recent times, cognitive scientists and evolutionary biologists have pushed back against social constructivism to insist on a single universal set of emotional capacities, though their assumptions and evidence have not gone uncontested either.

None of these debates—is emotion opposed to reason? is it a matter of mind or body? is it innate and universal or socially constructed and variable across cultures?—occurred as such in ancient India. This is not because Indians did not reflect on their experiences or theorize about them. On the contrary, the entries in this book invite the reader to see the spirited, subtle, and sophisticated theories and debates they did have about how to understand experience. But premodern Indian thinking about emotions is refreshingly innocent of these Western preoccupations. In the Indian discussions, we get fresh possibilities for thinking about human experience that operate, from the ground up, with quite different sets of assumptions and concerns.

Too often, Western thought occupies the role of universal theory, with non-Western cultures permitted simply to supply the data to be interpreted by that theory. But India has nearly three thousand years of investigating, categorizing, and reflecting upon human experience in ways every bit as sophisticated and critical as those developed in the West. This *Treasury* provides entries—that is, *entry points*—for particular terms for emotions and similar experiences to begin to demarcate the distinctive theoretical contributions Indian sources can make in understanding human experience.

Emotion Talk and an Ecological Approach to Emotion

This collection is based on my sustained immersion in Indian texts for over three decades as a student, scholar, and teacher. Over the years, I have collected words, passages, and ideas that have struck me as arresting, beautiful, or inspired. I have published scholarly studies on some of these emotion terms and the systems and narratives in which they occur. At the same time, I have come to feel that these ideas should reach further into the world than the narrow scholarly circles in which academics usually publish their work. Perhaps a wordbook or an anthology, this ancient Indian conception of a treasury, could be one way to bring them together and into the light.

I have included words and passages chosen for various reasons, reasons that are, in every case, deliberate and based on research and scholarly principles that are themselves not always fully visible in the entries. My principles of selection—I draw widely from what English speakers would call desires, passions, affects, dispositions, sentiments, and of course emotions—are based on what I think can help us understand this arena of human experience better, and which, albeit always in a necessarily partial and incomplete way, get at brilliant insights in the Indian texts. Some terms bring to the fore philosophical debates (Is remorse a reliable form of moral knowledge? Can hatred ever be justified? Should compassion be reserved for those whose suffering is undeserved?). Others open up rich veins of human feeling evoked by literature that might even arouse the experience, or an appreciation of it, in the reader (revolting depictions of bodily effluences in instructions to actors representing disgust, for example, or quite oppositely, the sweet anguish called love-in-separation favored by the poets). Some conceptual areas get very granular very quickly: ancient India had no single category matching the catch-all English conception of "love." Rather, there are many types of love differentiated at the outset as romantic, erotic, familial, ethical, religious, and so on. Some terms are meta categories (*rasa*, *bhava*, *vedana*) that indicate larger theoretical systems, the outlines of which we can only begin to discern in the context of a given entry. Some terms are profoundly elemental ideas in the history of Indian thought that suggest deep and abiding concerns (the three *gunas*, the all-pervading terms for desire, ideas of religious bliss and devotion, the nature of suffering, the humors of Ayurveda). Still others are here because I came across them, found them delightful, and simply wanted to share my discoveries. Other scholars would have reached for different passages and in some cases rather different entries altogether.

While my entries often bring forward philosophical and normative discussion about emotions, I have also been drawn to include textual passages and examples that evoke the phenomenality of a particular experience—that is, passages that convey *how it feels*. My entries often sidestep generalities to focus on the particular, much as the literary forms do on which many of the entries rely. The focus on the particular can itself help us get out from underneath some of the overgrown bracken of Western theory. While India offers many technical and abstract discussions of emotions (and many of these are present in the pages that follow), I give equal weight to literary, religious, and aesthetic treatments that do not describe or regulate so much as *evoke*. I want the affective nuances and subtleties of particular experiences to come through.

Of course, we cannot get access to emotions *directly* as they ebb and flow in any particular person's life. We must instead consider *talk* about emotions: what gets noticed in the untidy field of experience, and lifted up, named, described, suggested, or prompted in texts that are centuries or millennia old. We encounter emotion talk in texts that have varied purposes and aspirations, and thus find that the nature of such talk itself must attract our scrutiny. Medical texts have different ways of portraying and managing grief than court poetry; religious texts treat desire and erotic love more skeptically than does the *Kama Sutra*; aesthetic theorists appreciate anger and its cultivation in ways troubling to moralists. Emotions always occur in *contexts*, within scripts, narratives, normative orders of value, and systems of philosophical, moral, social, or political thought that inflect how they are to be described or regulated, indeed, that determine what even gets noticed to begin with.[4] Thus, as I draw as widely as I can from very different types of texts with an aim to begin to trace the contours of early Indian thought, I am ever attentive to the genres and purposes of these texts and how they shape the representation of any particular experience.

My interest in the *particular* and in the nature of the discourses describing emotions comprise two prongs of an approach developed with Chakravarthi Ram-Prasad that can be described as "ecological." This approach treats emotions (and other areas of experience) not as pregiven or self-contained fixtures of the world that show up here and there in our experience, but rather as constituted through the contexts and environments in which we humans always and constantly find ourselves. Just as *ecology* is the study of the relationships of organisms within their environments, where, in a nontrivial sense, organisms are products of their environments and vice versa, the study of experience involves attention to the processes and interrelatedness of noticed features of experience and their contexts.[5]

[4] Scholars of the Western classics have been perceptive to the contextual situatedness of emotions and the need for the scholar to attend to such contexts or "scripts," as Robert Kaster calls them. See David Konstan, *The Emotions of the Ancient Greeks: Studies in Aristotle and Classical Literature*, Toronto: University of Toronto Press, 2006, and R. Kaster, *Emotion, Restraint, and Community in Ancient Rome*, New York: Oxford University Press, 2005.

[5] Chakravarthi Ram-Prasad's *Human Being, Bodily Being* applies this ecological approach to the bodily nature of experience (Oxford: Oxford University Press, 2018).

In an ecology, the "same" thing looks different depending upon the context within which one frames inquiry: the same redwood giant is described differently as home to billions of microscopic creatures nestled in the mosses at its base than from the perspective of the birds nesting in its canopy, still more when it is considered as one node in a much larger forest, watershed, climate pattern, migration path for animals, or potential supply of timber. Its processes, interactions with its environment, and even its very structures and features vary depending on what is being studied and for what end. As dendrology becomes more advanced, even understanding what is tree and what is its environment can become difficult to untangle, a point itself salutary for advancing the scientific paradigms themselves. Nor should scientific descriptions be necessarily privileged, for the poet, storyteller, artist, and day hiker will suggest their descriptions and narratives that speak their truths. Fixed and essentialist notions of trees simply won't do, because good science, and indeed good poetry, can produce many, indeed, an unfixed number, of potential descriptions. These descriptions don't compete to promote one explanation as more accurate than others; these are nonrival and enriching descriptions of different aspects of the tree.

To us, emotions and other phenomena of human experience are also usefully seen as ecological in these ways: they are embedded in, or rather, constituted by, their environments; and both our observations and expressions of them are necessarily shaped by our perspectives and purposes at hand. Any emotion is a response to and an imposition on an environment, something irreducibly felt and known within and because of the circumstances in which it occurs. Of course, it is often hard to specify in advance the borders between the experience and the context, which is precisely the point. I am drawn to Alva Noë's question "Where do you stop and the rest of the world begin?"[6] and want to leave the question open.

The answers will always be different depending on the context in which the emotion is felt, noticed, and described, and the nature and purpose of the text doing the noticing. A neuroscientist might (usefully in some contexts) define grief in terms of specific chemical activity in a certain region in the brain, whereas the recently bereaved widow might define it in terms of the narratives and memories of a life spent with a particular and beloved spouse. As different as their accounts might be, both are right.

And so we must always attend to the contexts of emotions, and the nature and purposes of the descriptions, regulations, evocations, and normative instructions in which they occur. The epic heroine Draupadi is consumed with righteous anger (*manyu*) at her disgrace at court by the enemies of her husbands in front of men who should have protected and honored her. Her anger is not easily separated or even understandable apart from the moral and social details of these circumstances. To be sure, emotions can be abstracted from their narrative contexts and scripts, and certain texts do this adroitly and systematically, but their processes and purposes of abstraction can themselves become the objects of study. Why and under what constraints are certain experiences treated abstractly, and not others? Anger may be treated in general terms—inveighed against by moralists, listed as one of the universal emotions, appreciated in aesthetic terms, and so on—for specific purposes, but these purposes themselves require our notice. At the same time, we might also keep in view the nuanced phenomenological

[6] Alva Noë, *Out of Our Heads: Why You Are Not Your Brain, and Other Lessons from the Biology of Consciousness*, New York: Farrar, Straus and Giroux: 2010.

quality—that is, *how it feels*—of the particular anger captured only by a focus on the situational. Draupadi's anger and her situation are in some important sense irreducible to generalities. This *Treasury* attends to both registers: emotion talk that attempts to organize and give abstract treatment to emotions, and emotion talk that evokes highly particular instances of specific experiences.

The ecological nature of human experience suggests that it would be unwise to decide, in advance, on fixed or essential definitions of emotions. We need not decree that emotions or feelings are matters of mind *or* body, because mind and body are themselves no more fixed or pregiven than feelings are. Contemporary English speakers have had to resort to the neologism "hangry" to get at that distinctive variety of irritability that is neither entirely the physiological response to dinner arriving late to table, nor simply a matter of end-of-a-long-day tetchiness, but something of both, or in between. Perhaps much emotion talk is like this—where the complex task of trying to distentangle what is physiology, what is mood, disposition, and emotion, and what is context will tell us more about presumed definitions of these categories than about the phenomenon as it presents in experience.

I'd rather ask where and for what purpose does a given text decide to distinguish mind and body in the ways that it does—or even *if* it does, for I notice when texts don't presume such ontological distinctions at all. For example, readers will find experiences here that they might consider "physical"—tears, goosebumps, the "heart's soft core"—and might, following Cartesian dualistic assumptions, consider them as the bodily expression of the mental thing that is emotion. I myself won't go this far unless there is evidence in the Indian text itself that suggests that it chooses to make a distinction between what it considers "mind" and "body." Goosebumping might itself count as an emotion.

Similarly, we need not decide in advance that emotions are interior or exterior, individual or social, innate or learned, or any of the other distinctions so readily available in modern Western theorizing about emotion. I opt instead to see if and when such distinctions occur in the Indian texts themselves, and if they do, to what purpose. And where texts do make similar distinctions about experience, I remain open to the idea that these distinctions could be working simply to point out a feature of experience rather than attempting to settle in any final way on what it is.

As noted earlier, my entries often discuss emotions in highly particular ways as they are discussed or evoked in particular textual passages. I often aim less for a comprehensive general treatment of an emotion and more for the resonant and evocative valence that can be achieved only by depicting a particular state in a particular narrative. This disposition toward the particular, even the singular, is facilitated by the wordbook format. It is also a principled stance shared by some of the theorists we will be considering. The ninth-century literary theorist Anandavardhana, for example, takes up the question of how it is that poets can produce endless varieties of experience and feeling by attending to the particular as it is inflected by time, season, place, region, circumstance, and the vicissitudes of individual beings. He advises poets to seek the particular in a world of endless nuance and difference:

> Among sentient beings, such as men, animals, birds, there is obviously a great difference between those who have been raised in villages, forests, rivers, or the like. If one makes these distinctions in writing of them one

> will find an endless store of material. Thus, to take only humans, who could ever exhaust the manifold variety of customs and activities of persons from different countries and regions, especially of young women?[7]

The nuances of experience of diverse young women are best approached by the poet looking for shades of difference and multiplicity. The endless possibilities for variation allow for immeasurably finer and subtler poetic composition. It has also been observed that the "treasury of words," the word bank from which good poets have been making daily withdrawals from time immemorial, has limitless reserves to support this nuance.[8]

But a critic might counter that the facts of the world "come into denotation in their general, not their particular, forms." Words are categories that touch only generalities, and as general categories they conceal the elusive particularity of things. Indeed, certain Buddhist thinkers lobbed just this critique. But the aesthetic theorists were having none of it. Poetic expression is just that skillful concomitance of denoter and denoted, and if ways of being human are endless, then the poet's expressions of them must also be. In fact, they are doubly so when we consider the poet's imagination too. Properly conceived, the imaginative ways a poet can express experiences should not be seen to have a limit.

[7] *The* Dhvanyāloka *of Ānandavardhana with the* Locana *of Abhinavagupta*, translated by Daniel Ingalls, Jeffrey Masson, and M. V. Patwardhan, Cambridge, MA: Harvard University Press, 1990: 707–708. He is arguing against Dharmakīrti, a Mahayana Buddhist thinker who argues that language cannot get at the particular that exists only momentarily and thus is gone by the time the word for it is uttered; Dharmakīrti's view is quoted in the voice of the critic in the next paragraph.

[8] The *Gauḍavaho* (87) as translated and discussed by David Shulman, *More Than Real*, Cambridge, MA: Harvard University Press, 2012: 97: "Day after day, / from the beginning of time, good poets draw from the treasury of words, / and still its lock / remains unbroken."

My use of the traditional form of a wordbook deploys an Indian genre to suggest both possibilities. Words have always been taken as vital sources of knowledge in India even as thinkers argued with one another about whether they deliver particularities or universals. Read one way, this *kosha* offers an open-ended and profuse catalogue of many words with many shades of meaning to begin to get at the texture and multiplicity of particular experiences (indeed, composing open-ended and profuse catalogues was a task dear to the heart of many Indian thinkers!). When read in terms of the narratives in which words occur and the networks of other terms to which they are related in a modal or an ecological way, a word-based approach can help us keep in view the complex and relational particularity that we can discern in human experience. Read another way, however, these emotion terms, or perhaps some among them more than others, offer categories that allow for broader generalization, comparison, and questions about shared patterns of experience.

Classical Indian Languages

SANSKRIT TRADITIONS

The idea of the "classical" that I invoke in this book refers less to a narrowly drawn historical period and more to a broader conception of literary and intellectual works of a markedly high order, works whose genius ensured that people would preserve and revisit them time and again over the centuries. There are many ways to explore what might make a body of texts or ideas "classical," but I like the proposals of Sheldon Pollock when he suggests that India's "classical civilization" may be known in the "durability and distinctiveness" of its literary and philosophical traditions and practices.[9] In his capacity as editor-in-chief of the celebrated Murty Classical Library of India, Pollock puts forward a library of "classical literature":

> What do we think makes Indian works "classic"? It might in fact be their very resistance to contemporaneity and universality, that is, their capacity to communicate the vast variety of the human past. There will of course be many occasions for learning something about our shared humanity from these works, but they also provide access to radically different forms of human consciousness, and thereby expand the range of possibilities of what it has meant or could mean to be human.[10]

The Indian classics reach across space and time to teach us a wider conception of what it is to be human. At the same time, they pointedly resist assimilation into both European and modern conceptions of the universal.

I draw mostly from Sanskrit sources, but I also include a substantial number of Pali terms and a handful of Prakrit terms as well. Sanskrit's celebrated lexicon, the sheer enormity and precision of its vocabulary, together with the scope and centrality of its literatures and intellectual systems in aesthetics, philosophy, politics, medicine, and religion across southern Asia for millennia, put it at the center of the *Treasury*. Sanskrit was the language of most intellectual work in ancient India, and its corpus was, by conservative estimates, huge, many times the size of the Greeks'. The entries draw from all of its main knowledge systems and attempt to evoke the extraordinary power of its literary forms, which include

[9] Sheldon Pollock, "The Alternative Classicism of Classical India," 2015, https://www.india-seminar.com/2015/671/671_sheldon_pollock.htm.

[10] Sheldon Pollock, http://www.murtylibrary.com/why-a-classical-library-of-india.php.

the great epic stories, folk narratives, legends, and court poetry and drama.

Emotions don't reveal themselves to us in the Sanskrit materials in the way contemporary philosophers are conditioned to expect. There aren't any systematic treatises on emotions per se. But once we know how to look for emotion talk, we can find it everywhere—in the hymns and speculations of the Vedas and Upanishads; in the normative texts called *shastra* on morality, politics, social life, and religion; in the philosophical literature called *pramanavada*; in Buddhist and Jain texts of all sorts; in the Hindu ascetic traditions; in lyrical religious poetry like the *Bhagavad Gita*; in courtly literary texts and the aesthetic traditions that studied them; and of course, everywhere in the epics. I have drawn widely and lovingly from all these sources, trying to cast as diverse a net as my scholarly expertise and the many scholarly resources and tools I have deployed to help have permitted.

Within these genres, several are especially useful to mine for the *Treasury*, and certain foundational assumptions and patterns in Indian thought are helpfully set out in advance. We may begin with religion. Religious traditions in India can be seen as close studies of suffering, emotion, and desire. The ascetic traditions (Buddhism, Jainism, and the Yoga system, to name just the most prominent and ultimately enduring early examples) began with an acute sensitivity to suffering that in turn led to a disenchantment with life in *samsara* (endless rebirths) driven by karma (action), and the need to dismantle desire to achieve freedom (nirvana or *moksha*) from it (see the entry on *duhkha* for a basic précis of these insights). They offered rigorous therapies of the emotions to replace the turbulence of emotional life with peace, equanimity, and a kind of bliss that transcends desire. Within these broad structural assumptions and forms, the ascetic traditions, which in some cases grew to become world religions, developed intricate systematic psychologies. We will enjoy tracking the nuances and debates among these traditions in many of the entries that follow.

Much later than the initial textual output of the ascetic systems, a very different approach to emotionality referred to as *bhakti*, devotion, developed across traditions in India, but mostly within Hinduism. Often in explicit tension with the ascetic traditions, the exponents of *bhakti* celebrated emotion, particularly varieties of love and desire, as long as these were properly channeled to God. *Bhakti*, in the words of one of its most outspoken theorists, "trivializes *moksha*," preferring to sacralize the rich panoply of human feelings instead. While he is at it, this thinker rebuffs the "dried up" ritualists that have held sway in certain domains in Indian religion as well: *bhakti* should be kept from them much as one keeps one's treasure from a thief.[11]

In addition, I am drawn to the genres of *shastric* discourse—such texts as the *Laws of Manu*, the *Kama Sutra*, the manual of realpolitik called the *Artha Shastra*—because of this genre's attempt to render explicit the nuances of social life in both rich detail as well as highly ideological terms. Some *shastra* is "religious," while other texts may be considered "secular" (if these modern terms can be of any use in such a different intellectual context). *Shastra* is a distinctively Indian genre that is both descriptive and prescriptive, as it seeks to regulate the norms of a substantial variety of practices. The *Kama Sutra*, for example, describes and regulates the norms of sex, romance, and gender in ways that have obvious value for considering emotion talk. This body of

[11] Rūpa Goswāmi, *The Bhaktirasāmṛtasindhu*, translated by David L. Haberman, Delhi: Motilal Banasidass, 2003: 4–5, 8–9, 384–385; by "ritualists," Rūpa Goswāmi is referring to Mimamsakas, the foremost intellectual tradition espousing Vedic ritualism and interpretation.

shastric prescription is a disquisition on the idealized conduct of the cultured "man-about-town," in a way that locates emotions within a densely interactive material and social environment. Kautilya's *Artha Shastra* does similar work with the acquisition of power and wealth in advice to kings. And in the Dharma *shastras*, legal authorities like Manu and Yajnavalkya regulate the Dharma—that is, the etiquette, morality, law, and normative social order of all classes of the social body. These texts seldom thematize emotions as such but nevertheless manage emotion with great care and precision, often by way of lists and rules that rank and classify forms of experience. Indeed, the *shastric* proclivity for lists is a boon for my purposes because lists corral, define, and rank emotions in highly systematic and illuminating ways. Much formal Indian religious and philosophical thought is a kind of *shastric* discourse that offers very meticulous treatments of human psychology and social life.

It will surprise no reader familiar with India that the two great epics, the *Mahabharata* and the *Ramayana*, should furnish much human experience for our purposes. These monumental Sanskrit epics, and their stories within stories, have provided India with studies of character, disposition, and emotion for more than two millennia, and I follow many of these studies here. The *Mahabharata* tells of a great fratricidal war to end all wars; the *Ramayana* is a tragic love story between Rama and Sita that involves loss, recovery, and loss again. I have also sought to represent other Indian literatures ranging from the scrappy folk tales of the *Pancatantra* to the high court dramas of Kalidasa, from Sanskrit tales of the Buddha's life to the lyrical mysteries of Vedanta Deshika's devotional poetry. And everything in between.

Of particular relevance for Sanskrit thinking about emotions is the aesthetic tradition introduced by Bharata, the author of the first great treatise on dramaturgy who lived in the early centuries of the Common Era. Since aesthetics became a central arena for close scrutiny of emotion (as it was in premodern traditions in the West as well), I draw heavily from it, and so some general remarks about Bharata's system and its successors will be helpful here. While Bharata's treatise is a *shastra* on the performing arts, along the way it develops a complex theory of what we would call emotion and aesthetic feeling. The text supplies lists and descriptions of emotional states encountered in performing a play. Bharata's system inaugurated a long and highly sophisticated tradition of aesthetics we now call "*rasa* theory" that found its highest and most probing analyses centuries later among literary theorists (one of whom we've just met, Anandavardhana, but there were many others). For our purposes, two key terms—*rasa* and *bhava*—and the overall context of them will be essential for the reader to know.

First, among the many matters discussed by Bharata, a central question concerned how aesthetic response, the savor and the savoring (both *rasa*) of artistic pleasure, occurs. What makes a play pleasurable even when the players perform tragedy or painful human emotions? How can actors portray emotions in such a way that they and others will relish and appreciate them? To explain these processes, Bharata offered a formal analysis of how emotions are created and can be represented. The term "emotion" here is *bhava* ("way of being"), and while the two words do not overlap precisely, many of the experiences Bharata considers *bhavas* are instantly recognizable to English speakers as emotions. But the range of *bhavas* is quite a bit broader, as we can see from Bharata's lists. Bharata lists eight main *bhavas* that are thought to be "stable" in human experience (at least as it is to be considered in the context of aesthetic experience). These stable emotions (*sthayibhavas*) are attraction, amusement, grief, anger, determination, fear, disgust, and amazement. He then lists thirty-three "transitory" *bhavas*, many of which are emotions, such as despair, resentment, anxiety, shame, joy, and so forth, as well as such conditions as intoxication and exhaustion (for the full list, readers may turn to the entry on *vyabhicaribhava*, transitory emotions). And there are eight psychosomatic responses (*sattvikabhavas*) like weeping, sweating, goosebumps, and so on. Through work with these categories of experiences as well as the other elements of stagecraft, playwrights, actors, and directors produce their art.

Subsequent theorists wondered if Bharata's *shastra* was meant to provide an exhaustive list of emotions or whether other emotions might be accommodated in this set (for example, could "distress," which isn't listed, be included in "despair"?). Further, the idea of an exhaustive list itself was interrogated. A tenth-century literary theorist, Abhinavagupta, notes that people have wondered "how anyone could possibly number all the various states of mind" and "how any given number could capture this totality" of experiences people have.[12] He reminds us that Bharata was concerned with those states that actors and directors would need to know and perform, and so his model might not be an exhaustive theory of human nature per se. Bharata lists emotions that are particularly salient in the production of aesthetic pleasure.

This brings us to *rasa*, the emotional and aesthetic relish that prompts artists and keeps us going to plays and seeking out great literature. It is reasonable to assert that on questions of aesthetic sentiment—*how to produce it? what are its finer shades and varieties? what is the structure of human*

[12] *Abhinavabhāratī* 1.373, translated by Sheldon Pollock, *The Rasa Reader: Classical Indian Aesthetics*, New York: Columbia University Press, 2016: 207.

emotion on which aesthetic sentiment draws?—*rasa* theory goes further than any philosophical tradition of aesthetics in human intellectual history. Drawing on the meaning of *rasa* as "taste," Bharata offered a gustatory metaphor to define it: "just as connoisseurs eat and savor their fare when prepared with so many condiments and substances, so the learned fully savor in their heart the stable emotions when conjoined with the factors, transitory emotions, and reactions."[13] That is to say, a *rasa* is the *taste* of a stable emotion when the arts of the theater have represented that emotion along with the transitory emotions and the other elements of successful stagecraft. Since they interact with the repertoire of the eight stable emotions in order to savor them, there are eight *rasas* corresponding with them:

Rasas	*savor*	Stable Emotions
Erotic		Attraction
Comic		Amusement
Tragic		Grief
Violent		Anger
Heroic		Determination
Horror		Fear
Macabre		Disgust
Fantastic		Amazement

Thus, the erotic *rasa* savors attraction, the comic *rasa* savors amusement, and so on, with the *rasas* as the aesthetic experiences of emotions. One of the key explorations of *rasa* theory is the question of how it is that the private and "real" experience or *bhava* of one's own grief, anger, fear, or disgust may be highly unpleasant, and yet we relish the artistic representation and tasting of these same emotions. It is

[13] *Nāṭyaśāstra* 6.32–33. Pollock, *The Rasa Reader: Classical Indian Aesthetics*, New York: Columbia University Press, 2016: 51.

through the artistic refinement or manipulation of these emotions that we can savor the tragic, the heroic, the horrific, and the macabre. While not attempting to discuss this theory systematically—there are now excellent resources available for doing so[14]—the *Treasury* assumes at least this much background into its fundamental questions. I feature the *rasas* and stable *bhavas* in my entries (and many of the more "emotion-like" transitory and psychosomatic emotions as well).

PALI AND PRAKRIT

While Sanskrit secular texts as well as Sanskrit religious literatures of Hindus (of all varieties), Buddhists, and Jains are well represented in the *Treasury*, the Buddhist scriptures and commentaries preserved in Pali bring additional pleasures to our table. The Pali texts—Pali is a language and literature limited to the Theravada Buddhist tradition—provide some of the most intricate attention available anywhere to questions of psychology and the subtleties of emotion, and their contributions to the thoughtworld of classical India are not always fully recognized. It was in the Pali language that the most complete corpus of the early Buddhist teachings was preserved, and this corpus is devoted to the nature of human experience in highly meticulous and systematic ways.

Specifically, the Pali Abhidhamma texts offer phenomenological analysis of experiential life by attempting to list, classify, and define psychological states in a highly prolific and systematic way. Emotional phenomena, and their causal relations with other phenomena in the production of

[14] Chiefly, Sheldon Pollock's *The Rasa Reader: Classical Indian Aesthetics*, New York: Columbia University Press, 2016, and P. V. Kane, *History of Sanskrit Poetics*, Delhi: Motilal Banarsidass, 1961.

consciousness, are subject to intensive scrutiny and definition by a large corpus of canonical texts. Scholastics developed these ideas in Pali and in adjacent Buddhist traditions in Sanskrit (called Abhidharma) and Tibetan, for the next two millennia. These systems give us a completely different carving up of experience than anything in Western psychology, as will become evident in the entries drawing on them.

One important feature of Abhidhamma and Abhidharma literatures is that they define phenomena by modal analysis. For example, in the Pali system a standard list of phenomena present in one's field of experience in any given moment lists some fifty-six phenomena ranging from the barest processes of perception to rather more developed emotions and cognitive faculties. Any given moment of awareness will have an assemblage of these phenomena, each of which inflects the mode, valence, and strength of the other phenomena present, and together these phenomena construct the particular quality of the moment of awareness. (Incidentally, *rasa* theory can also be said to be "modal" in this sense—experience is made up of phenomena that in a dynamic way shape the modes in which other phenomena also present are felt and can be defined.) I see an "ecological" quality in this literature—indeed, I have learned to think ecologically from these Indian systems.

Entries from Pali sources are not limited to the Abhidhamma psychological genre, however; I draw also on Pali's considerable scriptural and literary corpuses, including some of the very earliest literary composition in India.

While occurring in just a handful of entries, Prakrit texts must be included as well. I find myself drawn to the austere but acute emotional landscape of Prakrit poetry. Prakrit occupies a curious position in the "language order" of classical India, as shown by Andrew Ollett, who calls it "the most important Indian language you've never heard of."[15] Its very name means "common," suggesting a more natural language when juxtaposed, as it always was, to the "refined" (*samskrta*) qualities of Sanskrit. But for all that, it was a courtly product, and the secular literature in this language, which began to come into view in the early centuries of the Common Era at the Satavahana court, was of a very high order. Indeed, Prakrit appears to have been a precursor to Sanskrit literary traditions of poetry (*kavya*) and the critical literary aesthetics that theorized it.

Prakrit literary composition, most notably the anthology of King Hala called the *Seven Centuries*, has a different emotional tone than Sanskrit. Its poems evince a sensibility simultaneously rustic and refined, spare yet suggestive, and artless while deeply erudite. Poems in Prakrit tend to feature (as objects of courtly and urbane representation) the emotions and sensibilities of rural and village folk; Prakrit is also the language that women and people of lower social position spoke in Sanskrit dramas such as those composed by Kalidasa (in fact, we should properly call such plays "Sanskrit and Prakrit dramas"). Variants of Prakrit were also the languages of many of India's earliest inscriptions, such as those of many of the edicts of the emperor Ashoka, indicating Prakrit's role as an early language of power and diplomacy. Last, a variety of Prakrit was also the chief scholarly and public language of the Jains, and their distinctive perspectives on human experience must be included in any lexicon on early classical Indian thought.

Absent here are the languages of India's classical Persian and Islamic civilizations as well as the vernaculars, many of

[15] Andrew Ollett, *Language of the Snakes*, Oakland: University of California Press, 2017: 14.

which have high literary and intellectual traditions as well. It is equally painful to omit Tamil, which has a literary corpus extending back to its early classical tradition adjacent to and interacting with Sanskrit. These languages and their lexica, had I the expertise to include them, would have greatly enriched the *Treasury*. And I do not draw at all from the modern subcontinent, as tempting as the hyperpolyglot that is contemporary India may be, nor do I partake of the delights of portmanteau Hinglish. I center on what might be loosely called early "classical" India as I draw from the deep storehouses of nearly two millennia of expression in these three literary traditions. If this *Treasury* encourages further work on emotions in other classical and modern Indian language worlds and textual traditions, then I shall gratefully come to consider it a success.

Even within these languages, I have not aimed to be exhaustive, either in providing a complete listing of emotion terms, or in canvassing all the possible sources on any given term. A kingdom's treasury should burst with jewels, but it cannot contain all of the treasures of the world. It should brim with the coin of the realm, but also contain rare gemstones, pearls, precious baubles, and curios accumulated by the court. I have included emotion terms that carry significant weight in the theoretical systems and literary traditions in which they occur. I would be remiss to omit the three *gunas*, the eight *rasas* and their counterpart *bhavas*, the Ayurveda humors, and so on, all of which are so fundamental to so much Indian thought. But I have also attempted to step over the well-worn grooves of expectation and include less obvious emotion terms that have attracted my notice for one reason or another, curiosities, as it were, that can help us see certain features of Indian thinking about human experience in a new light.

How to Read This Book

The *Treasury* is not a reference work; it is not a dictionary or encyclopedia of historical philology. Rather, it is a wordbook of literary and philosophical vignettes. My entries in some instances may seem idiosyncratic. I don't aim to offer an etymological or comprehensive historical account of each term, or a concordance of every mention of a term in a single text, much less attempt to track it in all texts. I often aim not for generalities that will cover most cases, but for the poignant anecdote that will sharpen the particular—noting, however, that it is through close attention to particulars that the contours of the thoughtworld of ancient India can begin to emerge most distinctively. Every entry is based on specific textual passages, but they may not always be the first texts that readers well acquainted with Indian literature will know. Specialists in specific areas of expertise will doubtless prefer that more of their beloved texts were included; it cannot be otherwise in a collection that draws so widely from so vast a textual world. Sometimes I have chosen to describe a term based on passages that raise philosophical questions and that may be illuminated by a comparative discussion with other theoretical treatments of similar emotions. In other cases, I have inclined in a literary direction, taking pleasure in how a poem or narrative brings into focus a particular experience, and ideally, helps us to feel it too.

I have aimed to make the *Treasury* readable for many different types of readers. I am first attuned to the general reader who may or may not have much background in Indian thought but who is interested in emotions and how they might be described in other contexts. For this reader, I have tried to keep much of the scholarly apparatus and technical discussions at bay, while still allowing the sophistication of the ideas to emerge. I use diacritics sparingly: general readers may get distracted by them and scholars don't need them. If a word has diacritics, readers can find it in parentheses when the word is first mentioned in the body of the entry and in the references section. Indian ideas about human experience deserve to be better known and we ought to remove specialist barriers wherever possible. Above all, I hope that my efforts make it possible that anyone interested in emotions and experience can gain access to the words, texts, and passages I explore here.

But the *Treasury* may be edifying for the specialist as well. It pulls together a range of phenomena and brings to bear some of the wealth of Indian thought concerning terms important to all of our work. Scholars who already know Indian material may find that thematizing emotion helps them see familiar texts and ideas in new light. Every entry is based on actual textual passages that are clearly cited, and I use my translations unless otherwise noted, though I very frequently use the very fine translations of others. For the scholarly sorts who want to track down my references and see for themselves the textual passages from which each entry is drawn, I have included scholarly citations under "References" for each entry. Readers less interested in these details may enjoy staying above the line.

Some will want to read the *Treasury* cover to cover, surveying the gems as they come up. Others may wish to look up particular terms, though they should be cautioned that the *Treasury* is not a dictionary, glossary, thesaurus, encyclopedia, or exhaustive history of emotions. All readers will find that every term can be usefully understood in relation to other terms, either words that are similar to the emotion under consideration, or those that might be antonyms of it. The facets of jewels in a chest reflect many other gemstones near and across from them. Often a term is part of a larger schema of emotions as an item on a list, or it may be a meta category that includes other phenomena—words are frequently synonyms of one another, even as texts often take great pains to parse their nuances. Amarasimha was also aware that words are always related to other words through complex webs (to switch metaphors) of semantic relations: his *Treasury*, despite unfolding in a linear way, was in fact a "knowledge web," indicating these relations between terms.[16]

We can take *karuna* as an example. This term for the hugely important feeling of pathos and sorrow is one of the *rasas* in Bharata's aesthetic theory, and the reader will be encouraged to see it in those terms. *Karuna* is also a key religious practice of compassion and comprises one of the "sublime attitudes" that define and locate it in an entirely different schema. It includes phenomena that lie close to it such as mercy and pity, and is just one of a large number of words for compassion. For these types of reasons, entries often urge that one "see also" other terms. Readers are encouraged to flip around and crisscross through the *Treasury* to see how, in an ecological way (to return to yet another metaphor), items are related to, and often helpfully defined by, other items.

[16] Sivaja Nair and Amba Kulkarni, "The Knowledge Structure in *Amarakośa*," *Proceedings of the Sanskrit Computational Linguistics—4th International Symposium*, 2010.

ENTRIES

A

abhaya

Fearlessness (Sanskrit and Pali)

"Where can fish and other creatures be taken where I might not kill them?" This anguished cry uttered by the eighth-century Buddhist monk Shantideva expresses shock and despair at the violence his life wreaks on the world. Living, eating, sleeping, working—they all involve killing, driving the other out, displacing them, asserting one's own place against theirs. The modern philosopher Emmanuel Levinas voices a distant but recognizable echo of Shantideva as he speaks of "one's fear for the Other" and "a fear for all the violence and murder my existing might generate, in spite of its intentional innocence." While Levinas alludes to the horrors of human history with its slaughter and oppressions and exiles, Shantideva feels acutely the destruction of animal life for the sake of humans.

Jains similarly tend to see humans as "red hot iron balls" destroying everything in their path. Yet every creature, from the lowliest worm to the highest deity in heaven, fears death. Even a strict vegetarian diet, Jains insist, entails the destruction of countless lives, insect and microscopic, in the harvesting of plants. As our growing understanding of the Anthropocene, this epoch of planet-wide human impact and its implications for all creatures and our own future, seeps in, Shantideva's question strikes a new note of horror.

It is from such sensitivity that the force of *abhaya*, fearlessness, makes sense. Fearlessness may put the English speaker in mind of courage, though of course, courage is bravery or fortitude *in the face of fear*, while fearlessness is the condition of not having fear in the first place. *Abhaya* is a feeling of security, the lack of a need to fear. It occurs when people consider how they might offer it to others. *How can I live so that other creatures need not fear me?* Fearlessness is achieved when others grant it.

In all three of the main religious traditions of ancient India—what we now call Buddhism, Jainism, and Hinduism—this assurance of security is configured as a gift (*abhayadana*). One vows to become sensitive to the impact of one's incursions on the world and bestows the restraint that would protect its living beings. The principled moral value of *ahimsa*, the vow of nonviolence perhaps best known in Mahatma Gandhi's movement, is a kind of *abhayadana*.

The gift of fearlessness has special significance when it is a king giving it. A king offering asylum, clemency, and protection can be said to bestow *abhaya*. Indeed, the king's protection and mercy confer his legitimacy. The lawgiver Manu states it bluntly: "a giver of fearlessness receives sovereignty." The powerful can graciously give security, but of course the ability to give others security is what gives them power. The paternalism of ancient Indian ideals of kingship configured security of person not as a *right* claimed by the individual but a benevolence extended by the powerful. The notion of the gift of fearlessness has found its way into the quite different, modern political discourse in the twentieth century, in the writings of Jawaharlal Nehru and Mahatma Gandhi, to remind leaders of nations of this ancient teaching. In the words of Nehru, "it was the function of the leaders of a people to make them fearless."

See also **anrishamsya; anukampa; bhaya**

REFERENCES
"Where can fish and other creatures" . . . *Śāntideva: The Bodhicaryāvatāra* 5.11. BCA: 34.
"one's fear for the Other" . . . E. Levinas, "Ethics as First Philosophy." In *The Levinas Reader*, trans. S. Hand and M. Temple, Oxford: Blackwell Publishers Ltd., 1984: 82.
"red hot iron balls" . . . As cited in P. S. Jaini, *The Jaina Path of Purification*, Delhi: Motilal Banarsidass, 1979: 178.
from the lowliest worm . . . *Dānādiprakaraṇa of Sūrācārya*, ed. A. Bhojak and N. J. Shah, Ahmedabad: L. D. Institute of Indology, 1983: 15.
"a giver of fearlessness" . . . Manu 4.232, *The Law Code of Manu*, trans. P. Olivelle, Oxford: Oxford University Press, 2004: 82.
"the function of the leaders" . . . J. Nehru, *The Discovery of India*, Oxford: Oxford University Press, 1980: 358.

abhijjha

Covetousness (Pali)

Religious texts in India seek to eliminate greed (*lobha*) and its affiliates: desire (*kama*), passion (*raga*), and the bottomless wanting (*iccha*) that are at the heart of the human condition. In Buddhism, when greed goes beyond mere desire into full-blown pining for someone else's property, we are in the territory of *abhijjha* (*abhijjhā*), covetousness. One hovers over another's property, hankering for it, and longing that it might "become mine." Though everywhere problematic as a motivation, ordinary greed isn't considered a full-blown *wrongdoing*, at least in terms of the ten bad deeds that function as a sort of ten commandments in Buddhism. But when it devolves into covetousness, it becomes a mental activity of craving others' things and it counts karmically. It is, in some estimations, as bad as stealing.

See also **byapada/vyapada; iccha; kama; lobha; raga**

REFERENCES

One hovers . . . The entire entry is taken from *Atthasālinī* 101. EX: 101.

ten bad deeds . . . See, for example, *Aṅguttara Nikāya* v. 273–299. NDB: 1525–1541. These are three physical deeds (taking life, stealing, sexual misconduct), four verbal deeds (lying, malicious speech, harsh speech, gossip), and three mental deeds (covetousness, malice, wrong view). See *byapada/vyapada* for malice.

abhilasha/ahilasa

Longing (Sanskrit/Prakrit)

Young heroines afflicted with the lovesick longing that is *abhilasha* (*abhilāśa*) remonstrate with their own hearts. Having fallen in love-at-first-sight with a king, Sagarika scolds her heart for its "obsessive longing for a person impossible to get": "How is it, cruelest of hearts, that you're not ashamed to run after a person you've only seen for a moment, abandoning this person—me!—you've grown up with from birth?"

Struck by an arrow from Kama, the God of Love, such heroines suffer the affliction of *abhilasha* (or rather, the softer sound of *ahilasa*, since these heroines speak Prakrit), considered the first of the ten conditions of lovesickness that, if left unremedied, can descend into edgy distress, raving, and, eventually, death (see *vipralambha*). But not to worry: by nature and literary convention, *abhilasha* will be fulfilled in due course, and this "longing to be together" will be realized. The hero will catch a glimpse of the heroine and fall into his own swooning *abhilasha*.

The palace dramas that celebrate *abhilasha* display a pattern of love-at-first-sight between a king and a young princess whose identity is initially unknown (either through amnesia or other contrivances of plot). Sagarika ("Ocean Girl") seems to come from nature far removed from the trappings of the court. But later she is revealed to have been a princess all along, and thus an entirely appropriate aristocratic bride for the king. In this way the play allows the audience to partake of the natural spontaneity and excitement of strangers meeting, while also seeing to it that their love will ultimately conform to, and thus reinforce, the narrow class strictures of courtly respectability.

See also **autsukya; madana; udvega; vipralambha**

REFERENCES

"obsessive longing" . . . Ratnāvalī 2.1–14. Trans. W. Doniger, *"The Lady of the Jewel Necklace" and "The Lady Who Shows Her Love,"* New York: CSL, 2006: 124–125.

"longing to be together" . . . In Bhānudatta's definition (*Rasamañjarī* 265, which also mentions the ten lovesick conditions. BRRR: 112–113).

The palace dramas . . . The observations in this pararagraph are drawn from the work of D. Ali, "Courtly Love and the Aristocratic Household in Early Medieval India," in *Love in South Asia: A Cultural History*, ed. F. Orsini, Cambridge: Cambridge University Press, 2006: 43–60.

abhimana

Conceit; Sense of Self (Sanskrit)

For religious thinkers, *abhimana* (*abhimāna*) is a type of conceit (*mana*) involving, as all conceits do, a manufactured sense of oneself, and it occurs on various listings of the types of pride. One of seven types of conceit in Buddhist thought, *abhimana* involves thinking one has distinctions that one doesn't. Other thinkers take it to be a deeper level of existential confusion. Theologian Ramanuja sees it as a primal and mistaken identification of oneself with one's body, causing us to adhere to a particular identity—human, female, male, and so on. Because this conception attaches to whatever worldly ends that identity pursues, *abhimana* leads us astray from pursuing the real happiness that is to be found in recognizing our true sense of self free of all constructed identities, and with it, our subservience to the intrinsic happiness that is God.

But other thinkers do not see *abhimana* in pejorative terms at all, and instead identify it with very rudimentary processes of self-awareness. Ancient Samkhya philosophy defines it as a basic "sense of self" underlying thought, emotion, and agency (see *ahamkara*, "I-making," with which it is identified). Drawing on these ideas, Vacaspati Mishra, a ninth-century polymath philosopher, came to define *abhimana* as "the awareness that one is empowered to act with respect to one's experiences or thoughts," a sense of ownership and agency that one is presiding over one's experiences. This sense of ownership present in one's experience—"I am feeling this"—is also a sense of agency—"I can do this." As such, *abhimana* is a crucial starting place for religious therapies of emotion in that one must become aware of oneself presiding over one's experiences to manage them.

Developing these ideas still further, the aesthetic theorist Bhoja sees *abhimana* as that which "produces the experience of the consciousness of pleasure" and the other emotions as "agreeable to the mind." In other words, for Bhoja, it is *rasa*, aesthetic feeling. There is an awareness of oneself desiring and experiencing the world through feeling, and then taking pleasure in it, that lies at the heart of aesthetic experience.

See also **ahamkara; atimana; mana; shringara**

REFERENCES

One of seven types . . . According to Vasubandhu, AKB v. 10, volume III, 1989: 784–785.

Ramanuja sees it . . . Rāmānuja's *Vedārthasaṃgraha* §143. Trans. J.A.B. van Buitenen, Poona: Deccan College, 1956: 297–298. I was aided in this understanding by C. Ram-Prasad, "The Happiness That Qualifies Nonduality: *Jñāna, Bhakti*, and *Sukha* in Rāmānuja's *Vedārthasaṃgraha*" (unpublished paper).

"the awareness that one is empowered to act". . . Vācaspati Miśra's *Sāṃkhyatattvakaumudī on Sāṃkhyakārikā* v. 24, RR: 112.

"produces the experience". . . *Śṛṅgāra Prakāśa,* introduction v. 8. Trans. S. Pollock, "Bhoja's *Śṛṅgāraprakāśa* and the Problem of *Rasa*: An Historical Introduction and Annotated Translation," *Asiatische Studien/ Études Asiatiques* 70, no. 1 (1998): 144. See also RR: 112.

adbhuta/abbhuta

Wonder; The Fantastic (Sanskrit/Pali)

When amazement is developed aesthetically, we have *adbhuta,* wonder at fantastic things. *Adbhuta* involves "a suspension of all of the senses," which I take to mean that one absorbs something lying beyond the senses in stunned amazement. In literature, *adbhuta* is the stuff of hyperbole, fantasy, misinterpretation, and apparent contradiction, all of which require the imagination to soar. In drama, *adbhuta* is prompted by seeing heavenly beings or fabulous temples and parks, attaining something deeply desired, or seeing magic tricks. Expect to feel horripilation, the goosebumps and hair standing on end we often find in Sanskrit texts. We experience wonder, literary critic Bhoja suggests, when we consider the trees of the gods: while earthly trees have sprouts, flowers, and fruit, heavenly trees are laden with silk clothes, jewelry, drinks, and palaces. "What a marvel!"

The gods and the great heroes furnish us with many examples of *adbhuta*:

> Though he had bridged the ocean in sport
> and slain ten-headed Ravana for fun,
> Rama only took pride in himself
> when Sita took him in her arms.

This lovely vignette suggests Rama's own astonishment that he is so loved, and by so lovely a woman. And Rama's self-effacing sensibility of being loved as his greatest feat prompts our stunned amazement. The depth of human emotion, we are coming to see, may itself be the greatest wonder of all.

The value of the marvelous is not lost on religious thinkers, of course. The Buddhist sources record the Buddha's miracles, described as "wonders and marvels," in a teaching that takes a surprising twist, prompting another, more elevated, example of wonder in the reader. The Buddha's disciple Ananda was once asked to recite the "wonders and marvels" of the Buddha, among them how he had lived in a fabulous pleasure heaven before his final life on earth; how his conception and birth were attended by immeasurable and brilliant rays of light flooding even the darkest recesses of the cosmos; and how at birth he, as a mere babe, took seven steps and announced his incomparability.

At the end of these fabulous reports, the Buddha adds an additional wonder and marvel: that for him, "feelings are known as they occur, as they are present, as they disappear; perceptions are known as they occur, as they are present, as they disappear; thoughts are known as they occur, as they are present, as they disappear. Remember this too, Ananda, as a wonder and marvel of the Buddha."

Here, what might at first seem to be a rather mundane form of awareness—being fully aware of what is occurring in one's own experience—is configured more properly as a miracle. We are brought down from the heights of cosmic spectacle to what is in fact the most extraordinary achievement of the Buddha: among all humans, he finally understood the content of his experience and could thereby master it. This surprising disclosure reconfigures the importance of what is to count as a wonder, and in doing so, prompts it.

See also **camatkara; rasa; vismaya**

REFERENCES

"a suspension of all the senses . . . and hyperbole, fantasy" . . . Rasataraṅgiṇī 7.44–45, 47. BRRR: 300–303. "Suspension of all the senses" is my translation, however (with thanks to C. Ram-Prasad, personal communication). The example of Rāma is Bhānudatta's.

In drama . . . Nāṭyaśāstra 6.75–76.

trees of the gods . . . Bhoja's *Śṛṅgāraprakāśa* 630. RR: 132.

"wonders and marvels" . . . Acchariya-abbhuta Sutta, *Majjhima Nikāya* iii.118–124. My translation, but see also BW: 50–54.

ahamkara

"Making I"; Ego (Sanskrit and Pali)

While not an emotion, *ahamkara* (*ahaṃkāra*) is so important and basic to Indian psychological theories that it must be considered here. Everyone has a sense of "I" as something that can be disassociated from the content of one's experience. I can look out the window and see the view, and be aware of myself doing so. When this reflexivity is fashioned into a person with an identity across time, we have *ahamkara*, "I-making," and from a very early period in India we find an appreciation first, of its presence, and second, of just how constructed and manufactured this ego or sense of self is. Much goes into constructing the first-person pronoun that we take as a given and reach for constantly. Though some schools of thought posited *ahamkara* as a vital mode of self, others took this ego-construction as problematic and sought to dismantle it.

Both the Upanishads and the ancient Samkhya philosophers speak of this sense of "I" at the center of one's awareness. In cosmological terms, an early Upanishad notices the all-pervasive "I." Once we become aware of it, it is present wherever we look for it: "I am, indeed, below; I am above; I am in the west; I am in the east; I am in the south; and I am in the north. Indeed, I extend over this whole world." Because my awareness of myself as an "I" can be everywhere—*I* am present as I perceive what is below and above wherever I look—I am all-pervasive in my experience. And this "I," according to the Upanishads, is a "self," a metaphysical reality.

The Upanishads are full of such striking observations of how we become aware of ourselves as a witnessing subject, and then they explore the nature and metaphysical status of the witnessing subject. The word *ahamkara* is made up of "I" (*aham*) and the verbal sense of "making" (*kara*), indicating the constructed nature of this sense of self. But an alternative and perhaps even more cosmically intriguing etymology would have it that *ahamkara* is the "sounding of *I*," perhaps echoing the first created being's calling out "I am here" at the beginning of the cosmos.

Samkhya philosophy sees *ahamkara* as generating a "twofold creation": first, the faculties of mind, agency, and the senses; and second, the more subtle sensory objects in the world. The *Samkhya Karikas* then identify this sense of "I" as a matter of conceit (*abhimana*), suggesting that at the very rudimentary levels of perception and cognition there is a manufactured, prideful sense of self. We *fashion* a sense of self, a mode of self-construction ever at work as we encounter the world, and we have a sense of presiding over our experience.

The notion of *ahamkara* as a conceit suggests to religious thinkers that it is a mistaken construal of who one is, refracted through our ignorance, desires, and aversions. Across the spectrum, the great thinkers identified this egoism and self-construction as the source of our cognitive distortions and moral failures. Pali Buddhist texts inveigh against "the I-making, mine-making, and underlying tendency to conceit" in human experience. The brilliant Advaitan Shankara sees *ahamkara* as a limited and idiosyncratic sense of personhood, decidedly not to be confused with *atman*, the true self. *Ahamkara*, he says, "should properly be called ignorance; it is the most noxious root of all faults and the origin of all evils." Even so worldly a thinker as the Dharma Shastra jurist Yajnavalkya finds this kind of pride to be a problematic and overweening sense of self. For all, the religious project is to dismantle this limited and pernicious ego and pride that constantly and everywhere projects itself.

See also **abhimana; mana; moksha; omana**

REFERENCES

"I am, indeed, below" . . . *Chāndogya Upaniṣad* 7.25. EU: 270–271.

"sounding of I" . . . This possibility was first suggested by J.A.B. van Buitenen, "Studies in Sāṁkhyā (II)," *Journal of the American Oriental Society* 77 (1957): 17. He suggests that *ahaṃkāra* is like *oṃkāra*, the sounding or cry of "om." As he points out, the sounding of "I" occurred first in the cosmogonic myth in *Bṛhadāraṇyaka Upaniṣad* 1.4, EU: 44–45; and from the primordial cry "I am here" issues all of creation.

Samkhya philosophy sees . . . *Sāṃkhya Kārikā* XXIV. These ideas were developed by Vācaspati Miśra's commentary (see *abhimana*).

"the I-making, mine-making" . . . As, for example, at *Majjhima Nikāya* iii.32. MLD: 906.

Shankara sees ahamkara . . . *Gītābhāṣya* of Śaṅkara, commentary on Gītā XVI.18. My translation, but see also BGC: 423. On *ahaṁkāra*, see also commentary on XVIII.53 (BGC: 490–491).

Yajnavalkya finds this kind of pride . . . *Yājñavalkya Dharmaśāstra* III.151–164. Trans. P. Olivelle, *A Treatise on Dharma*, Cambridge, MA: Harvard University Press, MCLI, 2019: 252–255.

akkhanti/akshanti

Impatience (Pali/Sanskrit)

In Pali Buddhism, *akkhanti* is "ferocity, irascibility, discontent, lack of forbearance, and lack of patience." This is impatience with other people and an unwillingness to put up with discomfort. People can be unwilling to listen to the Buddha's teaching out of *akkhanti* and petulance, thinking the rules are too stringent. Monks and nuns can be impatient with one another. Such impatience has very unfortunate consequences, and there are many disadvantages to allowing this emotion any space in one's psychic life: one becomes unloved and despised by many people, and given over to hostility and revenge. One will die confused and go to a low and punishing hell.

So *akkhanti* is to be guarded against. In Abhidhamma Buddhist psychology and the work it recommends for restructuring one's emotional life, *akkhanti* is analyzed as occurring at a very basic level of perception and assimilating information. It shapes, even before one is fully aware of it, how one sees a situation. And so it is at the level of perception that it must be fortified against. This is done through "restraint" as one guards what and how one comes to see. Certain practices of restraint work at the level of the sensory faculties, guarding the doors, as it were, of perception. Else, like a thief who slips into an unguarded city and plunders the treasures within, *akkhanti* can enter through the doors of perception and plunder one's good will and generous vision.

In Sanskrit, *akshanti* (*akṣānti*), and the variant *akshama*, is the undesirable feeling of hating the good qualities of others, and insofar as hatred is a burning sensation in the heart, this is painful. According to one authority, *akshama* is to be distinguished from the envy that is *amarsha* in that *amarsha* also involves the further feeling that one's own good qualities are being surpassed. Amara's *Treasury* lists indignation (*asuya*) and jealousy (*irshya*) as synonyms of *akshanti*, suggesting a cluster of terms interweaving many of the vile ways we look at one another. *Akshama* is the opposite of a quality of patience and forbearance called *kshama* that is everywhere admired.

See also **amarsha; appaccaya; asuya; dvesha; irshya; kshama/kshanti**

REFERENCES

"ferocity, irracibility" . . . *Vibhaṅga* 360. My translation, but see also P. A. Thiṭṭila, trans., *The Book of Analysis*, London: Pali Text Society, 1969: 468.

unwilling to listen to the Buddha's teaching . . . *Aṅguttara* i.236 tells of a monk filled with *akkhanti* and *appaccaya* (petulance) toward the Buddha's rules (NDB: 322–323); *Vinaya* IV.240 describes a nun teaching other nuns about *akkhanti* and other vices (I. B. Horner, trans., *The Book of the Discipline*, vol. III, Oxford: Pali Text Society, 2004: 210–211).

many disadvantages . . . *Vibhaṅga* 378–379. Thiṭṭila 1969: 489.

Abhidhamma Buddhist psychology . . . *Atthasālinī* 400–401. My translation and summary, but see also EX: 510.

hating the good qualities . . . According to the *Padārthadharmasangraha of Praśastipāda with the Nyāyakaṇḍalī of Śrīdhara*. Trans. G. Jha, Allahabad: E. J. Lazarus and Co., 1916: 561–562. *Akṣamā* is here one of several kinds of *dveṣa*, hatred, defined as heart-burning; *amarṣa* is also listed here, with this definition.

Amara's Treasury . . . *Amarakośa* 1.7.457.

amarsha

Envy; Resentment; Vindictiveness (Sanskrit)

When I saw all that blazing fortune at the Pandavas', I fell prey to resentment (*amarṣa*) and I am burning, though that is not my way. I shall enter the fire, or drink poison, or drown myself, for I shall not be able to live. For what man of mettle in this world will have patience when he sees his rivals prosper and himself decline?

In ancient India as in the West, envy is yellowish-green, the color Duryodhana, the eldest brother of the Kurus in the *Mahabharata,* turns as he utters these lines. Duryodhana has grown wan and sickly from resenting his rivals and cousins, the Pandavas. He has seen their opulent city in the wilderness. And though his father remonstrates with him that Duryodhana also enjoys his own kingdom and vast riches, and that his cousins wish him no harm, Duryodhana acknowledges and indeed welcomes his *amarsha,* arguing that it stirs martial ambition. He embraces his envy and stokes it by lingering on every detail of his cousins' prosperous palace and kingdom.

In Duryodhana's way of thinking, contentment yields complacency and can never produce greatness. So he nurtures his resentment until it leads him to embrace a perfidious plan to lure his cousin Yudhishthira to lose everything in a dicing match, which in turn leads ultimately to the catastrophic internecine war that is the story of this great epic. While he defends his *amarsha* as a manly virtue befitting his warrior aspirations, Duryodhana allows that it is a scorching and desiccating affliction: *amarsha* "has filled me, and burning day and night I am drying up like a small pool in the hot season."

See also **akkhanti/akshanti; asuya; irshya; matsara**

References

"When I saw all that blazing fortune" . . . *Mahābhārata* II.43.26–28. Trans. J.A.B. van Buitenen, *The Mahābhārata 2, Book of the Assembly Hall,* Chicago: University of Chicago Press, 1975: 110. On Duryodhana's envy, see G. Das, *The Difficulty of Being Good,* Oxford: Oxford University Press, 2009: ch. 1.

yellowish-green . . . Several times in this passage, Duryodhana's color, pallid and sickly, is noticed (II.45.7, 16).

"has filled me" . . . *Mahābhārata* II.43.21.

amhas

The Torment of a Tight Spot (Sanskrit)

This ancient term for the anguish of being hemmed in and trapped in a tight spot is best known in the Vedic scriptures (though *aṃhas* has cognates in its Indo-European cousins "angst" and "anxiety"). The nomadic peoples who recited the Vedas sought the freedom of open spaces, seeking the best pasture lands in the plains of northern India where the blackbuck ranges. Their hymns speak poignantly of the danger and anguish of confinement and constriction. For example, a Rig Vedic hymn to Pushan, a solar deity presiding over journeys and roads, pleads: "traverse the ways, Pushan, and keep away *amhas*, O Child of the Unharnessing. Stay with us, O god, going before us." The hymn goes on to beseech Pushan to go before them, clearing the path of fierce wolves and rapacious highwaymen, to make their journeys peaceful, profitable, and open.

REFERENCE

"traverse the ways" . . . *Ṛgveda* 1.42. Trans. W. Doniger O'Flaherty, *The Rig Veda: An Anthology*, New York: Penguin, 1981: 193–194. See also her comments on *aṃhas* on pp. 16–17, 118 n. 8; and see *Ṛgveda* 8.18.10.

ananda

Bliss (Sanskrit)

In the Upanishads, *ananda* (*ānanda*) is both the highest bliss humans should seek and the true nature of the self as it is, a state of utter peace and contentment unafflicted not only by suffering but also by the vicissitudes of desire and pleasure. Such bliss is not easily conceived, since our ordinary conceptions of happiness usually involve the gratification of our desires. But because desires subject us to the contingency of the world and our own shifting and restless whims, then bliss must be a deeper contentment free of them altogether.

The Upanishads reveal hidden connections—the "real behind the real." Most importantly, what is most real is the self (*atman*) that lies behind and yet witnesses all phenomenological experience, and the brahman, the ultimate reality that lies behind and yet witnesses all of the phenomenal world. The *atman* and brahman are highest bliss, and insofar as we truly know them and know ourselves as them, we enjoy such bliss.

The Upanishads are fascinated with altered states that may be likened to ultimate bliss. In dreams, for example, the self becomes a "creator" of worlds that it can enjoy: one "creates bliss, pleasures, and delight." One can revel in these worlds and then retreat, unaffected, from them, where nothing from the dream "sticks to one's person." But deeper than dreams is dreamless sleep where the self, while still breathing and capable of perceiving, remains untouched by the worlds, even those of its own making. In dreams, one may still be subject to fear, but in deep sleep all of that is gone. Deep sleep is the self complete unto itself: "when one is fast asleep, totally collected and serene, and sees no dreams—that is the self; that is the immortal; that is the one free from fear; that is brahman." And further: "this is one's highest bliss! On just a fraction of this bliss do other creatures live."

Sexual bliss is another analogue for the highest *ananda*, harkening back to the cosmogonic myth of the primal being splitting into two to experience enjoyment with an other; sexual union is returning to that original united wholeness through the merger of two. And so just as "a man embraced by the woman he loves is oblivious to everything within or without, so this person embraced by the self (*atman*) consisting of knowledge is oblivious to everything within or without." Here, "all desires are fulfilled, where the self is the only desire, and which is free from desires and far from sorrows." Sexual bliss is a return to plenitude and wholeness.

And so bliss, and the metaphysical realities that bliss reveals, are in turn revealed by these similar yet ultimately different states. In dreams, we become aware of an experiencer who creates worlds at will, which it can enjoy and then abandon; in deep sleep, one reposes in objectless contemplation, entirely content; and in sexual union, one returns to wholeness. Indeed, bliss is the true nature of our being that lies beneath the shifting sands of experience.

As the ascetic traditions developed, the idea that the supreme bliss of liberation renders all other happinesses null was carried forward by Hindus and Jains (Buddhists have similar ideas of highest happiness, usually *sukha,* but do not use *ananda* for this). *Ananda* remains the paradoxical happiness achieved by renouncing all desires and pleasures. In contexts of the much later devotional movements known as *bhakti, ananda* becomes the bliss that is God and devotion to God. For theologians in these traditions, the bliss associated with brahman, even if multiplied billions of times, would not amount to "even a drop of the ocean of the happiness of devotion."

See also **bhakti; moksha; sukha**

References

"the real behind the real" (satyasya satya) . . . Bṛhadāraṇyaka Upaniṣad 2.1.20. EU: 62–65.

"creates bliss . . . nothing sticks to this person" . . . Bṛhadāraṇyaka Upaniṣad 4.3.10, 15. EU: 112–114.

"when one is fast asleep" . . . Chāndogya Upaniṣad 8.1.1. EU: 284–285.

"this is one's highest bliss" . . . Bṛhadāraṇyaka Upaniṣad 3.3.32. EU: 116–117. I have changed the pronouns to the gender-neutral "one" instead of "his."

"a man embraced . . . far from sorrows" . . . *Bṛhadāraṇyaka Upaniṣad* 4.3.21. EU: 114–115.

carried forward by Hindus and Jains . . . For example, in Śaṅkara's commentaries on the Upaniṣads, see A. Fort, "Beyond Pleasure: Śaṅkara on Bliss," *Journal of Indian Philosophy* 16, no. 2 (1988): 177–189. For Jains, see Hemacandra's *Yogaśāstra* XII.51. YŚ: 195.

Devotional movements known as bhakti . . . See Rāmānuja's *Vedārthasaṃgraha* §140. Trans. J.A.B. van Buitenen, Poona: Deccan College, 1956: 294–295; and BR: 10–11.

anannatannassamitindriya

The "I-Will-Come-to-Know-What-Is-Unknown" Faculty (Pali)

Ever have the feeling that you should know about something, but you don't yet know what it is? But wait, if it is unknown to you, how do you know that you should know it? The Pali Buddhist tradition identifies this quandary and provides a faculty to explain it. A faculty (*indriya*—the word is related to the high god Indra, as that which governs) is an internal force in human experience that sometimes gently guides, and at other times sternly commandeers, one's awareness. This particular force is related to spiritual insight. In the early stages of the religious path, we may sense an inner prompting to learn the truths of the teachings, a voice that acknowledges unknowing and hopes for illumination. In a tradition that posits a deep primordial ignorance pervasive in the unregenerate human condition, this bridge from delusion to wisdom provides a necessary lifeline. Else how do we know that we are in ignorance of the very truths we should seek? We know because we have a faculty that allows one to utter to oneself: "I will come to know what is unknown" to me.

REFERENCE

I-will-come-to-know-what-is-unknown . . . anaññātaññassāmītindriya. Commentary on the *Vibhaṅga*, v.578–583. Bhikkhu Ñāṇamoli, trans., *The Dispeller of Delusion (Sammohavinodanī),* part I, Oxford: Pali Text Society, 1996: 154–155. The Sanskrit equivalent of this is *anājñātamājñāsyāmīndriya*, discussed by Vasubandhu (AKB, volume I, 1988: 162–163).

anrishamsya

Fellow-Feeling; Compassion (Sanskrit)

While the *Mahabharata* cannot be said to have a single message and at different points extols varying virtues as "the highest Dharma," the virtue proposed as the best *most often* in the text is *anrishamsya (ānṛśaṃsya)*, "good will, a fellow feeling, a deep sense of the other." *Anrishamsya* is one of the many words we have in Sanskrit for compassion and seems to have acquired a new emphasis in the *Mahabharata*; perhaps it was even newly minted in the epic. It is to be practiced by everyone as a general virtue and is especially important for kings.

Anrishamsya is a tenderhearted concern for those left behind, who might be vulnerable or neglected without one's notice. When King Yudhishthira enters the gates of heaven with only a faithful dog at his side, he refuses, out of *anrishamsya,* to proceed when told he must first abandon the dog. And Yudhishthira had displayed it on an earlier occasion too, when, given a boon to bring back to life only one of his four brothers, he chose Nakula, one of his stepbrothers. Why? Because of his compassion for Madri, Nakula's mother, who would be left with no sons at all were he to choose one of the older brothers, born of his own mother. *Anrishamsya* often appears with commiseration (*anukrosha*), crying out for another's pain.

But a king cannot practice nonviolence and compassion absolutely. The respected elder Bhisma, even while praising *anrishamsya* to Yudhishthira, says that "nothing great can be achieved through pure compassion," and that gentleness courts the disrespect of the people. It may be that, at least as the epic literature sees it, religious renouncers can fully observe the dictates of nonviolence (*ahimsa*), but kings, who are by nature and position sometimes required to be violent, should nevertheless aspire to feel *anrishamsya* whenever possible.

See also **anukampa; anukrosha; daya; karuna; nrishamsa**

REFERENCES

most often in the text . . . Alf Hiltebeitel counted the excellences said to be supreme duties (*paro dharmaḥ*) and found that the *Mahābhārata* claims this of *ānṛśaṃsya* eight times, more than any other virtue. *Rethinking the Mahābhārata*, Chicago: University of Chicago Press, 2001: 207.

"good will, a fellow feeling, a deep sense of the other" . . . These are Mukund Lath's words; Lath also notes that the *Mahābhārata* introduces *ānṛśaṃsya* as a new word. "The Concept of Ānṛśaṁsya in the *Mahābhārata*," in *The Mahābhārata Revisited*, ed. R. N. Dandekar, New Delhi: Sahitya Akademi, 1990: 113–119.

faithful dog at his side . . . *Mahābhārata* XVII.3.7–20.

he chose Nakula . . . *Mahābhārata* III.297.65–73.

"nothing great can be achieved" . . . *Mahābhārata* 12.76.18–19. Translated and discussed by U. Singh (PV: 74–75); see also page 69 and her discussion of *ānṛśaṃsya* in the *Arthaśāstra* and in the *Rāmāyaṇa* (110–120, 307–308, and 532 n. 126).

renouncers can practice total nonviolence (ahimsa) . . . Lath argues that the *Mahābhārata* teaches that kings cannot achieve *ahiṃsā* because they must practice an active life in the world, and so are to aspire to *ānṛśaṃsya* instead (118–119).

anukampa

Compassion; Trembling for Others (Pali and Sanskrit)

The idea of having compassion for all beings, what the early Buddhist sources referred to as "trembling for the world," is deeply ingrained in Indian religion. *Anukampa* comes from the verb to tremble or shake, suggesting the phenomenology of this word for compassion. The Buddha's life and teaching were said to have been "for the welfare and happiness of the multitude, out of *anukampa* for the world, for the good, welfare, and happiness of gods and humans." Buddhas and bodhisattvas have *anukampa* for all beings, not just for innocents, as they tremble also for the heedless, the misguided, the wrongdoers, and those attached to their own afflictions. An impartial and categorical feeling for others' pain is expected of all eminent persons.

Ideas about universal compassion make their way into political discourse with the emperor Ashoka, who picks up these themes and then vows, in an inscription etched on a sandstone pillar at Kosambi, to practice nonviolence and mercy (*daya*). Centuries later, another king, the glorious Samudra Gupta, is eulogized on this same pillar in a panegyric composed in highly ornamented Sanskrit, and rich in emotional description. (The pillar records, for example, the horripilation and tears of affection of the king's father at Samudragupta's coronation.) Today, the pillar stands in Allahabad, and on it Samudragupta's inscription is chiseled alongside Ashoka's (and, in time, an edict of the sixteenth-century Mughal emperor Jahangir comes to be added as well). Samudragupta's famous inscription praises his *anukampa* and bears testimony to his "soft heart that can be had toward anyone who merely bows down to him in devotion."

Great men are those whose hearts are tender and who can tremble for others.

See also **anrishamsya; anukrosha; daya; karuna; kripa**

REFERENCES

"Trembling for the world" . . . *Saṃyutta Nikāya* ii.274. CDB: 714

"for the welfare and happiness" . . . *Saṃyutta Nikāya* ii.274. CDB: 714.

bodhisattvas have anukampa . . . Asaṅga's *Bodhisattvabhūmi* II.1.2.1. BP: 497.

The Emperor Ashoka . . . Second Pillar Edict at Allahabad, ed. E. Hultzsch, *Corpus Inscriptionum Indicarum*, volume 1, Oxford: Clarendon Press, 1922: 156.

tears of affection . . . Allahabad Pillar Inscription, lines 7–8, ed. B. Chhabra and G. S. Gai, *Corpus Inscriptionum Indicarum*, volume 3, New Delhi: Archaeological Survey of India, 1981: 212. Affection is *sneha*. Upinder Singh is full of insights about this inscription (PV: 190–195).

praises his anukampa . . . Allahabad Pillar Inscription, line 25 (Chhabra and Gai 1981: 214).

anukrosha

Commiseration; Crying Out for Another (Sanskrit)

With *anukrosha* (*anukrośa*), we get yet another term for compassion. Often paired with *anrishamsya*, *anukrosha* involves a cry or a lament on someone else's behalf, and all beings, from Indra down to the animals, can feel it. After stripping the Demon King Bali from power, Lord Indra, the king of the gods, feels both *anrishamsya* and *anukrosha* for Bali. To be sure, just prior to this moment, Bali in his disgrace has chided Indra for his arrogance, pointing out that Time is the real slayer of us all and that their rivalry is eternal. Gods and demons are forever trading places in victory and defeat. Indra is moved by Bali's wisdom and graciously feels his pain.

And once a parrot felt *anukrosha* and *anrishamsya* for a huge tree standing in a forest. The tree had been home for the parrot its entire life, providing it food and protection. When the tree was struck by a hunter's errant poison arrow, it withered and died, and all the animals living in the tree abandoned it, except the parrot. This devotion captures the attention of Indra himself, who is astonished that a mere animal can feel *anukrosha*. The parrot tells him that "commiseration is the greatest characteristic of the dharma of good people, and it will always bring them joy." This unexpected observation—that there is a joy (*priti*) in the shared feeling of another's suffering—suggests that commiseration is not just the obligation of the dutiful to share other's pain, but that it has a happiness in it that comes from such love and devotion.

See also **anrishamsya; anukampa; daya; karuna**

REFERENCES

After his victory in battle with Bali . . . Mahābhārata 12.227.110. Mukund Lath first noticed the frequent pairing of *ānṛśaṃsya* and *anukrośa*. "The Concept of Ānṛśaṁsya in the *Mahābhārata*" in *The Mahābhārata Revisited*, ed. R. N. Dandekar, New Delhi: Sahitya Akademi, 1990: 115. See also Alf Hiltebeitel, *Rethinking the Mahābhārata*, Chicago: University of Chicago Press, 2001, 212–214; he is right, I think, to translate *anukrośa* as "commiseration."

And once a parrot . . . This story is told at *Mahābhārata* 13.5.1–31.

anumodana

Applauding and Rejoicing in Others' Virtue (Pali and Sanskrit)

Anumodana is a feeling of jubilation and rejoicing upon witnessing others perform good deeds or acts of worship. The feelings of exultation at observing others' spiritual advancement are encouraged as highly meritorious: when *you* give a gift or attain spiritual insight, *I* should celebrate. This counters envy and selfishness. In the *Perfection of Wisdom Sutras,* the Buddha himself is said to have achieved his awakening in part by rejoicing for countless eons at the merit of others.

Buddhist traditions have a ritually ordered sense of how one should celebrate others' doing well. Many Buddhists see almsgiving to monks as a community event in which everyone—not just the donor—should endeavor to touch the gift and say "well done," so that all might share in the merit and happiness of the gift. Giving is not a zero-sum game with a limited amount of merit redounding to the donor. Rather, it multiplies by the number of people who rejoice in it, just as a flame can be taken from one lamp to light many without diminishing the light of the first.

See also **kritajna/katannu; mudita**

REFERENCES

Perfection of Wisdom Sutras . . . *The Large Sūtra on Perfect Wisdom with the Divisions of the Abhisamayālaṅkāra,* trans. E. Conze, Berkeley: University of California Press, 1975: 269.

just as a flame . . . Suttasaṅgahaṭṭhakathā of Ariyawansa. M. Heim, *Theories of the Gift in South Asia,* New York: Routledge, 2004: 68.

anuraga

Affection and Attraction (Sanskrit)

While *anuraga* (*anurāga*) can be many kinds of affection, including that of a king for his courtiers and theirs for him, it receives the most sustained discussion when it is refers to romantic, sexual, and erotic attraction. And nowhere is it treated more meticulously in this meaning than in the aesthetic treatise of the brilliant eleventh-century scholar and intellectual King Bhoja. His chapter on *anuraga* in his treatise on aesthetics, *Illuminating the Erotic,* can illustrate one of the more delightful features of the *shastra* genre—its capacity to name, exhaustively (and perhaps also exhaustingly), the many varieties of experience and social arrangements.

In the course of his treatment of the ways literature evokes emotion and aesthetic experience, Bhoja's chapter on *anuraga* specifies that there are sixty-four varieties of this attraction:

> Affection, longing, regarding, yearning, wishing, hoping to win, desire, wanting, craving, ardent love, covetousness, fickle attraction, eagerness, faithful devotion, taking pleasure in, pregnancy craving, hopeful love, praying for, expectant desire, delighting in, caring, tenacity, binding, obstinate, considered, thoughtful, approved, partial, greedy, clinging, intense, powerful, deluded, purposeful, impetuous, amazing, passion, violent agitation, persevering, resolute, lustful, unconscious, reminiscing, intentional, a way of being, a kind of taste, sexual attraction, pleasurable, gallant, showing favor, tenderness, crying out for, all-conquering, intimate, subjugating, attachment, successful, complete, satisfied, with desires sated, fondness, loving, refreshing, and complete bliss.

This list contains synonyms that begin to suggest just how rich Sanskrit can be in covering this terrain (and English strains to offer terms for all of these nuances). Other descriptors are adjectives qualifying *anuraga*. And some words on this list have quite different meanings altogether, like delusion (*moha*) and faithfulness (*shraddha*). Here, they get deployed to introduce specific modalities of attraction—namely, deluded love or faithful devotion.

Bhoja gives verses that illustrate most of these kinds of *anuraga*. He then goes on to say that each of them can be further divided by eight, distinguishing each kind of attraction as eternal or temporary, reciprocal or unrequited, disclosed or hidden, and spontaneous or affected. Each of these eight kinds (of each of the sixty-four) can in turn be classified further according to another schema of eight: the subject of the attraction, the recipient, the foundation, the excitement, the social standing, the togetherness of the couple, the appearance, and the particular nature of the people involved. Now, each of these eight can be subject to further threefold classifications, as for example, discerning whether the subject is high, low, or equal status; the recipient is better, inferior, or equal; and the foundation of their attraction is ephemeral, of medium duration, or long-lasting. And so on.

Such divisions of three can be applied to each of the eight and we multiply them to arrive ultimately, Bhoja says, at 12,228 forms of *anuraga*! He then allows that other forms are also possible but illustrates merely 256 of them.

This is a most thoroughgoing treatment first, of the varieties and shades of human attraction, and second, of the inflections these incur from the many varieties of social relationships. While it may be that "our jaws are likely to fall slack at the hypertrophy of categories" delivered up by *shastra,* we can't fail to admire its precision in treating the spectacular range and variety of the human heart.

See also **kama; raga; ranj/rajjati; rati; shringara**

REFERENCES

including that of a king for his courtiers and theirs for him . . . See D. Ali, *Courtly Culture and Political Life in Early Medieval India,* Cambridge: Cambridge University Press, 2004: 105.

"Affection, longing, regarding" . . . See *Bhoja's Śṛṅgāra Prakāśa,* by V. Raghavan, Madras: Vasanta Press, 1978: 41–44, for this reference and Bhoja's other distinctions. For a similar style of "taming a subject" by enumerations and ramifying calculations with *kāma* in the *Kāma Sūtra,* see the discussion by W. Doniger and S. Kakar in KS: xxiii–xxv.

"our jaws are likely to fall slack" . . . As S. Pollock puts it in another context (that is, in his introduction to BRRR: xxxv).

anushaya/anusaya

Regret; Remorse; Underlying Tendencies
(Sanskrit/Prakrit)

The most spectacular public display of remorse (*anuśaya*) in ancient India may well be that of the emperor Ashoka who comes to rue the violence of the conquest that brought most of the Indian subcontinent under his rule. Nowhere was the bloodshed more horrific than what his forces wreaked on the people in Kalinga (in what we now call Odisha). In a most unusual public proclamation of remorse, his account of these events and his own grief at them is issued in a royal inscription on a rockface. Even by his own account, the genocide was appalling: "A hundred and fifty thousand people were deported, a hundred thousand were killed, and many times that number perished." These casualties weigh heavily on his mind and he feels "remorse, for when an independent country is conquered, the slaughter, death, and deportation of the people is extremely grievous" to him. He hopes that instead of victory by war, a new form of victory by Dharma, or righteousness, might now be effected and that he be forgiven.

While he urges restraint on his own power and future merciful rule by his descendants, Ashoka does make sure to warn the forest tribes "that he has power even in his remorse, and asks them to repent, lest they be killed." The political testimony of remorse, however heartfelt or pragmatic for establishing peace it may be, does not abrogate power or the threat of violence altogether.

In a totally different sense, *anusaya* is also a term used in Buddhist moral psychology for a class of phenomena known as "underlying tendencies," of which various lists are given; these are all negative psychological dispositions that drive problematic thought, feeling, and action, much like *asavas*, *kleshas*, and *samskaras*. Often a list of seven is described: the underlying tendencies to sensual desire (*kama*), to hostility (*patigha*), to holding ideological views, to doubt, to conceit (*mana*), to lust for existence, and to ignorance. They have to be dug out, much like a palm stump, because if they are simply cut off, they keep coming back.

See also **anutapa; asava/ashrava; hridayakrosha; kleshas/kilesas; pashcattapa; vippatisara**

References

"a hundred and fifty" . . . 13th Major Rock Edict, in R. Thapar, trans., *A Translation of the Edicts of Aśoka*, Delhi: Oxford University Press, 1997: 255.

"remorse, for when" . . . Thapar 1997: 255. While the inscription is to some degree effaced on the rock, the term for remorse seems to be "*anusaya*" as suggested in Alexander Cunningham, *Corpus Inscriptionum Indicarum, Vol. I, Inscriptions of Asoka*, Calcutta: Office of the Superintendent of Government Printing, 1877: 84.

"that he has power" . . . Thapar 1997: 256.

"underlying tendencies" . . . As at *Aṅguttara Nikāya* iv.9, iii.253–54. My translation, but see also NDB: 1003.

anutapa

Remorse; Repentance (Sanskrit and Pali)

One of the most unpleasant of human experiences is remorse. And among experiences of remorse, that felt by an evildoer on his deathbed may be the most acute. As with the "afterburn" that is *pashcattapa*, there is heat and burning in *anutapa* (*anutāpa*) perhaps especially at this hour.

A Buddhist text notes how one's past evil deeds "cling" to the mind right before death, and dark omens appear. The dying man "swoons, his thirst and fever increase, and the suffering of *anutapa* crushes him thoroughly." Little can be done at this point, and "crying aloud, frightened and distressed in mind, powerless and trembling because of his own evil deeds, the fool is taken to hell like a frog by a water-snake."

See also **anushaya/anusaya; hridayakrosha; pashcattapa; vippatisara**

REFERENCE

"swoons, his thirst and fever increase" . . . Saddharmopāyana, v. 288 and 291–292. Trans. A. A. Hazlewood, *Journal of the Pali Text Society* 12 (1988): 106.

appaccaya

Petulance (Pali)

Appaccaya, a petulant, surly sulk that makes one grumble, is in evidence when monks object to the Buddha's monastic rules as too stringent. They become churlish and sullen, complaining that the Buddha is too harsh over trifles, as when he insists that they limit their food intake and refrain from eating at night. The Buddha has a lesson for such monks: for those who see the rules as onerous tethers, the rules become like thick leather cords holding them down. But for those who see them as necessary but not burdensome constraints and decide not to resent them, the rules will not inhibit and shackle them and will instead seem like weak and fragile bonds. The sulk itself is a fetter that makes the rules seem more constraining than they actually are.

See also **akkhanti/akshanti**

REFERENCE

when monks object . . . Majjhima Nikāya i.449–50. MLD: 553.

asava/ashrava

Oozings (Pali/Sanskrit)

Like a cankerous sore that oozes, certain highly problematic desires and dispositions seep out from within, causing us the ethical problems and suffering that tie us up in the perpetual rebirth that is samsara. Or at least this is how Buddhist psychology talks about it. Most lists give four *asavas* (*āsavas*): sensual desire (*kama*), the desire for being, the tendency for wrong views, and ignorance. The oozings are usually synonymous with *kleshas*, the defiling afflictions that cause us suffering. They are not emotions as such, but they are so important to Buddhist thinking about the human condition that they must be included here. Buddhists consider the religious goal of nirvana to involve getting rid of the oozings—an *arhat*, or awakened person, is called "One Free of the Oozings."

The word *asava* is related to the verb "flow" or "discharge," and brings to mind not only seeping wounds but also fermenting fruit that comes to actively bubble and flow. And they run deep. One of them, ignorance, is so deeply part of experience in samsara that as one considers past lives, one finds that there is no first point at which one could say, "once there was no ignorance." Translators struggle with the right term in English for the *asavas*: cankers, intoxicants, depravities, taints, corruptions. I prefer "oozing" as the most visceral and accurate, and because it illuminates much about how Buddhist psychology conceives the deeply flowing and pervasive corrupting influences that taint human life. Because the *asavas* run so deep, the therapeutic work of meditation required to remove them is highly developed in Buddhist practice.

Jains also include *ashrava* (*āśrava*) in their psychology, but for them the direction of flow is the opposite. In their metaphysics, action in the world in all of its violence and impurity involves karma flowing "in" and sticking to the soul, thus keeping us trapped in samsara. Actions of body, speech, and mind are the "inflow" (*ashrava*), and spiritual liberation requires stopping this inflow and wearing off the existing karmic residue of past flows.

See also **anushaya/anusaya; kleshas/kilesas; samskara/sankhara; vasana**

REFERENCES

give four asavas . . . For example, *Dīgha Nikāya* ii.81, LD: 234. In the Sanskrit Abhidharma tradition, Vasubandhu moves between *āśrava*, *anuśaya*, and *kleśa* for this arena of experience, often defining them in terms of one another, and he offers various listings for these phenomena, some more finely grained than others.

"One Free of the Oozings" . . . That is, *khīnāsava*.

fermenting fruit . . . *once there was no ignorance* . . . *Atthasālinī* 48. EX: 63–64. See also *Dhammasaṅgaṇi* 1096–1112 on *āsavas*, trans. C.A.F. Rhys Davids, *A Buddhist Manual of Psychological Ethics (Dhammasaṅgaṇi)*, London: Royal Asiatic Society (1900) 1975: 291–296.

Jains also include ashrava . . . *Tattvārtha Sūtra of Umāsvāti*, 6.2, 9.1–2. Trans. N. Tatia, San Francisco: Harper Collins, 1994: 151, 213–219.

asha

Hope, and Often, Vain Hope (Sanskrit)

"Come here! Go!
Lie down! Get up!
Speak! Be still!"
Such is the way that the rich play with men
who are bitten by the demon of hope.

This wry sentiment suggests the painful side of hope that puts the poor man at the mercy of those who would play with his dreams. Hope is the demon that lures him into docile obedience yet forever holds back, just out of reach, its objects.

World-weary religious discourses tend to treat *asha* (*āśā*) as the type of hope that gets dashed rather than the hope that keeps us buoyant and optimistic. An ancient observation laments that as we age, our teeth and hair wear out yet our hopes for life and wealth do not wane. Hope is a "lifelong disease" and only those who can give it up altogether find happiness (*sukha*).

From at least the time of the Upanishads, hopes have been paired with "expectations" which seem to lie on a firmer foundation. For Shankara, *asha* is the craving for an object that may be attainable but is not definite, while expectations are attainable and definite. In a different distinction, Vedanta Deshika distinguishes between hope, which aims at an end, and worry (*cinta*), which concerns the means to acquire it. Perhaps precisely because hope doesn't trouble itself with exactly how its objects can be realized, it is so often crushed.

See also **cinta**

REFERENCES

"Come here!" . . . Ānandavardhana quotes this verse from *Hitopadeśa* 2.45 as an example of a certain literary figure, and it gets widely quoted in the literature (DL: 492–493 and n. 2).

An ancient observation . . . Vāsiṣṭha's *Dharmasūtra* 30.9–10; see P. Olivelle, trans., *Dharmasūtras: The Law Codes of Ancient India*, Oxford: Oxford University Press, 1999: 326.

The Upanishads . . . *Shankara* . . . *Kaṭha Upaniṣad* 1.8, EU: 374–375; see Śaṅkara's *Gītābhāṣya* on 16.12 in BGC: 421; and Ānandagiri's subcommentary as cited in IP: 120 n. 77, 78.

Vedanta Deshika distinguishes . . . As cited in IP: 120 n. 77.

ashru

Tears (Sanskrit)

Tears (*aśru*) are, so often, sadness itself. We see this in the three poems that follow. The first, a Sanskrit poem of love-in-separation, evokes the desolation of a traveler who finds himself still abroad when the monsoon season arrives. In the classical tradition, the monsoon season signals a time for couples to be reunited because travelers return home to wait out the rainy months when travel becomes impossible.

Night
turbulent overhead clouds
and a ripple of thunder.
The traveler
stung with tears
sings of a faraway girl.
Oh traveling
is a kind of death,
the village people hear it,
lower their heads
and suddenly quit their
proud tales
of adventure.

Hearing the tears in his voice as the traveler sings of his beloved, the village people stop romanticizing their traveling adventures. In a beautiful way, the gathering monsoon rains, invoked here not to celebrate the reunion of lovers but to lament their separation, presage the tears of our traveler.

Our second poem comes from the *Treasury of Well-Turned Verse* of Vidyakara, whose tender evocations of the misery of poverty demonstrate the aesthetic theorists' insistence that even the saddest of plights when rendered poetically can be savored in the aesthetic feeling called *rasa*.

> "Come, little one, weep not so long to see the other boys
> in their fine dress. Your father too will come,
> bringing a jeweled necklace and a suit of clothes."
> Close by the wall a penniless traveler stood
> and heard the mother's words. Sighing and with tears
> upon his lowered face he left his land again.

The impact of this vignette strikes when one realizes that the penniless traveler is in fact the father expected home with riches from his dealings abroad. This impact or "suggestion," (*dhvani*) is achieved by the power of the poem to suggest what is unsaid without saying it directly. Suggestion is the means that delivers the *rasa* or taste of aesthetic relish, as theorized by the ninth-century Kashmiri critic Anandavardhana. Part of how this poem does this is to mirror the tears of the little one and his father, where the father's tears, unseen by anyone but us, put lie to the mother's soothing words.

A final submission suggests that tears are helpful for releasing pent-up sorrow (*karuna*). The epic hero Rama has returned to the place where he had abandoned his innocent and beloved wife Sita many years before in the forest. He is overcome with tears, sobbing copiously as he ponders his pregnant wife alone and frightened. And he has no one to blame but himself for his grief. A river spirit observing Rama suggests that "those who are sorrowful must try to expel their sorrow, for

> When a flood puts pressure on a dam
> one counteracts it by releasing water
> and it is weeping that helps the heart
> hold out when it's overcome by grief."

In the hydraulics of emotion, tears allow some of the grief to discharge, stabilizing the heart that is otherwise bursting. Alas, only a few pages later we learn from Rama himself that the dam is so overrun by sorrow that he could not contain the tears if he tried.

See also **karuna; rasa; sattvikabhava; vipralambha**

REFERENCES

"Night" . . . From the *Amaruśataka*. BAM: 11.

"Come, little one" . . . *Subhāṣitaratnakośa* 1314. Trans. D. Ingalls, *An Anthology of Sanksrit Court Poetry*, Cambridge, MA: Harvard University Press, 1965: 360–361.

Suggestion is the means . . . See D. Ingalls's introduction to DL: 19.

"those who are sorrowful" . . . *Rāma's Last Act by Bhavabhūti*. RLA: 206–207.

only a few pages later . . . RLA: 210–211.

asuya

Indignation; Envy (Sanskrit)

Hoary authorities on the moral law referred to as Dharma Shastra proscribe *asuya* (*asūyā*) an indignation that is often a spiteful grumbling at others' virtues, success, or good fortune. The sage Vasistha commands that getting rid of *asuya* is incumbent on people of all social orders, and, together with practicing generosity, is conducive to a long life. Unlike Aristotle's indignation (*nemesis*), *asuya* is not limited to resentment at others' *undeserved* good fortune; the Indian texts do not bundle an appraisal of "just deserts" into the rivalrous emotions. *Asuya* can be felt regardless of whether or not one's rivals deserve their prosperity, and is discreditable either way.

In its most odious forms, *asuya* is the spiteful envy that is particularly problematic when giving gifts, and those who can master their resentment toward their recipients may win heavenly reward and even release from the cycle of rebirth. When giving gifts, one should not look too closely for faults in the recipient but instead give with a generosity not only of hand but of spirit.

There are shades and varieties of *asuya*, however, and the great poet Kalidasa knows them all. On the gentler end of the spectrum, a twinge of *asuya* shows up on the face of a young woman toward her companion in the following vignette. The scenario is that her companion is leading this young woman through a long line of potential suitors from whom she will choose her husband, and they have at last reached the candidate she truly loves. But her friend, though knowing this, does not let her linger, and rather cruelly moves her along to the next hopeful.

> The companion smiled, cane in hand.
> She could see what was going on inside
> her friend. So she said, "Dear Lady,
> let's move on to someone
> else." The bride threw her a look
> crooked with *asuya*.

"Crooked with indignation," as David Shulman translates this, compresses in one flash on the prospective bride's face a host of emotions at this moment: "indignation, anger, impatience, even perhaps a twinge of envy (for this princess is about to undergo a radical change in her life, and she may have some residual longing for the innocence of childhood that she must soon relinquish)." Kalidasa, with the luminous empathy, inspiration, intuition, and imagination that are the priceless tools of an inspired poet, Shulman argues, spots the truth of the conflicted turmoil in this young woman's mind at this moment, and lets us see it too.

See also **akkhanti/akshanti; amarsha; irshya; vyabhicaribhava**

REFERENCES

incumbent on people . . . "Abjuring slander, envy, pride, egoism, lack of faith, dishonesty, self-praise, reproaching others, hypocrisy, greed, delusion, anger, and *asūyā* is regarded as the Dharma for all stages of life." *Dharmasūtra* of Vasiṣṭha 10.30. My translation, but see also P. Olivelle, *Dharmasūtras: The Law Codes of Ancient India*, Oxford: Oxford University Press, 1999: 274. See also 6.8, 29.21 on the benefits of being "free of *asūyā*."

*Aristotle's indignation (*nemesis*)* . . . *Rhetoric* II.9.

look too closely for faults . . . *Asūyā* means that "one uncovers faults where there is virtue," *Dānasāgara* of Ballālasena, p. 30, as quoted in M. Heim, *Theories of the Gift in South Asia*, New York: Routledge, 2004: 47–48.

"The companion smiled" . . . *Raghuvaṃśa* 6.82. This verse and Shulman's insightful discussion of the way it illustrates Kalidasa's *pratibhā*, inspiration, is in *More than Real*, Cambridge, MA: Harvard University Press, 2012: 84–85.

atihasa

Too Much Laughter or Hilarity without Reason (Sanskrit)

King Brahmadatta is given a boon to be able to hear and interpret the language of all creatures. One day, he overhears an ant flattering his wife—among her many charms, she is narrow-waisted and broad in both bosom and hip, it seems. The ant's wife scoffs at this and says that just yesterday he had flattered another in exactly the same terms ("you say that to all the girls!"). The ant hastens to assure her that she is mistaken, and he coaxes her to yield to his flatteries.

Listening in, the king explodes in laughter at this exchange, incurring the umbrage of his own queen sitting with him in their pleasure garden. How he can burst out laughing at nothing? Laughter cannot spring from no reason at all. Surely, he must be laughing at her? Disgraced, she threatens suicide. His pleas that he overheard an ant couple talking are dismissed, for only gods have such powers. Brahmadatta's only way of mollifying his queen is to take up penance and put into practice wise teachings of renunciation. These lead to his abdication of the throne and eventual liberation, a situation that was hardly bargained for by his distressed queen, who is no more impressed by liberation than by inexplicable merriment.

See also **hasa; hasya**

REFERENCE

King Brahmadatta is given a boon . . . Matsya Purāṇa chs. 20–21. *Atihāsa* is mentioned in 21.20. Trans. B. D. Basu, *The Matsya Purana*, Allahabad: Indian Press, 1916: 65–68.

atimana

The Contempt of Vainglory (Pali and Sanskrit)

Intoxicated by my complexion,
by my figure, my beauty, and my fame,
puffed up by my youth,
I despised other women.

In these words, a former courtesan recalls the dual aspects of her own vanity: she was drunk with her own beauty and she despised other women. *Atimana* (*atimāna*) is the excessive self-regard that simultaneously looks down on others with contempt, a distortion of vision of both self and other. One is so puffed *up* with vanity that there is nowhere to look but *down*.

Vainglory pops up on various lists of conceit. Shankara sees it as "an exorbitant pride." The prefix *ati* added to *mana* makes it an arrogance that goes beyond any ordinary sense of self-worth. Buddhist lists catalogue *atimana* as a pride among pride, defined as "the swelling up of the mind in which you think of someone who is superior to you, 'I am better than her.'" It is a false sense of self, but also the putting down of others' qualities.

See also **darpa; garva; mada; mana**

REFERENCES

"Intoxicated"... *Therigāthā* 73. My translation, but see also C. Hallisey, *Therigāthā: Poems of the First Buddhist Women*, Cambridge, MA: MCLI, 2015: 50–51.

"an exorbitant pride"... Śaṅkara's *Gītābhāṣya* XVI.3. My translation, but see also BGC: 416–417.

"the swelling up of the mind"... BP: 90 n. 314. This is *mānātimāna*, pride among pride.

audarya

Magnanimity (Sanskrit)

Audarya (*audārya*) is the magnanimity of a generous giver who looks for no recompense or worth in the recipient and is instead simply grateful for the opportunity to give. It is a virtue that is also a feeling as one becomes suffused with the pleasure of wanting to give. If giving is alloyed with any other consideration, such as boasting or self-promotion about one's generosity, it is vitiated and turns to meanness.

Audarya comes to have fascinating theological valence in the medieval Shrivaishnava tradition of South India. One of this tradition's greatest thinkers, Vedanta Deshika, describes it as

> the quality of ignoring the receiver's inferiority or the giver's superiority, giving with pleasure, not expecting any repayment because the recipient is treated as one with a right to share. In addition, generosity means not being satisfied even when one has given on a large

scale. Therefore, the generous giver, like Lord Krishna, says that all petitioners are themselves "generous."

In this conception, God gives so magnanimously that he regards his beneficiaries as generous to accept from him.

This theology was initiated by the founder of Shrivaishnavism, Ramanuja, who celebrates the mutual generosity and gratitude between God and his devotees. God's magnanimity extends to being grateful for his devotees' humble offerings. Ramanuja's verses describe God's perspective on this relationship: "Even though I am Lord of all and my desires are ever fulfilled . . . I consume such an offering as if I had received something unimaginably dear."

See also **asuya; bhakti; kritajna/katannu**

REFERENCES

If giving is alloyed . . . *Vikramacarita* 6.9–10. FA: 604–605. This text is a careful study of *audarya*, with many case studies of it.

"the quality of ignoring" . . . Vedānta Deśika's *Gadyabhāṣya* on *Bhagavad Gītā* 7.18. Trans. J. Carmen, *The Theology of Rāmānuja*, New Haven, CT: Yale University Press, 1974: 193. See also V. Narayanan's "Reciprocal Gratitude: Divine and Human Acts of Thanksgiving," in *Spoken and Unspoken Thanks: Some Comparative Soundings*, ed. J. Carmen and F. Streng, Cambridge, MA: Harvard University, Center for the Study of World Religions, 1989: 23–31.

"Even though I am Lord of all" . . . Rāmānuja's *Gītābhāṣya* on 9.26. Carmen 1974: 193.

autsukya

Impatient Yearning (Sanskrit)

One could fill a separate *Treasury* with words for love and longing (see *anuraga* to get started). In a romantic tradition that carefully studies the anguish of lovers pining for their distant sweethearts, *autsukya* is a species of impatient yearning, closely related to longing (*abhilasha*). But where *abhilasha* is often love-at-first-sight, *autsukya* is the anguish of lovers who have been together and then cruelly sundered. It is marked by an impatience with the slowness of time until they meet again.

In the technical *rasa* literature, *autsukya* is a transitory emotion enhancing the *rasa* of love-in-separation (*vipralambha*). One gazes into the garden (the site of long-ago trysts) and sighs deep sighs; there is the lowering the face, droopiness, and a need to lie down. On this account, *autsukya* is a lethargic and resigned form of missing, but it can also manifest in dry mouth and anxiety. There is pallor and wasting away: bangles grow large on the limbs of such forelorn lovers as they grow thin with longing, and even soft moonbeams can pierce their delicate frames.

See also **abhilasha/ahilasa; anuraga; madana; udvega; vipralambha; vihara**

REFERENCES

gazes into the garden . . . See *Nāṭyaśāstra* 7.69–70 on *autsukya* as one of the transitory emotions.

a dry mouth . . . according to Rūpa Goswāmī, BR: 316–317.

avajna

Contempt (Sanskrit)

The dreadful and arrogant *rakshasa* known as Ravana becomes powerful by his fierce austerities, and he is granted a boon in which he will become invulnerable to *gandharvas*, *yakshas*, gods, *dainavas*, and *rakshasas* (in other words, all gods, demons, and supernatural beings). In his contempt—*avajna* (*avajñā*)—he disdains to mention humans, regarding them as too lowly even to consider. Of course, this contempt becomes his fatal weakness, for now it is only a human who can kill him. And the great *Ramayana* becomes this very story of Lord Vishnu descending to earth as Rama, a man, for the express purpose of saving the cosmos from the monster Ravana.

Two obvious lessons may be drawn from Ravana's boon: don't underestimate humans (or monkeys, as it turns out), and contempt goeth before a fall. These lessons are repeated throughout the epic traditions. As far as *avajna* goes, it may not be too far off the mark to suggest that contempt, and its close relations, anger, envy, and pride, drive the wars in the epics. These are stories of men competing for honor, recognition, and fame in high-stakes war games, and tracking the emotions involved reveals them to be the main drivers of these narratives.

Amara's *Treasury* lists a long string of synonyms: "contemptuous neglect, humiliation, disgrace, reviling, irreverence, despising, contempt, disrespect, and scorn." *Avajna* (and the related term, *avajnana*) and *avamana* occur most often, and both terms involve knowing and thinking of others in a way that involves looking down (*ava*) at them. For persons of higher stature (at least in their own estimation, but also in ways always indexed to social rank), to be looked down upon is simply intolerable, and the humiliation it brings must be avenged.

See also **amarsha; atimana; avamana; darpa; garva**

REFERENCES

he will become invulnerable . . . Rāmāyaṇa I.14.13–14.

Amara's Treasury *. . . Amarakośa* 1.7.453–454: *anādara, paribhava, parībhāva, tiraskriyā, rīḍha, avamānan, āvajñā, avahelana, asūrkṣaṇa.*

avamana

Disrespect; Insult (Sanskrit)

In practice, there is little difference between *avajna* and *avamana* (*avamāna*). Both are the contempt, derision, dishonor, and disrespect that cultures obsessed with status traffic in. (And which cultures are not obsessed with status?)

The *Ramayana* takes a very complicated turn when the hero Rama has vanquished Ravana and recovered his wife, Sita. Pervading the epic so far has been the love between Rama and Sita, and we have witnessed Rama's extreme love for her many times over. But when she is brought before him, something has changed in him: he feels a combination of "elation, desperation, and rage." He is now compelled by concerns of Dharma (righteousness), and he worries that it may not be seemly to take back his wife after she has been in another man's house, though he knows full well that she has been chaste and loyal to him. And so, in a scene excruciating for all who witness it, Rama repudiates Sita. He does so in terms of *avamana*.

The purpose of the war, he explains, was to wipe away the *avamana* that he had endured by having his wife stolen. It was about proving his manly valor and honor. It was not a matter of affection for his wife, but of "wiping out with his own fiery energy the *avamana* he had received." It was not for her sake, he insists, but for the sake of his reputation that he raised an army and fought so valiantly.

Needless to say, this devastates Sita and all present. She enters fire in an ordeal to prove her innocence, and only then does Rama take her back (at least for a while). When his reputation is later challenged again as malicious tongues wag about Sita, he repudiates her yet again, separating them forever.

Whatever we might make of this shift in Rama—and the Indian tradition has spent two millennia debating it—the focus on contempt and disrespect makes a certain narrative sense. If it was Ravana's contempt that started the whole thing (see *avajna*), here that contempt is wiped clean.

See also **avajna; mana**

REFERENCE

something has changed in him . . . *Rāmāyaṇa* VI.103. His "elation, desperation, and rage" (*harṣa, dainya, roṣa*) is at VI.102.16.

avega

Panic; Shock (Sanskrit)

When the wives of the enemy soldiers caught a glimpse of Rama's army advancing, their hands plucked their clothes and clutched their handmaids, their eyes darted to the faces of their husbands, and their feet itched to run away. This is *avega* (*āvega*), shock and panic. It occurs at the sudden arrival, as here, of invading forces. Natural calamities bring it about—high winds and rain; so do stampeding elephants, wildfires, and evil portents, such as meteor showers and eclipses. *Avega* is the movement of panic, not the paralysis sometimes induced by shock.

One can experience shock from good news too, and so *avega* is not just panic. When shocking but welcome news arrives, expect to see people spring up, hug one another, give fine presents, weep tears of joy, and horripilate.

See also **bhaya; samvega; trasa; udvega**

REFERENCES

wives of the enemy soldiers . . . *Rasataraṅgiṇī* 5.40–41. BRRR: 218–221.

Natural calamities . . . The rest of this entry is taken from *Nāṭyaśāstra* 7.63. *Āvega* is a transitory emotion (see *vyabhicaribhava*).

B

bahumana

Respect (Sanskrit)

Bahumana (*bahumāna*) is the esteem and high regard that makes human relationships go smoothly. It greases the wheels of the complex machinations of the court. Normally, we'd all like to be objects of *bahumana*. But we might reconsider when we view the dynamics of courtly romances. When the king emphasizes his *bahumana* for his queen, it can only be that she has been supplanted by a newer and younger woman in his erotic affections. These stories require the queen, the first consort, to be properly appeased when a new wife is brought into the household and this appeasement takes the form of ritual acts of respect. As one observer of the court puts it dryly: "Civilized men who are in love with some other woman are always extremely polite to their wives."

See also **irshya; manoratha**

REFERENCE

"civilized men" . . . *Vikramorvaśīya* 3.115. See V. Narayana Rao and D. Shulman, trans., *How Urvashi Was Won*, New York: CSL: 106–107; Urvaśī has just naïvely remarked on the king's *bahumāna* for the queen, and her friend points out what this politeness signifies. At 2.213, the king says that though he is in love with Urvaśī, he still "has a lot of *bahumāna* for the queen" (pp. 76–77).

bhakti

Devotional Love (Sanskrit)

Bhakti is a religious movement—involving institutions, communities, practices, theological reflection, literary work, and shifts of value—that swept across nearly all sectarian contexts in early medieval India. It flourishes to this day as the dominant form of religiosity in Hinduism. Here, I introduce only its affective dimensions as they are lavishly evoked and described in the literature. The term *bhakti* means "sharing," and is most often translated as "devotion." It is devotional love on both sides between God and humans, where feelings of many varieties of human love (such as love between parents and children, that between friends, and even erotic love) become sacralized.

Bhakti first comes to the fore in a systematic way in the *Bhagavad Gita*, in Lord Krishna's divine counsel to the tormented Arjuna as he faces the crisis of a war that will bring horrific destruction to his family on both sides of the battlefield. Among the *Gita*'s many messages in its capacious religious vision, the path of *bhakti*, adoration to God, emerges as the most prominent. This involves love for and with a personal god, Krishna, open to all who embrace him with their whole selves. Krishna tells Arjuna:

> Devoted to me,
> Keep your mind intent on me,
> Give honor to me,
> And sacrifice to me.
> In this way, you will
> Truly go to me,
> I promise,
> For you are my beloved.

All other religious practices and ideas—renunciation, yoga, sacrifice, learning, duty—can be cast as loving service to God, and in turn meet with God's infinite grace and love.

Commentators Shankara and Ramanuja developed these ideas and feelings into systematic theologies. Shankara sees *bhakti* as a kind of highest knowledge, a "gnostic discipline," that involves "a mystical search for oneness": God "gives the discipline of knowledge," whereby one comes to know the Supreme Self as one's own self. For Ramanuja, *bhakti* involves knowing the highest and very dear truth about God—"an extremely lucid perception," which is at the same time an intense feeling of love. This love (*priti*) is happy (*sukha*), blissful (*ananda*), and so intense that the devotee "cannot bear a moment's separation" from God.

Bhakti celebrates human emotion in all of its varieties as long as that emotion gets subsumed and developed in relationship to God. Rupa Goswami, a sixteenth-century figure in the Gaudiya Vaishnava circle of Krishna devotion, describes the Krishna devotee as "drenched with tears of joy, the hairs adorning his body stand on end, he is stumbling in ecstasy, his heart has blossomed wide open, and trembling with intense emotion." The scene for the archetypal love celebrated among these devotees is centered in the gorgeous forests of Vrindavan along the sapphire blue Yamuna river, where Krishna danced, sang, and played with rustic cowherd women. These women represent the ideal devotee, ready to drop everything—husbands, children, modesty, duty—to join Krishna's divine play in the forest at the sound of his flute. Their supreme love of God is the highest religious value: "a thrilled soul who dances with emotions caused by great *bhakti* burns up the misfortunes of hundreds of eons." Rupa Goswami quite brilliantly combines *rasa* theory with *bhakti* by sacralizing the emotions and aesthetic experiences decribed by Bharata—all true *bhava* and *rasa* can be understood as nuances in feeling love for Krishna.

In South Indian *bhakti*, we sometimes encounter an acute awareness of human frailty and dependence felt by the devotee in the face of God's infinite grace and compassion (see *daya*). Certain traditions encourage human agency and capacity in the relationship with God, while others see little possibility for these on the human side of the relation. Theologians came to contrast "monkey religion" and "kitten religion"—baby monkeys have to hold on to their mothers, while kittens get carried around limply by the scruff of their necks. Kitten *bhakti* often invites total surrender to the infinite mercy of the divine.

A sensibility of awe at God's compassion that strikes simultaneously with one's own incapacity infuses the poetry of these traditions, as we see in this evocation by another sixteenth-century figure, Appayya Dikshita (though in contrast to Rupa Goswami, Appayya was a Shiva devotee):

> Is there anyone who could fathom
> your depth, god of gods?
> All of creation, with all its colors
> and shades, comes from there.
> That being said, they also say
> that you can be grasped
> through love (*bhakti*). So through love
> and love only, I want to sing
> of you. You'll just have to put up with
> my monumental folly.

Leave the paths of knowledge, ritual, and moral duty to others, sings the devotee, for the special feeling of *bhakti* is for him the way to God.

See also **ananda; daya; prema; priti; vatsalya**

REFERENCES

"Devoted to me" . . . *Bhagavad Gītā* 18.65. Trans. L. Patton, London: Penguin Books, 2008: 201–202.

"gnostic discipline" . . . *"mystical search for oneness"* . . . C. Ram-Prasad, *Divine Self, Human Self*, London: Bloomsbury, 2013: 112.

"gives the discipline of knowledge" . . . *Bhagavad Gītā* X.10 and Śankara's commentary on it, BGC: 264.

For Ramanuja . . . Rāmānuja's *Vedārthasaṃgraha* §141–143. Trans. J.A.B. van Buitenen, Poona: Deccan College, 1956: 296–298; also *Śrī Rāmānuja Gītā Bhāṣya* as trans. in C. Ram-Prasad 2013: 65 and 125 n. 79.

"drenched with tears of joy" . . . Rūpa Gosvāmin, BR: 70–71.

"a thrilled soul who dances" . . . BR: 46–47.

"Is there anyone who could fathom" . . . Appayya Dīkṣita's "Self-Surrender" (*Ātmārpaṇastuti*). SPCM: 152–153; see also xx, xlviii–lvi.

bhava

Way of Being (Sanskrit)

While *bhava* (*bhāva*) is used across textual traditions often in a very general way much as we might use "emotion," here we consider its use in aesthetics, as it is a crucial idea in *rasa* theory and gets its most sustained treatment within it. Our definition—"way of being"—is of course far too imprecise, but it does the work of pointing out that *bhava* encompasses a good deal more than emotion, even when emotion is broadly defined (*bhavas* can include such conditions as fatigue, dreaming, and dying, for example). At the same time, discussion of *bhava* here is more limited than emotion, because aesthetic theory, at least in the earliest articulations of it, concerns artistic contexts and does not attempt to describe emotions per se. The ancient sage Bharata who first attempted to lay out *rasa* theory focused on emotions that prompt artistic expression and are produced in the theater.

Bharata defines *bhava* according to its verbal root, which is to "bring into being." The arts of the stage produce emotions by the characters, plot, registers of acting and so on, bringing into being "the poet's inner emotion." We might add that this idea is in keeping with how poetic expression was thought to first emerge in human history: a sage felt something terribly sad and spontaneously erupted into verse, his inner state *bringing into being* an expression pervaded with the feeling in form and content (see *shoka*).

Bharata then lists forty-nine specific *bhavas*, defining each according to its phenomenological qualities, how it is to be generated by aesthetic factors, the ways it is to be represented on the stage, and the kinds of situations that cause it to arise. Crucial to the theory is Bharata's division of the forty-nine *bhavas* into three types: "stable emotions" (see *sthayibhava*), "transitory emotions" (*vyabhicaribhava*), and "psychophysical responses" (*sattvikabhava*). The first of these are more basic and enduring, and, when combined skillfully with the other two types in a successful performance, produce the savor of them (see *rasa*). And because *rasa,* the aesthetic pleasure of savoring emotions, is the whole point of theater (and for later theorists, of literary art), Bharata defines *bhava* as what "brings into being the *rasas.*"

Subsequent thinkers did further work to understand exactly what *bhavas* are and how they are related to *rasas.* Abhinavagupta provides a definition of *bhava* much like how we might define emotion: "an experience pertaining to oneself and consisting of an awareness of pleasure and pain." He seems to be thinking about *bhavas* not only in aesthetic terms, but also in everyday life (see *sthayibhava*). The early modern figure Bhanudatta offers a definition of *bhava* as a "transformation that is conducive to rasa." *Bhava* is a change of state. He then adds that this transformation may be of two kinds: "internal" and "bodily," with the latter being an "involuntary physical reaction." These definitions have similar correlates with modern discussions in English about what is meant by "emotion."

See also **rasa; sattvikabhava; shoka; sthayibhava; vyabhicaribhava**

REFERENCES

which is to "bring into being" . . . *Nāṭyaśāstra* 7.1–3. RR: 54.
"brings into being the rasas" . . . *Nāṭyśāstra* 6.34. RR: 51.
"an experience pertaining" . . . *Abhinavabhāratī* 3.273. RR: xvi.
"transformation that is conducive to rasa" . . . *Rasataraṅgiṇī* 1.6–7; BRRR: 132–133.

bhaya

Fear (Sanskrit and Pali)

To deal with fear, we will look first at its phenomenology and then at powerful religious claims about its eradication. Last, we'll invoke a prayer to ward it off.

First, the *feeling* of fear: Rama, that brave and composed hero, is stricken with *bhaya* when he has chased a golden deer deep into the forest, only to find that he has been the victim of a ruse by a *rakshasa*, and that Sita has been left alone and may be in trouble. As the realization sinks in, "the hair on his body bristled with dread" and "consternation gave way to a feeling of *bhaya* that shot through him with sharp pangs." He can't get back to the ashram quickly enough, and he rushes back, tripping over roots, panicking. For her part, Sita has indeed been kidnapped, and she screams out for her husband as she is carried away. She had always been a woman with defiance and "a bright flashing smile." But as she is being dragged away by Ravana, "her face is drained of color under a crushing weight of *bhaya*."

Bhaya is the gamut of fear, from a sinking pit of dread to abject terror.

A central promise of Indian therapies of emotions held out that fear could be completely eradicated. A Buddhist practice can serve as our example. The Buddha insisted that all beings fear death, even those in the worst hells. (In India, hells are not eternal and one is reborn from them once one's evil karma is burned off.) But why would beings in hell fear death if death is a deliverance from their suffering? The answer is that fear of death and the means that usually take us there—violence and illness—is so deeply ingrained in human nature that we will always shrink from it. The only exception is the awakened person: by attaining nirvana, one becomes utterly free from fear. These thoughts suggest simultaneously the primal nature of fear, and the extraordinary ambition that is the religious goal. Fear can actually be completely eradicated.

Buddhist therapies of fear offer the renouncer a rigorous set of practices that gradually remove it. One must be a celibate renouncer for this, since the kinds of entanglements between Rama and Sita, for example, will always necessitate fear of loss. In a teaching titled "Fear and Dread," the Buddha is asked how a monk can cope with the fear and dread he will encounter as he sets off alone into the forest to meditate. He may find himself in the grip of fear, menaced by wild animals, evil spirits, or loneliness, all of which can rob him of his concentration.

The regime to deal with this fear involves purifying one's physical, verbal, and mental practices. By moral practice and thought, one can have a clear and focused mind poised to cope with whatever may come. And by not intending harm to others, one will likely avoid others' harm. Should one get startled by a rustle from the wind or if a peacock snaps a branch, one is to ask oneself: "Why do I always expect fear and dread? Why not stop right here and subdue the fear and dread before going further?" When fear comes, it must be noticed and seen to be a creation of the imagination, something we choose to construct. Once identified as such, it can be dismantled, leaving a peacefulness in its wake. Further clarification of one's thoughts and focus will further eradicate all kinds of fear—the startle reflex, the anxiety of dread, the worry of things to come.

These practices, at least in their full extent, may not be likely for many of us. Fortunately, we can invoke an ancient charm against fear, one that conveys its own enduring wisdom.

> As Heaven and Earth are not afraid, and never suffer loss or harm,
> Even so, my spirit, do not be afraid.
> As Day and Night are not afraid, nor ever suffer loss or harm,
> Even so, my spirit, do not be afraid.
> As Sun and Moon are not afraid, nor ever suffer loss or harm,
> Even so, my spirit, do not be afraid.
> As Truth and Falsehood have no fear, nor ever suffer loss or harm,
> Even so, my spirit, do not be afraid.
> As What Has Been and What Shall Be fear not, nor suffer loss or harm,
> Even so, my spirit, do not be afraid.

See also **abhaya; avega; bhayanaka; daruna; samvega; trasa**

REFERENCES

"the hair on his body" . . . *Rāmāyaṇa* III.42.20; 50.44–45. Trans. S. Pollock, *Rāmāyaṇa, Book Three, The Forest*, New York: CSL: 2006: 250–251, 304–305.

all beings fear death... *Milindapañha* 145–150. See I. B. Horner, trans., *Milinda's Questions*, volume I, Bristol: Pali Text Society 2015 (1963): 203–210.

"Fear and Dread" teaching... Bhayabherava Sutta, in the *Majjhima Nikāya* i.16–24. MLD:102–107.

"As Heaven and Earth"... *Atharvaveda* 2.15. Adapted slightly from R.T.H. Griffiths's translation, *The Hymns of the Atharva Veda*, Varanasi: Chowkhamba Sanskrit Series, 1968 (originally published 1895). The word used here for fear is not *bhaya*, but it comes from the same verb from which we get *bhaya*. I have omitted one verse in the original.

bhayanaka

Horror (Sanskrit)

The aesthetic development of fear (*bhaya*) is *bhayanaka* (*bhayānaka*). This is the feeling horror film aficionados enjoy. *Bhayanaka* relishes fright, suspense, panic, and terror. Characters in a play are frightened by hideous noises, ghosts, and battles, and feel suspense when they sneak into an empty house, find themselves alone in a dark forest, or discover that they have offended the king. Watching them, we feel *bhayanaka*. We partake of the characters' fears to an extent, while at the same time enjoying the remove provided by aesthetic distance. Horror's phenomenology involves "agitation of all the senses," an agitation visible when it is performed: hands and feet tremble (though the legs can also inconveniently freeze up and keep one from running away); there are heart palpitations, a parched mouth, and glancing uneasily about.

As a largely scholarly construct to explain this experience, the term *bhayanaka* is not often encountered in ordinary literature—though it is not entirely unknown (we see Lord Vishnu, in his terrible aspect, described as *bhayanaka*, terrifying). But the aesthetic that *bhayanaka* names is very well attested, perhaps nowhere more so than in the apocalyptic scene toward the end of the *Mahabharata*'s war when the warrior Ashvatthaman creeps into the enemy camp in the dark of night and massacres the sleeping enemies. He contrives this unchivalrous plan from seeing an owl swoop down, screeching, onto a banyan tree full of sleeping crows, and in frenzied and gratuitous violence, tear them all to pieces. The owl's butchery is so frightening, so horrific, and so ghastly that Ashwatthaman takes it as a message to do the same to his enemies. And many pages recounting his terrible carnage follow.

See also **avega; bhaya; bibhatsa; rasa; trasa**

REFERENCES

frightened by hideous noises . . . These are the causes of this *rasa* according to *Nāṭyaśāstra* 6.69–72. The descriptions of the performance of *bhayānaka*—hands and feet trembling, and so on—are given here as well. In Bharata's conception, *rasa* occurred in the character; only later did theorists see it as relished by the audience.

"agitation of all the senses" . . . *Rasataraṅgiṇī* 7.31. BRRR: 296–297.

Lord Vishnu . . . *Bhagavad Gītā* 11.27; *Mahābhārata* X.6.6.

Ashvatthaman . . . This scene is in *Mahābhārata* X. The owl omen is 10.1.35–49, trans. K. Crosby, *Mahābhārata, Book Ten, The Dead of Night*, New York: CSL, 2009: 12–15.

bibhatsa

The Macabre (Sanskrit)

It is curious that we can relish the disgusting in the aesthetic savor of *bibhatsa* (*bībhatsā*), the *rasa* of the macabre, not least because the metaphor clashes with the phenomenology. *Rasa*, taste, is what gets relished. But the phenomenology of both disgust and the macabre is recoiling and "spitting out" (see *jeguccha/jugupsa*). How can we relish something we want to spit out?

The aesthetic itself is certainly real: the *Mahabharata,* to reach for the most obvious example, lingers at great length on the aftermath of battles, where grisly and gruesome gore both revolt and fascinate. The text turns broken and rotting bodies, decapitated heads, circling vultures and jackals, disemboweled innards, and bloodsoaked fields into objects of artistic study, and audiences have relished these scenes for two millennia.

The aesthetics of disgust has been debated in Western aesthetics. Aristotle thought that because art can represent something true, even images of cadavers can be viewed with pleasure, since they can expand understanding. Jumping to Immanuel Kant, we find him puzzling over disgust, and ultimately denying it any aesthetic value: "there is only one kind of ugliness that cannot be presented in conformity with nature without obliterating all aesthetic liking and hence artistic beauty: that ugliness which arouses *disgust.*" David Hume agrees: there are things so "bloody and atrocious" (dashed "brains and gore") that they just cannot be softened into pleasure.

As modern philosophers Aurel Kolnai and Carolyn Korsmeyer work it out, the question is not only whether the disgusting is too foul and nauseating to prompt aesthetic experience, but also whether disgust is so visceral and immediate that it resists the mimetic distancing of art. Without such distancing, how could the aesthetic feeling be anything other than the instant recoil that is the experience itself? *How can we relish something we are trying to spit out?*

And there is a further oddity noted by many theorists and certainly implicit in *rasa* theory: the disgusting object seems to press itself on us even as we try to fend it off. Kant noted that in this "strange sensation . . . the object is presented as if it insisted, as it were, on our enjoying it even though that is just what we are forcefully resisting." He wants to blame the object, but surely it is we who are simultaneously attracted to and repelled by disgusting things. Plato supplies an extraordinary anecdote that can serve as evidence of this very phenomenon:

> I once heard a story which I believe, that Leontius, the son of Aglaion, on his way up from the Piraeus under the outer side of the northern wall, becoming aware of dead bodies that lay at the place of public execution at the same time felt a desire to see them and a repugnance and aversion, and that for a time he resisted and veiled his head, but overpowered in despite of all by his desire, with wide staring eyes he rushed up to the corpses and cried, "There, ye wretches, take your fill of the fine spectacle!"

Here is a man at war with his own eyes. But why on earth are we drawn to odious and loathsome sights that repulse us? It is becoming difficult to evade the conclusion that the aesthetic feeling that enjoys disgust draws on a deep convergence of attraction and repulsion so vividly portrayed in the wretched Leontius.

Let us turn back to *rasa* theory, this time through the eyes of twentieth-century philosopher K. C. Bhattacharyya. He is concerned with the aesthetic question of how it is that we can find aesthetic joy in the ugly. The answer lies in what aesthetic feeling is: a deeply involved, yet simultaneously distanced, "depth of the spirit." This trained artistic spirit negotiates ugliness with "the patient faith of courageous love." "There are spirits where joy is too deep to be killed by a repulsive experience and whose artistry is potent enough to evolve a beauty rich and strange out of presented ugliness." For such spirits, there can be an effort toward beauty informed by faith in beauty, and it converges with a love for the essential truth of the world, even in its ugly parts.

See also **bhaya; jeguccha/jugupsa; rasa**

REFERENCES

Nāṭyaśāstra 6.73–74, 7.26.

Aristotle thought that . . . Poetics, 6, trans. G. Else, University of Michigan: Ann Arbor Press, 1970: 20.

Immanuel Kant . . . Critique of Judgment (1790), trans. W. Pluhar, as cited in C. Korsmeyer, *Savoring Disgust*, Oxford: Oxford University Press, 2011: 45.

David Hume . . . "Of Tragedy," *Essays Moral, Political, and Literary (1777)*, ed. E. Miller, Indianapolis: Liberty Fund, 1987: 224.

Aurel Kolnai and Carolyn Korsmeyer . . . Kolnai's *On Disgust*, edited and with an introduction by B. Smith and C. Korsmeyer, Peru, IL: Carus Publishing Company, 2004; and C. Korsmeyer, *Savoring Disgust*.

Plato . . . Republic IV, 439e–440a. Trans. P. Horey, in *The Collected Dialogues of Plato*, ed. E. Hamilton and H. Cairns, Princeton, NJ: Princeton University Press, 1973: 682. Korsmeyer discusses this episode (*Savoring Disgust*, 41–42). Psychologists working on emotion document the same phenomenon: when asked if they want to see something disgusting, most lab subjects offer "a cautious 'yes.'" (J. Haidt, P. Rozin, C. McCauley, and S. Imada, "Body, Psyche, and Culture: The Relationship between Disgust and Morality," *Psychology and Developing Societies* 9, no. 1 [2007]: 123).

K. C. Bhattacharyya . . . "The Concept of Rasa," *Indian Philosophy in English: From Renaissance to Independence*, ed. N. Bhushan and J. Garfield, New York: Oxford University Press, 2011: 195–206. This piece was originally published in 1930.

brahmaviharas

Sublime Attitudes; "Divine Abidings" (Pali and Sanskrit)

In early Indian religion, mystics and contemplatives experimented with altered states of awareness that give access to other dimensions or realms, including those inhabited by the deities. This idea is the background to the meditation states known as the *brahmaviharas* (*brahmavihāras*), "divine abidings," as they developed in the early Buddhist scriptures. Meditation that cultivates certain expansive and happy states of mind allows one to inhabit or live, even if temporarily, the experiences of certain kinds of deities, in this case, the deities in the Brahma heavens. These sublime attitudes, emphasized particularly in the Pali tradition, are four: lovingkindness or friendliness (*metta*), compassion (*karuna*), sympathetic joy (*mudita*), and equanimity (*upekkha*). When the meditator becomes highly developed in these experiences, he or she "abides" in a divine or sublime awareness.

The divine abidings are varieties of love. The first is a loving friendship that through disciplinary cultivation can expand the affection one feels for one's loved ones ultimately to all beings. As lovingkindness expands in quality and scope, the meditator attains "freedom of the loving heart" and is no longer shackled by prejudice and resentment. Compassion is the awareness of others' suffering and the desire to stop it, conceived as a wide and deep expansiveness as well. Sympathetic joy is the capacity to share in others' happiness and good fortune without the ugly constrictions of envy. And equanimity is smoothing out the gullies of partiality and preference to feel for all beings in an impartial way.

While these experiences clearly have moral implications, they are conceived in the early Buddhist tradition as practices to achieve spiritual liberation. They were also called "immeasurables" in that their practice is never complete—one can always expand them further, either through deeper development of habit or by broadening their scope to include ever more beings toward whom one feels such love.

The divine abidings were picked up by other traditions besides Buddhism. In the Yoga system, they are also considered therapies that remove resentment, cruelty, envy, and indifference as one works to create a lucid and calm mind.

According to Patanjali, "calming of awareness arises by cultivating lovingkindness toward those who are happy, compassion for those in pain, sympathetic joy for those who are virtuous, and equanimity for those who are not." As in Buddhism, these practices break down barriers between self and other to universalize these distinctive forms of fellow feeling by removing problematic dispositions. They then become great "strengths."

Not to be outdone, an authoritative Jain text mentions four similar practices, recommending "friendliness toward all living-beings, delight in the distinction and honor of others, compassion for the miserable, lowly creatures, and equanimity toward the vainglorious." And we find mention of the divine abidings in Caraka's medical text, where they are ideal dispositions of the caring physician: "the doctor should have lovingkindness and compassion for the sick, sympathetic joy for those recovering, and equanimity toward those for whom nature is taking its course."

See also **karuna; metta/maitra; mudita; upeksha/upekkha; yoga**

REFERENCES

as they developed in the early Buddhist scriptures . . . See the "Tevijja Sutta" in the *Dīgha Nikāya* (i.250–251) for mention of the *brahmavihāras* (LD: 194–195). They are elaborated most fully in chapter IX of the *Visuddhimagga*, from which I draw here (PP). Chapter 13 of the *Vibhaṅga* is focused on them, where they are referred to as "immeasurables" (*appamaññā*).

"calming of awareness" . . . *Yoga Sūtra* 1.33, my translation, but see also YSU: 38. Commentator Vācaspati Miśra develops this verse to explain how each removes its opposite. At *Yoga Sūtra* 3.23, they are "strengths" or "powers" (*bala*); YSU: 66.

"friendliness toward all living-beings" . . . *Tattvārtha Sūtra of Umāsvāti* 7.6. Trans. N. Tatia, San Francisco: Harper Collins Publishers, 1994: 172. Equanimity here is *mādhyasthya*, staying [balanced] in the middle.

"the doctor should have" . . . *Caraka-Saṃhitā* IX.26; see CS: 190–191.

byapada/vyapada

Malice (Pali/Sanskrit)

Vyapada (*vyāpāda*), Amara's *Treasury* tells us, is "plotting harm"; it is the ill will that schemes to ruin others. If, as the Pali Buddhist sources claim, hatred and anger (*dosa* in Pali and *dvesha* in Sanskrit) lie at the root of so much of our suffering, *byapada* (*byāpāda*) goes one beyond them. *Byapada* is the willful thought of malevolence that issues from hatred and anger. It is the full manifestation of them into a mental action where the dark thought is voiced (at least to oneself) of actually wishing harm to befall one's enemy. I can dislike, even intensely, a certain politician, say, but it only constitutes *byapada* or malice if I actively wish for his destruction. As such, *byapada* is one of the ten bad deeds of Buddhism that must be eradicated if one is to achieve moral and religious progress.

Byapada is considered one of five "fetters" that hold back one's spiritual progress. Even more technically, *byapada* is a particular kind of awareness in the Abhidhamma system that occurs in certain unhealthy and unskillful types of consciousness; it is the result of an "unwise bringing to mind" of something or someone disliked, and so to get rid of it will require changing the focus and quality of one's attention. It is to be countered by joy, because malice is incompatible with joy and the same moment cannot hold both (see *piti*). Meditation instructions urge the development of happy and expansive thoughts to displace *byapada*.

See also **abhijjha; brahmaviharas; dosa; nrishamsa; patigha; piti**

REFERENCES

Amara's Treasury . . . 1.5.324.

ten bad deeds . . . See references for *abhijjha*.

five "fetters" . . . See, for example, *Saṃyutta Nikāya* v. 94, CDB 1591–1592. The five fetters are sensual desire, malice, sloth-and-torpor, flurry and worry, and doubt. See separate entries for *uddhacca*, *kukkucca*, and *kama*.

in the Abhidhamma system . . . It can occur as a *cetasika* in a certain kind of immoral thought associated with distress, as, for example, in *Dhammasaṅgaṇi* 84.

"unwise bringing to mind" . . . *Sammohavinodanī* 271. Trans. Bhikkhu Ñāṇamoli, *The Dispeller of Delusion*, part I, Oxford: Pali Text Society, 1996: 333. "Something disliked" refers to what one is hostile toward (*patigha/pratigha*).

countered by joy . . . *Visuddhimagga* IV.86, PP: 138–139.

C

cakshuraga

Eye-Love (Sanskrit)

Any respectable storehouse of gems includes, as suggested at the outset, rare curios, baubles really, that are no less charming for being infrequent. Such is "eye-love" (*cakṣūrāga*), love or affection at first sight. It appears in *Rama's Last Act* when two young cousins who do not know that they are related meet and feel instinctive admiration and friendship for one another. Bhavabhuti, the playwright of this searing exploration of Rama's abandoning of Sita, is fascinated throughout the play by bonds forged inexplicably, the ways affection occurs without reason, and love that defies all external factors.

When the two cousins—who happen to be the sons of the brothers Rama and Lakshmana—meet, they wonder if their instant affection for one another is the result of chance, or whether it is owing to an "ancient friendship" forged in a previous birth, or if they are, as turns out to be the case, relatives somehow hidden from one another. But before their relationship is revealed, an observer says

> It is a common characteristic of the soul that a given person should feel a natural affection for another given person. Worldly men have a figurative expression for this starry friendship—"eye-love." And therefore it's written that this is something real, however unfounded and inexplicable it may appear to be.

There is no way to counteract
a predilection that has no cause.
There is some thread of affection that knits
living things together deep within.

This lovely idea suggests that bonds of inexorable attraction stitched deep within become evident when eyes first meet.

The passage suggests another idea relevant for our writing about words written about emotions. Bhavabhuti makes his character suggest that because there is a term for this experience, and because it is written about, *it must be something real.* This is a theme he weaves throughout his drama as he inserts into the play observations about how literature makes life intelligible, and thus real. The opening lines of the play pay "reverence to language, a deathless thing, a part of the soul," and then, picking this up, the final lines of the play extol Bhavabhuti himself as a "master of the sacred mystery of language." Words are powerful and eternal, connected to the soul because they conform to truth, or rather, in the hands of great poets, *create* the truth: "In everyday life, a good man's words correspond with facts / But in the case of a primal seer the facts conform with his words." Eye-love is real because the poets have taught us about it.

See also **prema; sneha; vasana**

REFERENCES

"It is a common characteristic of the soul" . . . RLA: 298–299; "affection" is *sneha*. Note that this is Pollock's translation, but I have changed his translation of *tārāmaitrakaṃ cakṣūrāga iti* from "being starry-eyed" or "love at first sight," (which involve interpolations from the commentators) for a more literal translation of "this starry friendship—'eye-love.'" Perhaps the friendship was written in the stars?

"reverence to language" . . . *"master of the sacred mystery"* . . . RLA 2007: 64–65, 388–389. See also Pollock's discussion of this device in his introduction, RLA: 38–39.

"In everyday life" . . . RLA: 76–77.

camatkara

Aesthetic and Spiritual Wonder (Sanskrit)

The word *camatkara* (*camatkāra*) is an onomatopoeia—"making the sound of *chamat*," a smacking of the lips or clicking the tongue in surprise and exhilaration—an experience aptly described as both "earthy and numinous." Its phenomenality is the quick intake of breath impacting the mouth that can occur in either aesthetic or spiritual wonder. It is sometimes also considered gustatory, where it is savoring enjoyment so directly and fully that it cannot meet with interruption or satiation. Such rapture involves "trembling, horripilation, and frissons."

This fillip of wonder comes to be developed into a quite elevated category in both aesthetic and religious contexts by the great Kashmiri polymath, Abhinavagupta: it is the savoring also called *rasa* in aesthetic experience, and it is the savoring of the bliss of mystical insight. In aesthetic literary experience, when a sensitive reader realizes that "something special has suddenly flashed before him," he is struck by this "sudden delight." This wondrous delight is the very aim of poetry, for when a poem succeeds in delivering its impact, the sensitive reader feels *camatkara*, and is fully enraptured.

While Abhinavagupta does not reduce religious experience to aesthetic rapture (or vice versa), he likens one to the other. The *camatkara* experienced in mystical awareness is an intensification involving "cognition, bliss, and wonder," and transcending the momentary rapture induced by beautiful poetry. Here, *camatkara* is the bliss of fulfillment and relish that occurs when the ordinary world falls away and is replaced suddenly "by a new dimension of reality" that marks religious experience. One savors in wonder the fullness of highest reality and one's own participation in it.

Literary theorists in Andhra, David Shulman shows, added to the conversation. Where Abhinavagupta emphasizes an element of previous experience (often the sublimated experiences and memories of the *vasanas*) that makes *camatkara*'s "click of delight" possible, other thinkers focused on the qualities of the poem. The phonic and semantic properties of poetic expression disrupt us and force an impact. A beautiful poem in Telugu both claims and demonstrates this:

> An arrow shot by an archer
> or a poem made by a poet
> should cut through your heart,
> jolting the head.
> If it doesn't, it's no arrow,
> It's no poem.

See also **rasa; samvega; vasana; vismaya**

REFERENCES

an onomatopoeia . . . "earthy and numinous" . . . RR: 333 n. 5.

"trembling, horripilation, and frissons" . . . *Abhinavabhāratī* 273, trans., RR: 195. See also Raniero Gnoli, in *The Aesthetic Experience According to Abhinavagupta*, Varanasi: Chowkhamba Sanskrit Series Office, 1968: 60–61, also xlv–xlvii.

"something special" . . . This is the only reference in Ānandavardhana to this term, but it comes to be substantially developed by his commentator Abhinavagupta. See DL: 721.

"cognition, bliss, and wonder" . . . As analyzed by R. Torella, *The Īśvarapratyabhijñākārikā of Utpaladeva with the Author's Vṛtti* (Serie Orientale Roma LXXI): 118–119 n. 23.

"by a new dimension" . . . As described by R. Gnoli in his introduction to his translation of *Abhinavabhārati*, xlvi.

David Shulman shows . . . This paragraph is indebted to D. Shulman, "Notes on *Camatkāra*," in *Language, Ritual, and Poetics in Ancient India and Iran: Studies in Honor of Shaul Migon*, ed. D. Shulman, Jerusalem: Israel Academy of Sciences and Humanities: 257–284. The *beautiful poem in Telugu* is by Nannĕ Coḍa, translated by Shulman, 273.

canda

Ferocity (Sanskrit)

Candika—the Fierce One—is among the most common epithets for Devi, India's great goddess. Her ferocity and violent impetuosity in battle saves the world from wicked demons. To be sure, ferocity is only one aspect of her nature, as she is also benevolent and compassionate. But it is her ferocious rage that gets celebrated most in the great hymns and legends about her. Devi is famous for having done what no male god could do, singly or collectively, when she slayed Mahisha, the awful buffalo demon, crushing him with her foot and beheading him. When the red of her raging eyes flows outward and settles into the blood streaming from Mahisha's wounds, we see Candika's *canda* (*caṇḍa*). The fury of her terrifying aspect is such that we must wonder why Mahisha didn't immediately give up his life on first catching glimpse of Candika's face, with knitted brows, like Death itself.

See also **kopa; raudra; rosha**

References

red of her raging eyes flows outward . . . Caṇḍīśataka, verse 40. Trans. G. Quackenbos, *The Sanskrit Poems of Mayūra with Bāṇa's Caṇḍīśataka*, New York: Columbia University Press, 1917: 305.

we must wonder why . . . Devī Māhātmya, as translated and discussed by T. Coburn, *Devī-Māhātmya: The Crystallization of the Goddess Tradition*, Delhi: Motilal Banarsidass, 1986: 293; see also 94–98.

capalata

Fickleness; Rashness (Sanskrit)

In erotic contexts, *capalata* (*capalatā*) is the restless inconstancy of lovers that results in great heartache for their beloveds. An onomatopoeia, *capalata* is moving and flitting about. It is the havering between passion and hate that makes people "undiscriminating, harsh, and impetuous." A man's fickleness can lead him to take a second wife, or, turning the table, his *capalata* may help the wife rationalize taking her own lover.

Capalata can also be the reckless rashness of impulsive men, perhaps more a vice or character flaw than a single episode of emotion. Bharata says that it leads men to do harsh things like rebuking others or killing without any forethought. Wise people see this habitual behavior and know that it issues from an irresolute man.

See also **vyabhicaribhava**

REFERENCES

havering between passion and hate . . . That is, *rāga* and *dveṣa* in this quotation by Rūpa Goswāmin, BR: 320–321 (though the translation here is mine). Here, he is defining it in the context of it being one of the transitory *bhāvas* in aesthetic theory.

a man's fickleness . . . Vātsyāyana's *Kāma Sūtra* 4.2.1, 5.4.4. See KS: 98, 116.

Bharata says . . . *Nāṭyaśāstra* 7.59–60.

cinta

Anxiety; Worry (Sanskrit)

Fate is a cruel
and proficient potter,
my friend. Forcibly
spinning the wheel
of anxiety, he lifts misfortune
like a cutting tool. Now
having kneaded my heart

like a lump of clay,
he lays it on his
wheel and gives a spin.
What he intends to produce
I cannot tell.

In this poem, the preeminent female Sanskrit poet Vidya ties anxiety to Fate. Anxiety is the worry we have when we don't know enough, when the future is uncertain, and when Fate, with intentions both opaque and perverse, grips us in his hands.

Cinta (*cintā*) overlaps with *shanka* and both can cover the broad field that is worry. But *cinta* is more of a single-minded brooding and ruminating, at least according to one authority. It is the needless fretting over something that one cannot control.

But *is* worrying needless? Does anxiety have any use? It would seem to be needless if Fate decides all. The *Hitopadesha* says, "What is not to happen will never happen, and what has to happen will not be otherwise. Why don't you use this as an antidote against the poison of *cinta*?" But, on the other hand, if our anxiety prompts us to take care, and if our efforts have some say in what is to become of us, then is it truly needless? The same text cites exactly the same verse in a different context to illustrate a case where a bit of taking care could be life-saving.

See also **kukkucca; shanka**

REFERENCES

"Fate is a cruel" . . . Vidyā, BAM: 30–31.

singleminded brooding . . . According to Bhānudatta in *Rasataraṅgiṇī* 5.24. BRRR: 212–213.

"What is not to happen" . . . *Hitopadeśa*, prologue and 4.31–34. FA: 68–69, 450–451.

D

dainya

Desperation; Humility (Sanskrit)

Dainya is "a condition of wretchedness or extreme misery." While some might define it as gloom—literally, the lack of brightness—this is rejected by Bhanudatta. Gloom comes from perceiving something in one's external sensory sphere, but *dainya* is more fundamental to one's condition. It comes from falling into destitution or losing a loved one, and can be felt in the pinch of hunger or some other bodily affliction. People taken over by *dainya* stop properly cleaning themselves, lose self-respect, and fall into depression.

Dainya can also be the humility and servility that poverty brings, and it is not easy to disentangle the condition from the emotion. Vidyakara's *Treasury of Beautifully Spoken Jewels* gives voice to the plight of the desperate, revealing the resignation and loss of dignity that is *dainya*, here translated as "humility."

> Begone, oh shame. Firm-mindfulness, give over,
> and human self-respect; why mock in vain?
> Humility casts off all virtue
> and accepts a host of faults;
> But what she orders is what I shall do.

See also **ashru; dina; duhkha/dukkha/duha; kripa; nirveda; shoka; vishada**

REFERENCES

"a condition of wretchedness" . . . *Rasataraṅgiṇī* 5.21. BRRR: 210–211. *Dainya* is a transitory emotion. "Gloom" is *anaujjvalya*, lack of brightness (translated by Pollock as "somberness").

"Begone, o shame" . . . *Subhāṣitaratnakośa* 1502. Trans. D. Ingalls, *An Anthology of Sanskrit Court Poetry*, Cambridge, MA: Harvard University Press, 1965: 392. This is from the chapter on *nirveda*.

dambha

Sanctimoniousness (Sanskrit)

Dambha is more of a vice than an emotion, but in certain treatments it has affective qualities that draw our notice. *Dambha* is the hypocrisy of ostentatiously pious persons, and the biting satire of eleventh-century Kshemendra hangs it out to dry. No form of sanctimoniousness in religion is left unscathed: ritualists, ascetics, priests, brahmans, yogis, and moralists are revealed to be villains, cheats, and rogues. Smug in their religious pieties, such persons are driven by greed to become conjurers, deluding others in order to accrue wealth and high opinion. *Dambha* enters peoples' hearts in many guises to distort them, but once recognized as such, its spell is broken. Of his work, Kshemendra says

> My labor is in no way meant for those who are tainted even slightly by the symptoms of the disease that is the conceit of sanctimoniousness.

The satirist means no ill—he has no wish to scold the sanctimonious, but simply to warn others. But wait, perhaps he slyly addresses them after all:

> Someone shamed by laughter will not persist in his wrongs. To help him, I myself have made this effort.

The laughter provoked by the well-meaning satirist may be the ultimate cure to this unfortunate disease.

See also **mada; mana; ussuka**

REFERENCE

eleventh-century Kshemendra . . . Kṣemendra's "Grace of Guile," in *Three Satires: Nīlakaṇṭha, Kṣemendra, and Ballaṭa*, trans. S. Vasudeva, New York: CSL, 2005: 92–129, especially 126–127. Kṣemendra's comments on his work are quoted and discussed in Vasudeva's introduction, 19–20.

darpa

Arrogance and Bravado (Sanskrit)

While *darpa* can be a neutral term for pride, it can also be a manly and arrogant swagger, such as that of the ideal Kshatriya warrior and king. The poet Bhavabhuti shows this as he lets us into the thoughts of Rama as he first meets his son, Kusha, whose real identity is at first unknown to him.

What remarkable manliness in this Kshatriya boy.
His glance shows he doesn't care a straw
for any creature in the universe
he moves with impetuosity
and causes earth itself to bow.
Although still in his youth he bears
a weightiness like a mountain's.
Is this the heroic *rasa* approaching
Or is it Pride incarnate?

It is both; Kusha's brother tells this courageous and virile young man to swallow his *darpa* and be polite in front of Rama.

Arrogance can get one into trouble because it tends toward disrespect for elders and dereliction of duty. The ancient

Dharma Shastra authority Apastamba warns: "when a man is elated, he becomes proud; when he is proud, he violates the Law; and when the Law is violated, of course, he goes to hell once again." A student should instead honor those in a higher station than he. Shankara, citing this authority, notes the state of exultation in *darpa*, and says that a brahman student must abandon it and other forms of egoism. There is a feeling of excitement or elation—*hrista*, related to the word *harsha*—driving *darpa* that leads to this inflated sense of self.

See also **atimana; garva; harsha; mada; mana; vira**

REFERENCES

The poet Bhavabhuti . . . RLA: 338–339 (VI.74–76). The "heroic *rasa*" is *vīra*. This is a good example of Bhavabhūti's "deliberate intermingling of aesthetic theory with emotional description," the use of the language of artistic representation of emotions to talk about real or lived emotions, as beautifully described by G. Tubb. ("The Plays of Bhavabhūti," *Innovations and Turning Points: Toward a History of Kāvya Literature*, ed. Y. Bronner, D. Shulman, and G. Tubb, New Delhi: Oxford University Press, 2014: 412–413).

Apastamba warns . . . Āpastamba's *Dharmasūtra* I.13.4, trans. P. Olivelle, *Dharmasūtras: The Law Codes of Ancient India*, Oxford: Oxford University Press, 1999: 23.

Shankara . . . Śankara's commentary on the *Bhagavad Gītā* XVIII.53, BGC: 490–491. See also his definition of *darpa* as causing one to transgress Dharma (on XVI.18, BGC: 423).

daruna

Dreadful (Sanskrit)

We normally think of emotions as something inside us. But words, omens, threats, and situations can also be saturated with them. Such is the case with *daruna* (*dāruṇa*) Consider the circumstances surrounding Sita's abduction in the forest by the monster Ravana. Ravana set up a scheme where his confederate lured Rama away hunting what he thought was a magical deer. When Rama kills the deer, it turns back into a *rakshasa* and calls out, in Rama's voice, to his brother Lakshmana to save him—a "dreadful" cry. Meanwhile, Lakshmana was supposed to stay and protect Sita, but Sita became so frightened for Rama's safety that she spoke harsh and "dreadful" words to him to make him go help Rama. Lakshmana was so angered and hurt by these words that he left her side to rush to Rama. And far from the ashram, Rama begins to realize what has happened as he hears a jackal's cry—a "dreadful" omen. He is nearly undone by fear and madness as he hastens back to her.

And Sita is in trouble. All of these dreadful words and happenings culminate in her ghastly kidnapping by the vile Ravana.

See also **bhaya; preyas; vaira**

REFERENCE

circumstances surrounding Sita's abduction . . . Rāmāyaṇa III.55.2, 57.14, 57.25. Trans. S. Pollock, *Rāmāyaṇa, Book Three, The Forest,* New York: CSL: 2006: 328–329, 338–339. Rāvaṇa too notes that his enmity with Rāma is *dāruṇa* (see *vaira*).

daya

Mercy; Compassion (Sanskrit/Prakrit)

Daya (*dayā*) occurs in an asymmetrical relation of the powerful conferring mercy on the powerless or unworthy. When bestowed on the unworthy, it entails an awareness of culpability and clemency simultaneously. Religious poets praise the *daya* of God who bestows mercy on even the worthless. The feminine aspect of God's extraordinary compassion, Lakshmi, is sometimes called Daya, the Goddess of Mercy, to bring out the core theological understanding of Shrivaishnavism: male and female, justice and compassion, are at one in the divine. The feminine aspect, Daya, steadies and restrains God's stern hand of justice.

The Srivaishnava poet Vedanta Deshika, who wrote of his personal intimate love of God in three languages, Sanskrit, Prakrit, and Tamil, is a master at evoking and invoking *daya* (and Daya). He speaks in this Sanskrit verse of his acute sense of worthlessness and concomitant wonder of God's mercy, a forgiveness God offers despite, or perhaps even because of, knowing all.

Finding me—
an ocean of ignorance, chief beast among
the sinners, breaker of all rules
  the emperor of worthless fools—
how can you,
    O Lord of Gods,
who knows all things,
conceive of a better vessel
for your
    mercy.

Steven Hopkins suggests that for Deshika, the idea of the "worthless fool" is a theological principle that suggests that it is precisely the wretched reprobate who has no recourse but total surrender who is most pure in his devotion and most securely saved by God's merciful grace. Deshika expands the same idea in a Prakrit verse:

What is outside the scope of your knowing,
  O Acyuta,
beyond the reach of your mercy,
  what burden too heavy
for your strength?
      Are you not then

the most perfect means
  to our most perfect end,
both the means and the goal?

The extent of human frailty is matched only by the scope of the all-knowing mercy that saves it. All human effort and agency in one's own salvation is surrendered to God whose immeasurable compassion washes away all burdens.

See also **anukampa; karuna**

REFERENCES

sometimes called Daya . . . As beautifully rendered by Vedānta Deśika in the *Dayāśataka*, SPCM: xl–xlvii, 82–149.

"Finding me" . . . Vedānta Deśika's *Devanāyakapañcāśat*. Trans. S. Hopkins, in *An Ornament for Jewels: Love Poems for the Lord of Gods by Vedāntadeśika*, New York: Oxford University Press, 2007: 65.

the "worthless fool" . . . See S. Hopkins, *Singing the Body of God: The Hymns of Vedānta Deśika in the South Indian Tradition*, New York: Oxford University Press, 2002: 213.

"What is outside the scope" . . . Vedānta Deśika's *Acyutaśatakam*. Hopkins 2007: 79. Hopkins notes that *dayā* bears comparison to the Tamil *arul*, which combines grace and mercy, as we see, for example, on pages 42–43 in his volume.

dhairya

Composure (Sanskrit)

When his beloved wife Sita is kidnapped by vile Ravana, Rama almost completely unravels. This stately, righteous, and almost impossibly self-possessed hero remained unruffled at losing his kingship, being sent into exile, and battling hostile adversaries in the forest. But he is flung into inconsolable grief, desolation, and lamentation when he loses Sita, the person whom he loves the most. As he pieces together a plan to find her, he makes an ally of the monkey Sugriva, a heroic figure who has suffered his own misfortunes, not least also losing his wife to another. With delightful irony, this monkey firmly chastises the man-god Rama for his loss of composure (Rama has collapsed on the ground in an unbroken stream of tears as he recounts how he lost Sita).

Sugriva calls Rama to task for losing his *dhairya*: "Remember your own natural composure. Such faintheartedness is unworthy of a man like you. I, too, have met with great misfortune through the abduction of my wife, yet I do not grieve in this fashion, nor do I grieve over her, though I am just an ordinary monkey. How much less should you, who are great, disciplined, and resolute?"

Rama slowly gathers himself up, wipes his tears, and resumes his usual fortitude.

See also **bhaya; daruna; dhriti; utsaha; vilapa**

REFERENCE

"this monkey firmly chastises" . . . *Rāmāyaṇa* IV.6.16, 7.5–8, 8.6. Trans. R. Lefeber, *Rāmāyaṇa, Book Four, Kiṣkindhā*, New York: CSL, 2005: 52–59. This episode also repeatedly mentions the fortitude (*dhriti*) that Rāma needs to reclaim.

dhriti

Fortitude; Contentment (Sanskrit)

In some contexts, *dhriti* (*dhṛti*) is a virtuous approach to life rather than an emotional episode, but it is also one of the thirty-three transitory emotions that can be represented on the stage, particularly in portraying heroism and righteous conduct. Views are mixed about whether this stoic unflappability is "a contentment even in the face of pain," or whether it is "the notion that it is not in fact pain." Is one content (*samtosha*), perhaps even happy, come what may? Or is *dhriti* a lack of emotion, a matter of reconfiguring one's thinking through a sort of cognitive therapy, to be rid of negative emotions, so that one does not feel fear, grief, or depression?

Some say *dhriti* is an "enjoyment" of what one has, and a lack of regret for what one does not have in the first place. One critic finds it exemplified in Lord Shiva. True, "his ornaments are ash, his abode the woods, his mount an aged bull, his cloak a hide." But does he have any less enjoyment for that? Is he not "the Great God," known as the "very God of gods"?

See also **dhairya; samtosha; tushti; yoga**

REFERENCES

"a contentment even in the face" . . . Bhānudatta gives both interpretations, and the example of Shiva is his. (*Rasataraṅgiṇī* 5.31–33; BRRR: 214–217.) "Enjoyment" is *bhoga*.

does not feel fear, grief, or depression . . . *Nāṭyaśāstra* 7.56.

dina

Desolation (Sanskrit)

Dina (*dīna*) is the misery felt by the aged king Dasaratha when an ancient and forgotten promise to his wife Kaikeyi is called in and he is forced to exile his eldest son, Rama. In her cruelty, Kaikeyi makes this demand on the eve of Rama's coronation, and the righteous thing to do, as Dasaratha sees it, is to honor this promise, though it destroys him. In the pathos that follows until Dasaratha dies of grief, he is *dina*, desolate.

Dina means grief, ruin, utter desolation. The *Ramayana* logs many pages of anguish in the wake of Kaikeyi's outrageous demand, drawing heavily on Sanskrit's rich lexicon of pain. Dasaratha, his family, and the entire population feels anguish (*arta*), devastation (*vyatha*), grief (*shoka*), despair (*vishada*), wretchedness (*kripana*), suffering (*duhkha*), lament (*vilapa*), and mourning (*parideva*), to name just some of the torments described. *Dina* gets at the utter disintegration into which Dasaratha falls. This majestic king slumps, desolate, mouth parched, speechless, eyes brimming with tears, "heaving heavy sighs, racked with grief and remorse, all his senses numb with anguish, his mind stunned and confused." Pages later, we will watch this once mighty and heroic king perish of this annihilating desolation.

See also **duhkha/dukkha/duha; kripa; nrishamsa; parideva; shoka; vilapa; vishada; vyatha**

REFERENCE

"racked with grief" . . . *Rāmāyaṇa* II.16.1–7, for this particular episode, where *dīna* is mentioned, but see also, for further representative examples, II.11.13 and II.31.28, trans. S. Pollock, *Rāmāyaṇa, Book Two, Ayodhya*, New York: CSL, 2005: 86–89.

dohada

Morbid Desires, Especially Pregnancy Cravings (Sanskrit and Prakrit)

While technically, *dohada* can be any strong desire, these strange and sometimes morbid obsessions are most often the overwhelming and not-to-be-denied cravings of a pregnant woman. Stories abound with these hankerings. Sometimes, they give expression to the deepest longings of the woman; at other times, they foreshadow the nature of the child in the womb. In some cases, the *dohadas* are quite benign, as they intimate the extraordinary nature of the child to come.

But in every case, it is clear is that the *dohada* must be satisfied: the jurist Yajnavalkya insists that one must satisfy the pregnant woman's craving, else the fetus is imperiled.

Such cravings are psychologically intriguing when they give voice to the woman's deepest desires. In a famous *jataka* story, a pregnant crocodile demands the heart of a monkey else she will die, and her husband must go to great lengths to try to get it and prove his devotion. In other stories, it is not easy to tell how much the perverse craving is the woman's and how much it belongs to her unborn child. In a Jain tale, a queen is overwhelmed with a desire to cut out the heart of her husband and drink his blood. Through a clever stratagem, the king manages this without dying, but they think it wise to abandon the child at birth, and they do so in the usual way of floating him up a river.

The famous story of King Ajatasattu in the Buddhist tales records how even in the womb, he prompted an unremitting desire in his mother to drink blood from the right knee of her husband, the king. The king, being a kindly sort, opens his knee with his sword and catches the blood in a golden dish, and she drinks it. The queen wants to try to end the pregnancy, surmising that this desire is a harbinger of a vicious prince who will someday threaten his father. But the king is too fond of his unborn child and prevents this. In time, the child does grow up to become the most famous patricide in Buddhist tradition.

See also **iccha; udana**

References

jurist Yajnavalkya . . . Yājñavalkya Dharmaśāstra III.79. Trans. P. Olivelle, *A Treatise on Dharma*, Cambridge, MA: Harvard University Press, MCLI, 2019: 236–237. *Dohada* is likely a Prakrit term that got absorbed into the Sanskrit lexicon; here, the text refers to the Sanskrit, *dauhṛda*, suggesting a morbid heart; the Pali is *dohaḷa*. See H. Durt, "The Pregnancy of Māyā: I. The Five Uncontrollable Longings (*Dohada*)," *Jour-*

nal of the International College for Advanced Buddhist Studies 5 (2002): 43–66. Or the Prakrit *dohada* could be the equivalent of Sanskrit, *dvi-hṛda*, "having two hearts," suggestive of both the condition of pregnancy as well as the psychological complexities in these tales. See M. Bloomfield, "The Dohada or Craving of Pregnant Women: A Motif of Hindu Fiction," *Journal of the American Oriental Society* 40 (1920): 1–24.

jataka story . . . Suṃsumāra Jātaka (#208); see also Chaddanta Jātaka (#514).

a Jain tale . . . *Harivaṃśapurāṇa* 33.47–92, as cited in P. S. Jaini, "Fear of Food: Jaina Attitude on Eating," *Collected Papers on Jaina Studies*, Delhi: Motilal Banarsidass, 2000: 289, 295 n. 24.

King Ajatasattu . . . As told in the Thusa Jātaka (#338), and elsewhere.

domanassa

Distress (Pali)

This term features particularly in Buddhist psychology as a type of mental pain distinguished from physical pain. *Domanassa* is both a pain that the mind produces and something felt "in" the mind. *Domanassa* is considered a "faculty" of the mind in that it implements certain operations of the mind, such as attention and imagination, to cause us distress. Indeed, that it is self-caused is one of its cruelties. We dwell on painful things and expand them with our limitless powers of invention. On the other hand, since it is generated by the mind, it is manageable, at least in theory. A key source of it is covetousness, *abhijjha*, wanting what is not ours to have, and this can be tamed. People who have cut off all attachments may still have physical pain, but they have figured out how to be free of all mental distress.

The great Pali Buddhist commentator Buddhaghosa says that *domanassa* is characterized as a crushing of the mind, and its function is to harass the mind. "Those who are gripped by *domanassa* tear their hair, weep, thump their breasts, twist and turn, hurl themselves upside down, take the knife, drink poison, strangle themselves with ropes, walk into fires, and endure many kinds of suffering." It distresses the mind but crushes the body too. *Domanassa* may include some of what we might call clinical depression, but it can also occur in episodes of extreme grief and loss.

See also **abhijjha; duhkha/dukkha/duha; somanassa**

REFERENCES

such as attention and imagination . . . These ideas are supplied by a commentary on Vasubandhu, *Vibhāṣā*. (L. de La Vallée Poussin, volume II; trans. into English by L. Pruden, Berkeley, CA: Asian Humanities Press, 1988: 732 n. 235).

covetousness, abhijjha . . . Vibhaṅga 195. Trans. P. A. Thitiila as *The Book of Analysis*, London: Pali Text Society, 1969: 253.

Buddhaghosa . . . See *Visuddhimagga* XVI.51 for this paragraph. This is my translation but see also PP: 510.

dosa

Hate (Pali)

As Buddhists see it, three toxic roots are at the bottom of all human suffering: greed, delusion, and *dosa*, our subject here, a feeling of hate, anger, aversion, or repulsion. The term is something of an umbrella covering, according to one authority, this considerable range: malice, repulsion, repugnance, hostility, ill temper, agitation, indignation, antagonism, wickedness, malevolence, heartfelt antagonism, anger, irritation, vexation, belligerence, being offensive, injuring, being harmful, enmity, antipathy, violence, rudeness, and disaffection.

Dosa is cognate with Sanskrit *dvesha*, and much that is said of it applies to the Pali term. But in view of the enormous importance placed on this experience in Indian religion, allowing a separate entry for *dosa* permits some of the Pali Buddhist thought about it to emerge (but be sure to see also *dvesha*). In this tradition, to feel *dosa* is problematic morally, of course, but equally problematic is its corrosive and injurious effect on oneself: "when greed, *dosa*, and delusion arise from within, they harm the wicked-minded person, just like when the bamboo fruits." This botanical metaphor refers to how bamboo destroys the parent plant when it flowers and fruits. The Buddha invites his disciples to examine their experience to see how the arising of *dosa* generates their own "suffering, harm, and discomfort." Once one has learned how to detect it, one can see that underneath the energy that animates hate and anger there is an underlying pain. Since Buddhism aims at eradicating suffering, it targets this toxic experience to eliminate this most insidious kind of pain.

And so, much Buddhist contemplative practice is aimed at uprooting—another botanical metaphor—this destructive and painful experience. Its antidote is lovingkindness, which consists of the concrete thought and hope that others be happy (see *metta*). If one can replace one's *dosa* toward one's enemies with hopes for their happiness, one achieves a happier, calmer, and less agitated mind. Of course, this is easier said than done, and the texts provide numerous methods and strategies for getting rid of this painful affliction.

See also **byapada/vyapada; dvesha; metta/maitra**

REFERENCES

malice, repulsion . . . Dhammasaṅgaṇi 189–90.

"when greed, dosa, . . . suffering, harm, and discomfort" . . . Saṃyutta Nikāya i.98, CBD: 189.

dovacassata

Stubborn and Difficult to Fix (Pali)

The Victorian English translations of this obscure gem from the Pali Buddhist sources—"contumacy," "the being refractious," and "captiousness"—are almost as delightful as the Pali word itself. *Dovacassata* (*dovacassatā*) is a condition of resisting the teachings of the Buddha, and the texts define it as "contrary, hostile, disrespectful, dismissive, inconsiderate, and lacking deference." People can be intransigent in the face of the teachings and thus impervious to and contemptuous of authority. The Buddhist texts instead prize malleability: one should be like gold in a goldsmith's hands, pliant, workable and bright, and yielding to the right sort of molding. As with gold, this requires the removal of impurities, grit, and alloy that otherwise make one hard, unyielding and, well, refractious.

See also **appaccaya**

REFERENCES

Victorian English . . . C.A.F. Rhys Davids, trans., *A Buddhist Manual Psychological Ethics (Dhammasaṅgaṇi)*, London: Royal Asiatic Society, 344. This is her translation of *Dhammasaṅgaṇi* 228.

"contrary, hostile" . . . *Dhammasaṅgaṇi* 228.

like gold in a goldsmith's hands . . . *Aṅguttara Nikāya* iii.253–254. NDB: 335–336.

duhkha/dukkha/duha

Pain; Suffering; Misery (Sanskrit/Pali/Prakrit)

Duhkha (*duḥkha*) is the cornerstone on which the renouncer traditions of India were built. Mentioned only briefly in the Upanishads, *duhkha* is fully elaborated in the early Jain and Buddhist sources and becomes foundational for Indian religion thereafter. As a young man, Siddhattha Gotama, raised in luxury in a palace fortified to shut out the true nature of the world, escapes it to discover in sequence an old person, a sick person, and a corpse. Each new revelation stuns him, and he leaves home as a renouncer to come to terms with the inevitable decay, loss, and death that life involves, a bleak sense of misery that he called *duhkha.* He experimented for years with therapies of desire and emotion to eventually claim to have transcended *duhkha* entirely—a discovery and transcendence that made him the Buddha.

If a single lifetime invariably brings loss, life after life in the unending cycle of rebirth in samsara brings unremitting loss; ideas about *duhkha* in early India developed simultaneously alongside ideas about samsara, endless rebirth. The Buddha is said to have asked once:

> What do you think, monks, which is more: the stream of tears that you have shed as you roamed and wandered this long course, weeping and wailing because of being united with the disagreeable and separated from the agreeable—this or the water in the four great oceans?

The answer, given the beginninglessness of samsara and the eons upon eons in which we have been reborn in infinite lives within it, is of course the tears we have shed. Similarly, can there be found a spot of earth where in some past life we haven't shed blood, sunk down, and died? In a teaching in the Jain Prakrit sources, a young man, Mriga, describes the *duha* we face in samsara, as we have been born not only in every walk of human life, but also in many lives as animals and in hell:

> An infinite number of times have I suffered hopelessly from mallets and knives, forks and maces, which broke my limbs.

> Ever so many times have I been slit, cut, mangled, and skinned with keen-edged razors, knives, and shears.

Perhaps even worse than contemplating the physical sufferings and death we have endured is facing the interminable loss of our loved ones. A mother who fell into deep despair at the death of her little daughter, Jiva, is instructed that over countless lives in the past she has wept also at the cremation grounds for 84,000 daughters who also happened to be named Jiva. Time is just that huge. And the numbers are against us: left unaddressed, the losses of *duhkha* will continue in the future without end, just as they have marked all our previous lives. Unless one seizes the opportunity now to get off the wheel of samsara with its inexorable violence, one is submitting to a potentially infinite future of such miseries.

Such considerations, reiterated incessantly by ascetic teachers of the era, prompted people to give up worldly aspirations and take to the forests to learn how to be rid of *duhkha*. Such therapies begin with recognizing the brute fact of *duhkha*—Jiva's mother has an epiphany at realizing the sheer length of time she has suffered the loss of so many daughters, and her epiphany is itself liberating as she disentangles herself from the grief. More formally, these teachings of *duhkha* constitute the Buddha's "First Noble Truth," and from it is formulated a path out of it to become free entirely from all suffering. Once one recognizes *duhkha*, one can identify its cause—*trishna*, that is, craving, desire, attachment—from which springs all of our suffering. Vanquishing *trishna* cuts off the *duhkha* that follows from it.

These teachings were mainstream by the time the *Mahabharata* deploys them to grieve the sorrows at the end of its great war. *Duhkha*'s centrality to the human condition, and the role of *trishna* causing it, must be reckoned with in all Indian religious systems thereafter.

No Indian philosopher taught that every second of life is *duhkha*, of course. We also experience *sukha*, pleasure and happiness. But the key insight about *dukkha* is also an insight about *sukha*—namely, that underneath the moments of hedonic happiness that we do manage to snatch is an underlying unease at their impending loss, an unease that is itself a variety of *duhkha*. The transience and contingency of *sukha* is itself *duhkha*: happiness "has many contradictory visages; with a hundred troubles in the accomplishment of its desires, it is always overcome by suffering, like honey by poison; it is to be treated as suffering." Since the conditions on which our happiness rests include our own moral actions (karma), and since we are fallible beings driven by *trishna*, these will pull us down sooner or later.

In one way or another, the religions of early India worked out therapies to address and transcend suffering, an achievement variously referred to as *moksha* or *nirvana* (though the *bhakti* traditions will find this freedom from suffering in God). Regardless of the differing conceptions and practices developed to achieve this, all posit that suffering can be left entirely behind. Religion, if it is going to bother at all, should be audacious. And if it is going to help us, it must deal forthrightly with the bleakest and darkest hours of our condition. The Indian traditions spotted this early on and spent the next 2,500 years solving our basic existential problem.

See also **moksha; nirvana/nibbana; parideva; shoka; sukha; trishna**

REFERENCES

"What do you think, monks" . . . *Saṃyutta Nikāya* ii.179. BW: 218; see also p. 219 for the similar analogy with blood.

"An infinite number of times" . . . *The Uttarādhyayana Sūtra from the Jain Sūtras*, trans. H. Jacobi, Sacred Books of the East 45 (1884), ch. 19,

verses 61–72. *The Uttarādhyayanasūtra*, ed. J. Charpentier, Uppsala: Appelbergs Boktryckeri Aktieboleg, 1992: 149.

A mother who fell into deep despair . . . *Therigāthā* 51–53. Trans. C. Hallisey, *Therigāthā: Poems of the First Buddhist Women*, Cambridge, MA: Harvard University Press, MCLI, 2015: 38–39. One of the cruelties of the story is the irony that *Jīvā* means "life."

the Mahabharata *deploys them . . .* As, for example, *Mahābhārata* 12.174. Trans. A. Wynne, *The Book of Liberation*, New York: CSL, 2009: 4–19.

"has many contradictory visages" . . . These are the words of the Vaiśeṣika Śrīdhara in the *Nyāyakaṇḍalī* (pp. 16–17), trans. and discussed in C. Ram-Prasad, *Knowledge and Liberation in Classical Indian Thought*, New York: Palgrave, 2001: 81.

dvesha

Hate (Sanskrit)

Perhaps the most perceptive observation about *dvesha* (*dveṣa*) is given in the *Yoga Sutras*: "hate follows from attachment to suffering." But why would one be attached to suffering? And yet in our perverse way, we often nurture hate despite its toxic and aversive nature. We suffer, which is bad enough, but then we hold on to that suffering by hating it or its objects, which only generates the further suffering that is aversion. In a Buddhist metaphor, we are like a person struck by two darts: the first dart hits us from outside and is a painful sensation of the sort that is probably unavoidable in life. But the second dart is our holding on to it with a negative response—often hate or aversion—that strikes us painfully a second time; there is an element of assent in pain. This second dart is manageable, however, and religious therapies can dismantle it altogether and save us from its suffering.

The ascetic traditions often clustered hate with two other banes of human existence—greed (*lobha* or *raga*) and delusion (*moha*)—that drive all human suffering. To be rid of all three is to be awakened and released entirely from the round of rebirth. In these systems, *dvesha* is an aversion that comes from past recollection of an undesirable object. We bring to experience a history of reactions and when something painful strikes us we react in hate. Nurtured, this reactive aversion to things, people, or states of affairs can swell into full loathing, all too often directed at persons.

Buddhists are supposed to work diligently to head off hate by practicing forbearance (*kshanti*) or lovingkindness (*metta*), replacing hate with these antithetical experiences. Forbearance is the "perfection" of not reacting in hate to whatever provocations come our way. Shantideva insists that there can be no peace, happiness, sleep, or security as long as the dart of hate is stuck in the heart; it disfigures us, making even our friends shrink from us, so an aspiring bodhisattva must work tirelessly for forbearance.

For Shankara, the therapy of hate is cognitive because hate is based on a fundamental ignorance. Because we falsely identify ourselves with the body, when something or someone assaults our body, we react, thinking ourselves harmed when in fact, the self (*atman*) is distinct from the body and untouched by its suffering. Correcting this delusion is the key to ridding ourselves of the vicissitudes of both hate and attraction.

See also **amarsha; dosa; klesha/kilesas; kshama/kshanti; metta/maitra; patigha; raga**

REFERENCES

"hate follows from attachment to suffering" . . . *Yoga Sūtras* II.8: *duḥkhānuśayī dveṣaḥ*; see YSU: 46.

a person struck by two darts . . . *Saṃyutta Nikāya* iv.208–209, CBD: 1264–1265. The term here is *paṭigha* rather than *dosa* (Pali for *dveṣa*), but the language of attachment (*anusaya*) and the idea is similar to the *Yoga Sūtra* claim.

dvesha is an aversion that comes from past recollections . . . This is widely found; see, for example *Nyāyasūtra Bhāṣya Vārṭika* on *Nyāyasūtra* 1.1.10, trans. G. Jha, volume I, Delhi: Motilal Banarsidass, 1999:

217–218. See also *Nyāyasūtra* 4.1.3, where the commentary defines *dveṣa* as *amarṣa*, resentment, and 3.2.41, where it said that recollection in turn is shaped by many things including attraction and aversion (*dveṣa*) (Jha, volume IV, 1999: 1433; and volume III, 1999: 1371–1372). Aversion and memory work together in a feedback loop to pattern and entrap our experience.

forbearance (kshanti) . . . Śāntideva rails against *dveṣa* in chapter 6 in BCA: 50–64; see specifically 6.2–4. Buddhaghosa recommends loving-kindness (*metta*) as the antidote to hate (see *brahmaviharas* for reference), while Śāntideva focuses on *kṣanti.*

For Shankara . . . Bhagavad Gītā XIII.2–6 and Śaṅkara's commentary. BGC: 332–339.

E

eshana

Instinctual Drives and Legitimate Pursuits (Sanskrit)

The ancient teachings of the Upanishads suggest several possibilities for what it was that emerged first in the beginning of the cosmos. A nothingness, Death itself, somehow present at first evolves into life as a first Being appears. The Being finds himself, or in some cases *itself* (we find both masculine and neuter terms in the various accounts) alone, and begins to desire. The Being desires a second being with which to copulate, and it is this drive for an Other, and all that comes with it—sex, offspring, life—that populates the world. It is through Desire that the one becomes two and then the many.

Insofar as such cosmogonies reveal what is primal in human nature, we find *desire* driving our experience. The *Brihadaranyaka Upanishad* specifies three *eshanas* (*eṣaṇās*), desires or drives: the desire for children, the desire for wealth, and the desire for the world beyond. Already in the Upanishads, these desires are problematic: the text says that when one sees these for what they are, one will cast off the world and become a mendicant.

The notion of deeply seated desires comes to be pervasive in Indian thought. Desire is *the* central human problem from the standpoint of the ascetic religious systems because it leads to suffering. The Buddha prefers to speak of *tanha*

(Sanskrit *trishna*), enumerating three kinds of craving at the root of all suffering: for sensual pleasure, for existence, and for annihilation. In sharp contrast, desire is lavishly celebrated in the erotic and aesthetic traditions. Vatsyayana, author of the famous *Kama Sutra*, sees sensual desire (*kama*) as a basic human need, like food, with a potential for faults and problems but necessary for sustaining our lives.

For a sober but affirmative treatment of human instincts, and a subtle reworking of them into valued human aspirations, we can turn to the Indian medical texts. Like modern scientists studying infants in the lab to determine what is innate, the physician Caraka notes that newborns come to us already able to cry, suckle the breast, laugh, be afraid, and so on, without any learning. We aren't "blank slates" at birth. Echoing the Upanishads, he suggests that humans are driven by three primal *eshanas*: the pursuit of life-breath, the pursuit of wealth, and the pursuit of the world beyond. For him, these are not only part of the normal healthy human endowment but are also the legitimate ambitions, wills, drives, and aspirations that, when well-regulated by moral norms, should inform our projects. Ayurveda offers a therapy for wellbeing that would align our instinctual drives with these socially desirable pursuits.

See also **iccha; kama; trishna**

References

the desire for children . . . Bṛhadāraṇyaka Upaniṣad 3.5.1, EU: 82–83. For cosmogonic hymns in this text, see 1.2, 1.4, EU: 36–39, 44–47.

craving . . . for sensual pleasure . . . Tanhā (Sanskrit *tṛṣṇā*) is divided as such in the Buddha's very first sermon: *Saṃyutta Nikāya* v.421–424, CDB: 1843–1847. "Sensual pleasure" here is *kāma*.

basic human need, like food . . . Vātsyāyana's *Kāma Sūtra* I.2.37–38, KS: 12.

able to cry, suckle the breast . . . "There is the manifestation of crying, suckling the breast, laughing, being afraid, etc. which are not learned," see also CS: 216; chapter XI, verse 30.

the pursuit of life-breath, pursuit of wealth, and pursuit of the world beyond . . . *Agniveśa's Caraka Saṃhitā*, XI.3; for a discussion of these, see HB: 31–33.

ambitions, wills, drives, and aspirations . . . With these four possibilities, Dominic Wujastyk offers a range of translations for *eṣaṇā* in Caraka's text, *The Roots of Ayurveda*, London: Penguin, 2003: 22–23.

G

garva

Haughtiness (Sanskrit)

Words for pride and arrogance are plentiful in the sources—*garva, mana, mada, darpa, atimana*—and these are often used synonymously. With *garva*, we find an emphasis on the hauteur of the highly placed, whether their superiority is owing to high status, wealth, beauty, youth, erudition, power, or influence. *Garva* is the haughtiness of one's sense of superiority vis-à-vis others and is deeply entwined with contempt. It is displayed, according to Bharata, by one's insolence to others, by scorning and offending them, not answering or refusing to greet people, looking downward (literally, "at the shoulders"), whirling about, mocking and deriding others, and being disrespectful to elders. In contrast to other forms of pride and arrogance, it is not that the superiority of the haughty person is in question: one is not trying to fly above one's station because one is, in fact, highly placed. Rather, the arrogance comes from derision and contempt toward others.

Much of this resonates with Charles Darwin's description of the proud person who "exhibits his sense of superiority over others by holding his head and body erect," is "swollen and puffed up" and "looks down on others, and with lowered eyelids hardly condescends to see them." I think that the "looking at the shoulders" in Bharata's description captures this sense of refusing to raise the eyes to the other's face noticed by Darwin as well. And there are peacock-ish behaviors of whirling about.

While typically *garva* attracts censure, sometimes the haughty affectations of pretty women are admired by the poets, perhaps because their very conceitedness itself signals their supposed superiority.

See also **atimana; avajna; avamana; darpa; mada; mana; urjasvi**

REFERENCES

by scorning and offending them . . . This is from Bharata's *Nāṭyaśāstra* 7.67.

Charles Darwin's description . . . *The Expressions of the Emotions in Man and Animals*, Oxford: Oxford University Press, 1998 (1872): 262–263. J. Sinha also quotes Darwin in relation to *garva* (IP: 240).

haughty affectations of pretty women . . . Aśvaghoṣa admiringly describes the beautiful Sundarī as having *garva* in *Saundarananda* (4.3) and describes such feminine haughtiness as entrancing for men (7.24). HN: 80–81, 138–139.

guna

Disposition; Psychosomatic Modes (Sanskrit)

The word *guna* (*guṇa*) can mean so many things and not all of them are relevant to our purposes. Where the *gunas* are pertinent is when they refer to the modes that reality takes as humans experience them in temperament and emotion.

According to an ancient philosophical school called Samkhya, the world of experience—bodies, minds, physical stuff, the textures of time and the seasons, and so on—involves the interaction of its three basic *gunas*, or modes: *sattva*, *rajas*, and *tamas*. The Samkhya texts speak of *sattva* as that which is "agreeable, brilliant, buoyant, and shining"; *rajas* as "disagreeable, active, stimulating, and moving"; and *tamas* as "despondent, restraining, heavy, and encompassing." The world is constantly changing and dynamically creative because of the interactions of these modal qualities. While much, much bigger than what we mean by emotion, the *gunas* can be conceived as psychic and moral aspects of reality as they are experienced in mood, temperament, and emotion.

The emotional valences of these three modes—agreeable (*priti*), disagreeable (*apriti*), and despondent (*vishada*)—are instructive on how emotions interact in ways that I would describe as "ecological." The *gunas* "mutually arise, depending on, producing, and complementing" one another, according to the texts. This specifies that their operations are inextricably relational, situational, and dynamic. A commentary offers a useful example. One and the same lovely and admirable woman is agreeable to her husband, disagreeable to her jealous co-wives, and a source of despondency to men who can't have her. The "essence" or "nature" of this particular woman changes in relation to each of these three people; she manifests variously in relation to different others. This suggests that not only are the modes and valences of emotional life intersubjective, but the *natures* of the subjects in question are dynamically variable, and indeed, *constituted*, through this relationality. We become who we are, at least in part, through how we are experienced variously by others.

There is more to know about this extraordinary system. The phenomenological world characterized by the *gunas* is termed *prakriti*, nature, and is one-half of a dualistic metaphysics in which the other principle is *purusha*, spirit (or, more literally, "person," but in a specialized sense). Samkhya's divide between *prakriti* and *purusha* might at first glance look similar to the Cartesian dualism of body and mind. Far from it. This system treats mind and body together as part of *prakriti*, the created and creative order of nature wherein all phenomena we would associate with emotions are aspects of the interactions and combinations of *rajas, tamas,* and *sattva.* Then there is a plurality of *purushas* that are entirely aloof from these workings of the mind, emotion, bodily experience, and material reality. They look on as impartial witnesses or spectators, utterly free and disentangled from the workings of phenomenal life. This metaphysic posits a component of the human person that exists apart from all thought, feeling, impulse, instinct, and action, a pure consciousness somehow free from the contingencies and determinations of the phenomenal world.

In various forms, this idea of an aloof person or consciousness runs deep in Indian thought and courses through its many quests for freedom, since ultimate freedom is precisely this disengagement from all that is conditioned and contingent and thus subject to loss and pain. The philosophical and therapeutic path of Yoga, a system closely affiliated with Samkhya, aims at achieving just this realization that the *purusa* is, in fact, utterly untethered to the depredations of the manifest and everchanging world of nature and emotion. Beyond this particular spiritual project, the notion of the three *gunas* shaping temperament was widely attested, from the *Bhagavad Gita* to the aesthetic philosophers.

See also **priti; rajas; sattva; tamas; vishada; yoga**

REFERENCES

Samkhya texts speak . . . Sāṃkhyā Kārikā XII–XIII. My reading of the *guṇas* as "modes" of reality rather than the usual "constituents" of *prakṛti* (which implies a part and whole relationship) draws on K. B. Ramakrishna Rao, "The *Guṇas* of *Prakṛti* According to the Sāṁkhya Philosophy," *Philosophy East and West* 13, no. 1 (1963): 61–71. As the example of the woman shows, for Sāṁkhya, "substances are not different from qualities, and vice versa" (70). C. Ram-Prasad adds the useful idea of the *guṇas* as "valences," drawing out how we experience these changing aspects of the stuff of nature. ("Madness, Virtue, and Ecology:

A Classical Indian Approach to Psychiatric Disturbance," *History of the Human Sciences*, April 2021: 10–11.)

A commentary offers . . . Vācaspati Miśra's *Tattvakaumudī* on *Sāṃkhyā Kārikā* XII–XIII. My translation, but see also G. Jhā, Bombay: Tookaram Tatya, 1896: 40–45.

plurality of purushas . . . See G. Larson, *Classical Sāṃkhya*, Delhi: Motilal Banarsidass, 1979: 168–171.

H

harsha

Elation; Thrill (Sanskrit)

Harsha (*harṣa*) is a rush of happiness and joy at attaining what one had hoped would occur: one's beloved appears, a child is born, the king grants his favor, good fortune strikes. The face lights up and one horripilates, gushes sweet words, hugs everyone, and may produce tears and sweat. It is a condition of arousal, elation, thrilling, and goosebumps (see *romaharsha*, the thrill when hair stands erect). *Harsha* and its derivatives (*hrista*, thrilled, and *praharsha*, delight) are perhaps the most frequently encountered words for joy, gladness, and delight in the epics. Often, warriors going into battle are, at least at the beginning, pumped up with the exhilaration of *harsha*, though this can shift quickly as the brutality of the fight sets in.

In the *Ramayana*, Sita has been kidnapped and is wasting away in the garden of her captor when the monkey emissary Hanuman arrives to check on her and convey Rama's message that he is coming to save her. Sita "experienced unequaled *harsha*, and in her *praharsha* she shed tears of joy from her eyes with their curling lashes. The lovely face of that wide-eyed woman, its long eyes all red and white, lit up, like the moon, the lord of stars, when released from Rahu, demon of the eclipse." The *harsha* that elates her wipes away the extreme sadness and anguish she had been enduring, and she becomes like the moon emerging from the darkness. We see her again like this when Hanuman returns with Rama in battle and she is finally released from captivity.

See also **ananda; piti; priti; romaharsha**

REFERENCES

one's beloved appears . . . Nāṭyaśāstra 7.61–62. *Harṣa* is a transitory emotion (*vyabhicāribhāva*).

"experienced unequaled harsha" . . . Rāmāyaṇa V.33.78. Trans. R. Goldman and S. Sutherland Goldman, *Rāmāyaṇa Book Five, Sundara*, New York: CSL, 2006: 292–293. See also VI.101.11–15.

hasa

The Smiles and Laughter of Mirth (Sanskrit and Pali)

Hasa (*hāsa*) gives us a single term that we don't have in English—the feeling that ranges from the gentle smile to the giggle, from the hearty guffaw all the way to the doubling over in hysterics. English "amusement," "mirth," and "hilarity" get at pieces of this range, but none does the full gamut that *hasa* does. Authors find that *hasa* is a "blooming of the mind" in delight and pleasure like the unfolding of a flower. We expand a bit in laughter, slackening the tightness of our cares.

The full phenomenality of funny is evident in Bharata's six types of *hasa* that we shall consider in turn and with examples from the literature. In an important way, these show that the feeling *hasa* is inseparable from the smiles and laughter that constitute it.

First, we have *smita,* the restrained smile that shows no teeth but is evident in the open eyes and slightly raised cheeks. Second, there is *hasita*, a laughing smile that reveals the teeth as well as fully grinning eyes and beaming cheeks. These two forms of amusement may be felt, according to Bharata, by the highest grades of people. Sages in heaven watching the antics of adolescent Krishna as he steals yogurt and flees old women pursuers, permit a mild smile to grace their lotus faces. The demure Parvati was shy and frightened on her wedding night with Shiva. To put her at ease, he got his attendant *ganas* to pull funny faces "to make her smile despite herself."

Third, we find the slightly less genteel *vihasita*, a giggle or chuckle sweetly sounding, with eyes and cheeks contracted, and a flush creeping over the face. When she overhears the young Krishna call out to his chums to steal the yogurt because his old auntie "is snoring," the same auntie, only pretending sleep, chortles with this laugh.

As the level of hilarity rises, we go down the social hierarchy. Coarser persons can be subject to *upahasita*, loud guffawing with head and body narrowing and shuddering, nostrils flaring, and eyes squinting. The demoness Shurpanakha, rejected in her advances by both Rama and Lakshmana, wrongly and ludicrously accuses Sita of this violent jeering, where in fact, Sita had only smiled.

By the time one succumbs to *apahasita*, the guffawing is altogether inappropriate; head and shoulders heave and eyes get wet. The gruff sage Narada roared at seeing Lord Krishna performing a divine dance for old cowherd women. The implication seems to be that the object of the humor is as ludicrous as the laugher is unseemly.

Atihasita, literally "too much" hilarity, is yet another degree altogether. The laughter is paroxysmal as one is overwhelmed with tears, a violent scream rends the air, and hands clutch at splitting sides. Krishna's playmates convulsed with *atihasita* when a daft and wrinkled monkey took Krishna's teasing as a proposal to marry her. (Though, see the entry on *atihasa*, which can also mean inexplicable laughter).

The emotion *hasa* is savored in the comic *rasa*, *hasya* (see next entry). Here is not the place to offer a theory of humor, but we find *hasa* and *hasya* produced by displays of incongruity, impropriety, and inversion ("misplaced ornaments, uncouth behavior, odd dress"), and by ridicule, since it is generated by "mimicking others' actions, meaningless chatter, displays of malice or fatuousness." We laugh, it seems, at other people.

Hasa is highly socially coded, configured by and performing social norms and boundaries, often by breaching them. Decorous sorts can seldom fully relax and expand into hearty mirth, as Bharata permits only rubes to roar with laughter. But if it is true that the chance to let go in a good belly laugh is one of the few truly precious things in life, perhaps it is the so-called rustics who get the last laugh.

See also **atihasa; hasya; smita**

REFERENCES

a single term that we don't have . . . C. Ram-Prasad, "The Emotion That Is Correlated with the Comic: Notes on Human Nature through Rasa Theory," in BRH: 193–212.

"blooming of the mind" . . . This definition is frequently given in a range of texts, as discussed in IP: 184–185. The flower simile is given by the *Kāvyamīmāṁsā*.

Bharata's six types of hasa . . . *Nāṭyaśāstra* 6.51, 54–60.

Sages in heaven . . . This example of *smita* is given by Rūpa Gosvāmin, and he gives the examples here of *vihasita*, *apahasita*, and *atihasita* as well. He lists *avahasita* for *upahasita*, with much the same meaning. BR: 552–555.

"to make her smile" . . . *Kumārasaṃbhava* 7.95. BK: 294–295. Here the word is *hāsaya*, a form of *hāsita*.

The demoness Shurpanakha . . . This is in Kalidasa's *Raghuvaṁsa* 12.37.

"misplaced ornaments" . . . *Nāṭyaśāstra* 6.49.

"mimicking others' actions" . . . *Nāṭyaśāstra* 7.9.

hasya

The Comic (Sanskrit)

Hasya (*hāsya*) is the *rasa* of *hasa*: where *hasa* is laughter, *hasya* is, literally, "what is laughable." Our focus becomes the humorous—what should be laughed at. Sanskrit literature has all genres, high and low, of the risible: satire, political farce, parody, pun, comedies of manners, grotesquerie. And to be sure, Bharata's prohibiting the most genteel social classes from the most enthusiastic laughter (see *hasa*) is contravened by the imperatives of comedy, which are to get us all laughing. One bawdy comedy opens by giving its audience permission to laugh: "a merry tale does not dash the hope for heaven, so with a glad heart the wise should set aside hypocrisy, and just laugh." The playwright's job is to make kings, courtiers, and rustics alike laugh, and the heartier, the better.

The *hasa/hasya* pair differs from some of the other *bhava* and *rasa* pairings that suggest more distance and some disjuncture between the *bhava* and the *rasa*. My own personal grief of bereavement is entirely unwelcome, but I can relish the feeling of tragedy of another's loss in the theater. But with *hasa* and *hasya*, the comic is fully congruous and of the same nature as the *hasa*, as the joke is the same in each—"the funny gag works in the living room as it does on the stage." The comic makes us laugh, and we savor both the laughter and the humor.

For the poets, the comic invites us to share in something humorous, as it gives us a perspective or a vantage point that subverts supposedly more serious matters. A poem by King Bhoja provides an example:

> My friend, you'd better move your blouse
> to cover this fresh line of scratch-marks

on your breast—aren't you supposed
to be still angry with him?

This vignette relies on several tropes in the literature: the woman's friend is speaking to the jealous woman who was at one point angry with her man, but the scratch-marks disclose a recent bout of passionate lovemaking that shows that she didn't manage to stay angry long, despite her performance of pout. We share in the friend's teasing and knowing eye.

We can even share in the teasing of the great gods:

"This Shankara, universally acclaimed for abstinence,
now bears his wife with half his body, afraid to be without her.
And people say *he* conquered *us*?" With this, the god of love
squeezed his wife's hand, and laughed—and may his laugh protect you.

Lord Shiva, here called Shankara, was at one time a serious yogi until he was seduced by the lovely Parvati, and then their lovemaking shook the cosmos and entangled their bodies into a single half-male, half-female divine reality. Here Kama, the god of love who had at one time been attacked by Shiva, now mocks him for this supposed failing that demonstrates Love's triumph. And we smile too.

See also **atihasa; hasa; rasa; smita**

REFERENCES

what should be laughed at . . . Hāsya is the gerundive of the verb *has*. L. Siegal's *Laughing Matters*, Chicago: University of Chicago Press, 1987, has a wide-ranging exploration of premodern Indian humor and comedy.

"a merry tale does not dash" . . . Ram-Prasad, quoting "The Kick (*Pādatāḍitaka*)," verse I.10, in "The Emotion That Is Correlated with the Comic: Notes on Human Nature through Rasa Theory," in (BRH:

199). For a full translation of "The Kick," see C. Dezsö and S. Vasudeva, *The Quartet of Causeries*, New York: CSL, 2009.

"the funny gag works in the living room" . . . Ram-Prasad, 198, discussing the *Abhinavabhāratī* on *Nāṭyaśāstra* VI.49.

"My friend, you'd better move" . . . *Śṛṅgāraprakāśa*, trans. S. Pollock, "Bhoja's *Śṛṅgāraprakāśa* and the Problem of Rasa: A Historical Introduction and Annotated Translation," *Asiatische Studien / Études Asiatiques* 70, no. 1 (1998): 171.

"This Shankara" . . . *Śṛṅgāraprakāśa*, RR: 132.

hiri/hri

Shame (Pali/Sanskrit)

This variety of shame is considered an asset of the virtuous and may be contrasted with the crippling effects of other types of shame. *Hiri* (Sanskrit *hrī*) is the valuable sense of shame we have in mind when we disapprove of those who lack it, those "shameless" reprehensible people who evince no regard for social propriety or common decency. We expect people to be abashed at their flagrant misdeeds, and we deplore their obtuse insensitivity to their own disgrace. While other varieties of shame (see *vrida* and *lajja*) can get at the ignominy and humiliation of wrongdoing—particularly when it has been exposed—*hiri* is the sense of shame that checks our bad tendencies *before* they can issue in action. It thus acts as "a guardian of the world," as the Pali texts have it, a "beautiful" moral sentiment that protects the world from our incursions upon it. Buddhists pair it with the allied force of "apprehension" (*ottappa*), a fear of one's capacity for wrongdoing that similarly protects the world.

Hiri is described in social terms, as a self-awareness one has when one considers the appraisal of others and how they would see one in morally compromising behavior. It can have elements of disgust, as it is what allows us to recoil viscerally from vile actions. It can also be linked to nonmoral embarrassment, such as the modesty or shame felt at being seen in a state of undress. Humans are strikingly sensitive to how they are seen by other humans. *Hiri* is the sense of being abashed by the seeing eye of others, even if one is only imagining it.

See also **lajja; ottappa; vrida/vridita**

REFERENCE

"guardian of the world". . . For a systematic discussion of *hiri* and *ottappa*, see M. Heim, "Shame and Apprehension: Notes on the Moral Value of *Hiri* and *Ottappa*," in *Embedded Languages: Studies of Sri Lankan and Buddhist Cultures*, ed. C. Anderson, S. Mrozik, R.M.W. Rajapakse, and W. M. Wijeratne, Colombo: Godage International Publishers, 2012: 237–260.

hridaya

The Heart (Sanskrit)

> The heart (*hṛdaya*) is the abode of all beings; the heart is the foundation of all beings. For it is on the heart that all the beings are founded. So clearly, Your Majesty, the highest brahman is the heart. When a man knows and venerates it as such, the heart never abandons him, and all beings flock to him; he becomes a god and joins the company of gods.

This Upanishadic wisdom locates the essence of our being in our hearts, and suggests that when we fully understand this, we find our power.

In many premodern traditions, the heart-mind is the locus of thought and emotion. In ancient Chinese thought, *xin* is both heart and mind. While perfectly capable of making anatomical distinctions about the heart and the brain, and between cognitive and affective experience, many Indian and Chinese thinkers saw these processes as coming together in the heart. Indian thinkers would have found Mencius's observations congenial to their own conceptions:

> The organs of hearing and sight are unable to think and can be misled by external things. When one thing acts on another, all it does is attract it. The organ of the heart can think. But it will find the answer only if it does think; otherwise, it will not find the answer. This is what Heaven has given me.

For Mencius, thinking and feeling are not in conflict, nor are they conflated, with one another; like the other organs, the heart is stimulated by feeling, but it also has the capacity for thought. There is an intelligence in the heart given to us as part of our natural endowment.

Indian thinkers too took the heart to be the source of intentionality and consciousness, as is said explicitly in the medical texts, and it can be a seat of moral knowledge (see *hridayakrosha*). At the same time, the heart is often the locus of emotion; grief and anxiety often present more powerfully in the chest cavity than in the gray matter between the ears. When Arjuna falters at the battlefield at the horror of fighting his relatives, Krishna scolds him for this "weakness of the heart."

We know the truth of the heart when hearts break. For broken hearts, often those of nonhuman animals also, can lead to death. Jane Goodall, and other researchers working closely with animals, report similar findings. When the young man who was to become the Buddha left home on his valiant steed Kanthaka, he finally had to say goodbye to this magnificent horse. Kanthaka was so bereaved that he lay down and died of a broken heart. Much later in the Buddha's life, the Buddha retreated for a rainy season from the cares of his new monastic institution and the petty squabbles of his monks. He stayed in the woods and was attended by a wonderful elephant, Parileyyaka. When it came time for the Buddha to leave the forest retreat, his dear friend Parileyyaka wept and died of a broken heart.

See also **hridayakrosha; hridayamarman; sauharda; shoka**

REFERENCES

"The heart is the abode" . . . *Bṛhadāraṇyaka Upaniṣad* 4.1.7, EU: 108–109.

"The organs of hearing and sight" . . . The *Mengzi*, trans. and discussed by C. Virág, "The Intelligence of Emotions? Debates over the Structure of Moral Life in Early China," *L'Atelier du Centre de recherches historiques* 16 (2016): 5. My understanding of Mencius and *xin* is based on her discussions here and in her *The Emotions in Early Chinese Philosophy*, New York: Oxford University Press, 2017.

in the medical texts . . . Vāgbhaṭa's *Aṣṭāṅgahṛdaya* as trans. by Dominic Wujastyk, *The Roots of Ayurveda*, London: Penguin, 2003: 202, 276. *Citta* and *cetanā* are located in the heart. Wujastyk notes that Bhela, an early Ayurveda author, is "perhaps unique" to disagree, and instead finds the head to be the locus of the mind (*manas*) (202 n. 12).

"weakness of the heart" . . . *Bhagavad Gītā* 2.3.

valient steed Kanthaka . . . Kanthaka's story is told in *Jātaka-nidāna* i.65. Pārileyyaka's story is told in the Dhammapada commentary, trans. E. W. Burlingame, *Buddhist Legends*, volume I, Cambridge, MA: Harvard University Press, 1921: 176–183.

hridayakrosha

Cry of the Heart (Sanskrit)

A cry of the heart (*hṛdayakrośa*) is a voice that calls out, often inconveniently, when one has done something wrong. It issues from the heart region. We would probably call it the pangs of conscience to get at the phenomenality of it, though we would want to resist importing the Christian associations that the notion of conscience introduces. Perhaps better to look to the British moral sense theorists and borrow the Earl of Shaftesbury's "moral sense," a sensitivity built into our nature that tells us right from wrong.

The Mimamsa philosopher Kumarila entertains a debate about whether a cry of the heart, in itself, can be a valuable moral sentiment. Some might argue that the presence of a cry of the heart indicates an inner moral guide. The fact that one is subject to a cry of the heart upon sleeping with the wife of one's teacher, "though it might bring her great pleasure," suggests that such doings cannot be moral. Conversely, one might think that the absence of painful inner censure from one's core must surely mean that one has not acted wrongly. This is a time-honored sentimentalist ethic: since humans are endowed with moral sentiments, feelings can be valuable guides to moral knowledge. But Kumarila, a dyed-in-the-wool Vedic traditionalist, is having none of it: neither reason nor feeling can be a guide to morality, for scripture alone is authoritative.

The French *cri du coeur* is a protest similar in its sincerity (and so, "heartfelt"), but is a different idea. Its distress is not the sharp pang of conscience, but that of injustice where the heart itself speaks against oppression, asserting the fundamental human right to not be hurt. The idea gets its furthest philosophical development in the thought of Simone Weil: "At the bottom of every human being, from earliest infancy until the tomb, there is something that goes on indomitably expecting, in the teeth of all experience of crimes committed, suffered and witnessed, that good and not evil will be done to him. It is that above all that is the sacred in every human being." The heart cries out this truth.

See also **anutapa; hiri/hri; pashcattapa**

REFERENCES

The Mimamsa philosopher Kumarila... This discussion takes place in the *Ślokavārtika* 2.244–49. Trans. G. Jha, Delhi: Sri Satguru Publications, 1983: 59. I am grateful to John Taber for his help with Kumarila.

in the thought of Simone Weil... Quoted from her essay, "Human Personality."

hridayamarman

The Heart's Soft Core (Sanskrit)

In the final scenes of Valmiki's *Ramayana*, the divine hero Rama, responding to malicious gossip casting aspersions on his beloved wife's virtue while she had been kidnapped and held in the house of the vile Ravana, turns his pregnant Sita out into the forest alone, where she eventually bears their twins. Rama and Sita, whose love story the *Ramayana* has also evoked in tender detail, are never to be fully reunited. The moral and emotional pain of this stunning ending gets its most sensitive and anguished reconsideration centuries later in a play by Bhavabhuti. The playwright exposes Rama to the full force of his censorious eye and treats the innocent Sita with great compassion. But he also takes great care to reveal the heart-wrenching anguish that the tragedy entails for Rama, for their hearts had been deeply intertwined since they were first wed. Rama sheds copious tears (see *ashru*) at the memory of his abandoning Sita and his guilty anguish at her plight. And Bhavabhuti reveals how this sorrow has assailed Rama's "heart's soft core" (*hṛdayamarman*) more than half a dozen times in the play as the process of his sorrow unfolds.

A *marman* is a tender, vital spot in the body; the heart's *marman* is the tender vital heart flesh that, in sensitive people, is so easily torn. Rama again and again describes his heart's soft core as pierced by the arrowhead, knife, or poisoned dart of his grief. Though scarred over, the heart's soft core bursts apart repeatedly at every memory of his loss. More philosophically, Rama suggests that such painful tearings by the cruelties of samsara "make sensitive people feel such revulsion that they're ready to give up all objects of desire and seek peace in the wilderness."

See also **ashru; avamana; hridaya; shoka; vilapa**

REFERENCES

their hearts had been deeply intertwined . . . This is evident from the start in Vālmīki's *Rāmāyaṇa* I.76.15–17: they keep one another ever in their hearts; their "innermost hearts spoke clearly to the other"; and Sītā "knew his innermost heart especially well." Trans. R. Goldman, *The Rāmāyaṇa, Book One*, New York: CSL, 2009: 366–367.

"make sensitive people feel" . . . RLA: 74–75. Readers can find Rāma's soft vitals getting further rent on pp. 98–99, 156–157, 188–189, 212–213, 246–247, 350–351. A witness, Sumantra, also experiences the tearing of the heart's soft core on pp. 302–303, modeling the reader's response to the tragic *rasa*, Bhavabhūti tells us repeatedly, that this play is invoking.

I

iccha

Wanting (Sanskrit)

In a lexicon full of words for desire in its many shades, varieties, and objects, *iccha* (*icchā*) is a very basic form of wanting. In the philosophical literature, *iccha* is the pull of attraction that is the opposite of *dvesha*, the push of aversion; it is the wanting that encompasses all other varieties of desire.

> *Iccha* is wishing for something not yet obtained either for one's own sake or another's. It arises from the connection of mind and self relating to such things as pleasure or memory. It is the motivating cause of effort, memory, righteousness, and unrighteousness, and here are the types of it: sensory pleasure, longing, passion, volition, compassion, dispassion, fraud, and emotion.

This is to say that *iccha* occurs as the mind (*manas*) takes in sensory information and connects with the self (*atman*) in pleasure or memory of pleasure. Memory is both a cause of *iccha* and a source of it. We long for not only what is right in front of us but also that which we remember enjoying. In turn, such memories propel further desires.

Iccha drives the effort, the springs of action, as the commentary goes on to explain, that we require to keep our organism in equilibrium. We balance as best we can wanting what we need and being repelled by what is harmful in order to preserve life. *Iccha* is the desire that sets in as we first open our eyes in the morning, and then it drives all of our efforts, good and bad. *Iccha* is the desire for pleasure and the desire to act; the desire that is passion and the desire that turns back, dispassionate, from something problematic; and it is the desire to deceive that is fraud, and the desire to help that is compassion.

See also **dohada; dvesha; eshana; kama; lobha; raga; rati; trishna; vancha**

REFERENCE

"Iccha is wishing" . . . *Padārthadharmasangraha* 8.15, 8.17. My translation, but see that of G. Jha, *The Padārthadharmasangraha of Praśastipāda with the Nyāyakaṇḍalī of Śrīdhara*, Allahabad: E. J. Lazarus and Co., 1916: 560–564. "Sensory pleasure," is *kāma*; "longing" is *abhilāśa*; "passion" is *rāga*; "compassion" is *kāruṇya*; "dispassion" is *vairāgya*; and "emotion" is *bhāva*. We also see the *icchā/dveṣa* binary at *Bhagavad Gītā* 7.27; we also commonly see the binary as *rāga/dveṣa*.

ingita and akara

Affect and Expression (Sanskrit)

These are the palpitations, slight flushes, beads of sweat, movements of the eye, and quivering changes of voice that shrewd observers can detect—and crafty dissimulators can affect—in the arts of surveillance described in the *Arthashastra*, the ancient treatise on statecraft compiled by the sage Kautilya. In an unguarded countenance, the inner feeling can make its way to the surface and be detected by shrewd observers. Conversely, people can master the arts of semblance and guise to conceal and deceive: hate may masquerade as love, joy as dejection, fortitude as dread. Kautilya, ancient precursor to Machiavelli, cautions the king to deploy agents trained in the gestures of concealment to study envoys and ministers for signs of subterfuge. Secret agents must avoid women and drink, and always sleep alone for fear that their countenances can reveal state secrets when indisposed. The wise minister in the employ of such a king learns also to scrutinize the gestures and signals of the king himself to detect his shifting favor, as though his life depended on it (which it probably does).

Studies of *ingita* (*iṅgita*) and *akara* (*ākāra*) are by no means confined to the machinations of realpolitik, and prove equally useful in the romantic sphere, where they are often meant to reveal more than to conceal. The *Kama Sutra* meticulously details the arts of female flirtation and advises the man-about-town to carefully observe the affects and expressions of the woman he woos to see if she shares his erotic feelings. Both at court and in courtship stating bluntly how matters stand is intolerably vulgar. Yet knowing others' emotions is of great strategic importance. And so watching the eyes and gestures of others becomes a science and an art.

See also **kama**

REFERENCES

agents trained in the gestures . . . Arthaśāstra 1.15.6–10. For a discussion of *iṅgita* and *ākāra* among other gestures and signs in courtly contexts, see D. Ali, *Courtly Culture and Political Life in Early Medieval India*, Cambridge: Cambridge University Press, 2004: 193–201.

avoid women and drink . . . Arthaśāstra 1.16.21–23.

scrutinize the gestures . . . Arthaśāstra 5.5.5–6.

The Kama Sutra *. . . Kāma Sūtra* 3.3.23, 3.3.25–29, 3.4.34, KS: 84–85, 88.

irshya

Envy; Jealousy (Sanskrit)

The first blast of jealousy, and the one following it, the
grief and the fire in the heart—we banish it!
Just as the earth feels dead, feeling more dead than a
corpse, just like the feeling of one dead is the dead
feeling of a jealous mind.

> That fluttering mind that has found a place in your heart—from it I set free your jealousy, like hot vapor from a bag of skin.

This potent charm against jealousy (or perhaps envy) comes to us from the ancient book of spells known as the *Atharva Veda*. It evokes at once the movement and heat of *irshya* (*īrṣyā*) as it enters the heart, and the deadness it leaves deep inside.

I find that it makes for an absorbing pastime to imagine the ancient Vedic peoples who sought such charms. Who was it who paid a magician to utter this ritual incantation to free his body from this hot vapor? Of whom was he jealous? Or was it a woman? And did the charm work?

Sanskrit sources do not always make the distinction between envy and jealousy that one sometimes sees in English. *Irshya* can be both: resentment at (or suspicion toward) rivals for their (potential) success with one's beloved, and resentment toward others for what they have. We see jealousy in the *Kama Sutra*, where both men and women get jealous at the first indication of a rival. And we find envy in Duryodhana: as he burned with the resentful envy of *amarsha*, the warrior villain of the *Mahabharata* is also described as being "scorched by *irshya*."

And while we find multiple words loosely sharing the semantic range of jealousy, envy, and resentment, the philosophical tradition aims also for precision. One scholar distinguishes envy (*irshya*), jealousy (*asuya*), and resentment (*amarsha*) in this way: *irshya* is the desire to prevent others from acquiring things to be shared; *asuya* is the inability to stand others' good qualities; and *amarsha* is the incapacity to forbear offense (it is the opposite of *marsha*, forgiveness). As we see in the case of Duryodhana's bitter cast of mind, the mere fact of his rivals' success is enough to count as an offense and a humiliation to him (see *amarsha*).

See also **akkhanti/akshanti; amarsha; asuya; matsara; vancha**

REFERENCES

"The first blast of jealousy" . . . The first two verses are my translation of *Atharvaveda* 6.18; the last is Whitney's translation with slight modifications (changing "thy" to "your"); W. D. Whitney, *Atharva-Veda Saṁhitā*, Cambridge, MA: Harvard Oriental Series, 1962: 293–294. I am aided also by R.T.H. Griffiths's translation, *The Hymns of the Atharva Veda*, Varanasi: Chowkhamba Sanskrit Series, 1968 (originally published 1895). For more charms, see entries on *bhaya* and *vancha*.

in the Kama Sutra . . . *Kāma Sūtra* 5.4.54, 6.1.12; KS: 119–120, 133. See also *Arthaśāstra* 3.3.9 for a "jealous wife."

"scorched by irshya" . . . *Mahābhārata* 1.129.10.

irshya is the desire . . . *Nyāyasūtra Bhāṣya Vārṭika* on *Nyāyasūtra* 4.1.3. Trans. G. Jha, volume IV, Delhi: Motilal Banarsidass, 1999: 1435–1436.

J

jeguccha/jugupsa

Disgust (Pali/Sanskrit)

Disgust is one of the basic emotions (*bhavas*) listed in the aesthetic theory initiated by Bharata. When refined in artistic performance, it can be relished in the macabre (see *bibhatsa*). Bharata says that *jugupsa* (*jugupsā*) is prompted by "hearing or seeing what is not amenable to the heart," and on the stage it should be represented by the actor "shrinking back in all limbs, spitting, contorting the face, and experiencing anxiety in the heart." To perform disgust, the actor "should cover the nose, shrink the body, and shudder." In the stereotypes on which theater relies, disgust is coded for gender and class: "women and low persons" are particularly given to it.

But the *object* of disgust is not usually indexed by social class. Bharata's treatment of the macabre mentions battlefields and cremation grounds, suggesting that the disgusting is found in the death and decay of the human body. Later commentators describe bodily substances as conditions for disgust—stinking flesh, blood, marrow, and so on, and the presence of worms in these. At its most basic, *jugupsa* concerns human animality and vulnerability: blood, bodily discharges, worms, maggots, and decay—what some social psychologists today call "core disgust."

There is little evidence that *jugupsa* can be the moral disgust that worries contemporary philosophers like Martha

Nussbaum, who sees disgust for other people (variously women, criminals, members of races other than one's own) as ethically problematic considering the social, political, and ideological purposes it is so often put to serve. *Jugupsa* is not often deployed in this way in the sources; people certainly disapprove of the wicked and depraved, but individuals' moral failings seldom make them objects of *jugupsa*, and *jugupsa* is not a label slapped on classes of people.

In the hands of celibate renouncers, disgust is sometimes cultivated for ascetic purposes: Buddhist sources outline detailed practices of studying the thirty-two parts of the body (body hairs, head hairs, nails, and so on) to generate a sense of revulsion for the body; these aim at detachment from desire and carnality. More severely, meditations on ten different types of rotting corpses lying in cremation grounds (the bloated, the chopped up, and so on) are described in lurid detail to counter lust and vanity, and to make the meditator aware of the urgency and inevitability of death. Disgust (*jeguccha* in Pali) as such is not thematized in these "meditations on the impure," but the term does occur in the course of these rather extraordinary ascetic therapies.

While there is no gendered element to these meditations, there is a strand of Indian religiosity in other contexts that cultivates disgust specifically toward women's bodies and the sexuality women represent, a disgust that doubtless had social implications in the patriarchal institutions and gender hierarchy of all of these religions. In the male gaze from which most of our sources are drawn, women's bodies are projected to be at once alluringly attractive and dangerously vile. In the highly poetic renderings of the Bodhisattva's renunciation of the world, disgust toward women's bodies plays a crucial role. The Bodhisattva recoils from the sleeping women in his harem right before escaping the palace and renouncing household life, and he likens their sleeping bodies to bodies sprawled in a cremation ground. He finds them "disgusting" and resolves to leave the palace that night.

In a very different religious framework, Rupa Goswami describes a pious male worshipper of Krishna who has turned from his licentious ways, so that now, "when he sees the face of a woman, he wrinkles up his face, becomes rigid, and spits." While in theory, disgust with sexuality and the body is supposed to be beyond gender, it so often is overlaid on the specific bodies of women.

See also **bhava; bibhatsa**

REFERENCES

Bharata says . . . Nāṭyaśāstra VII.26.

Later commentators . . . See IP: 200–201.

philosophers like Martha Nussbaum . . . Nussbaum's *Hiding from Humanity*, Princeton, NJ: Princeton University Press, 2004, is an important philosophical consideration of moral disgust and shame; see also W. Miller's *The Anatomy of Disgust*, Cambridge, MA: Harvard University Press, 1997, on the modern history of the social, moral, and political uses of disgust. One exception to the general lack of moral disgust can be found in the *Rāmāyaṇa* (IV.54.7): the monkey Aṅgada, deploring the moral turpitude of his uncle Sugriva, is disgusted (*jugupsita*) by him; Sugriva, though, for all his failings, is a heroic character.

cultivated for ascetic purposes . . . Meditations on the thirty-two body parts can be found in the *Visuddhimagga*, PP: chapters VI and VIII.

He finds them "disgusting" . . . Lalitavistara 15.39. Liz Wilson explores the conflation of the erotic and the repugnant, and their superimposition on the female body in *Charming Cadavers*, Chicago: University of Chicago Press, 1996: see especially 68–70.

"when he sees the face of a woman" . . . BR: 610–611.

K

kama

Sensual Pleasure and the Desire for It (Sanskrit and Pali)

Readers can find plenty of entries in these pages that disparage *kama* (*kāma*), but here we celebrate it. For the early ascetic religions, *kama* and the craving it leads to are the source of all suffering. But even within these traditions, later tantric developments reconsidered the energies of *kama* and came to harness *kama*'s power for dramatic transformation. And mainstream Hinduism has long given *kama* its proper due as a legitimate pursuit in promoting the three "aims of human life": sensual pleasure, prosperity, and morality—though sometimes a fourth is added, liberation (*moksha*), which transcends the other three. Most authorities see a hierarchy in these aims to be invoked when they conflict, with *kama* considered the least important. But all agree that each has its own intrinsic value and legitimacy and should be pursued within its own terms at certain stages in life and as circumstances allow. It is in this context that the *Kama Sutra*—a *shastric* guidebook for doing *kama* well—is to be understood.

Popular culture in the West has a blinkered grasp on Vatsyayana's *Kama Sutra* as merely a titillating catalogue of sexual positions. Rather, the text is a fascinating glimpse of courtly culture—or at least a certain elite male fantasy of it—in early medieval India, centered on the exploits of the playboy, the "man-about-town," whose wealth, status, and privilege promote a life of leisure and amorous pursuit. His primary ambition in life is to seek out those "who incline to the ways of the world and regard playing as their one and only concern."

As a *shastra*, the *Kama Sutra* is full of descriptions and prescriptions (and it can sometimes be hard to tell the difference between the two) for the complex practices and relationships to be navigated in the romantic and erotic sphere of life. But why, the text itself asks, does one need a manual for sex? Surely passion can find the way. We see that animals get along just fine without reading textbooks on sex. The answer is straightforward: "because a man and a woman depend upon one another in sex, it requires a method." Anything that involves complexity in human relationships needs instruction on technique to perform well. Sexual practice is a skill, and skill is learned with methodical *shastric* instruction that shares the wisdom garnered over the ages on the subject. Moreover, Vatsyayana's commentator adds, humans, unlike animals, engage in sex not just for reproduction, but also for enjoyment; a man can be led to climax without much skill involved, but to ensure that the woman is pleased, proper methods should be studied. Indeed, he goes further: should anyone find success in this sphere without having studied the methods, it could only be a matter of pure chance, like a bookworm accidentally eating a perfect letter-shaped hole in a page.

Shastra on *kama* thus enhances pleasure and helps one avoid its perils. While there are certainly pitfalls to be found in the pursuit of pleasure, *kama* is "a means of sustaining the body, just like food." *Kama* is also a reward for diligence in the other aims of life—ethics and the proper pursuit of wealth and power can and should yield pleasure. The text is to be studied by both men and women along with the sixty-four arts, which include singing, dancing, musical instruments, flower arranging, teaching mynah birds to talk, writing plays and poetry, and athletic pursuits. These genteel pursuits are the graces of this courtly life of pleasure.

For all the ways the text evokes an ancient Indian playboy fantasy, the *Kama Sutra* documents the sometimes grim social, economic, and political realities in which sexual liaisons take place, a world of polygamy, class hierarchy, political machinations, adultery, economic disparity, sexual violence, and everywhere, the vulnerability of women. But while Vatsyayana shows how power and social convention shape the ways people will experience *kama*, he does not allow them to exhaust its possibilities: he is often keen to discover where pleasure and love can occur *despite* the social norms and institutions that constrict them.

Take love marriages, for example. Vatsyayana dutifully logs the *shastric* ideal that prizes above all the respectable match made by parents where considerations of class, status, wealth, and family connections prevail. His gimlet eye does not fail to note that in these formal courtships, the young woman is treated "just like any other piece of merchandise" as she is displayed before potential husbands. But he also casually drops in that "some people say that a man will do well with a woman who catches and binds his mind and heart and his eyes," and that such a man should consider no other woman; "the best alliance plays the game so that both sides taste one another's happiness and treat each other as individuals." True, the love match is not conventionally considered the ideal form of marriage, but wait, perhaps it is "the best of all, because it gives happiness (*sukha*), costs little trouble, and involves no formal courtship, since its essence is mutual love (*anuraga*)."

The tender ministrations and courtship that happen *after* the wedding in the ten days building up to the final consummation is a time of gentle courtesies and escalating foreplay where the man slowly woos the young woman. This is in keeping with the central premise of the text that *kama* is enhanced when both parties enjoy it and learn its arts. To this point, a central preoccupation concerns women's pleasure. In a body of lore largely preserved by men, the text records male debates about the nature of women's sexual pleasure. Is it like that of men? Are women and men different in ways that impact their desire and its culmination? And, in any case, how can one actually come to know the nature of someone else's experience? Vatsyayana comes down decisively on the side of interpreting men and women as members of the same species with the same essence; they seek similar sensual pleasure, whatever their differing methods owing to their physical bodies. But the physical differences do entail that lovemaking should endeavor to help women reach climax before men to ensure that they achieve pleasure before the show ends.

On the tradition's own account, the authorship of the *Kama Sutra* is actually a bit complicated. Vatsyayana is the author, but he draws on earlier scholars, one of whom was said to have been cursed by Lord Shiva to become a woman; later, Shiva turned her back into a man but not before he had learned "both flavors," and helped to compose the chapter on courtesans. Another tradition has it that the courtesans of Pataliputta commissioned their chapter and so had an important role in formulating it. Regardless, in the courtesan chapter we see things from the calculating eye of the courtesan, or rather the high-ranking and celebrated courtesan-de-luxe, as she balances money, sex, love, and power. For these elite and powerful women, at least, the gaze is reversed as they take the measure of the men in their society and endeavor to set the terms of their entanglements.

For me, the most charming thing about the *Kama Sutra* is its encyclopedic attempt to be comprehensive while at the same time resisting any notion that this subject can ever be fully contained. To be sure, the text engages in a seemingly exhaustive listing of all manner of topics related to flirtation, courtship, and sexual practice in ways that give the air of a complete treatment. But Vatsyayana will never let such lists have the last word: even when it comes to a single set of erotic practices—say, the many ways one can leave nail scratches marking one's lover in a passionate grip—there is an infinite variety of possibilities. Vatsyayana is the first to admit that there is only so much a textbook can do in this sphere. "Because the things people can imagine are infinite, and there are infinite kinds of dexterity, and one can learn anything by practice and repetition, and passion is at the very heart of scratching with nails, who could survey all the forms?"

See also **anuraga; priti; raga; rati; trishna**

References

"aims of human life" . . . These are *kāma, artha,* and *dharma,* discussed by the *Kāma Sūtra,* chs. 1–2, KS: 3–13; they each have their bodies of *shastra.* (The fourth aim, only sometimes mentioned, is *mokṣa*). See W. Doniger, *Against Dharma: Dissent in the Ancient Indian Sciences of Sex and Politics,* New Haven, CT: Yale University Press, 2018, for a fascinating take on the relationship of these *shastras.*

"who incline to the ways of the world" . . . *Kāma Sūtra* 1.4.39. KS: 21. Throughout this entry, I use this translation.

"because a man and a woman" . . . *Kāma Sūtra* 1.2.16–20. KS: 9–10, with the commentary of Yashodhara in the footnotes; see also p. 3 n. 1 for the bookworm simile.

"a means of sustaining the body" . . . *Kāma Sūtra* 1.2.37. KS: 12. The sixty-four arts are at 1.3.

"just like any other piece of merchandise" . . . *Kāma Sūtra* 3.1.14; the other references in this paragraph are 3.1.76, 3.1.22, 3.5.29–30, KS, 76–78, 93 (with slight modifications to the translation on p. 93).

happen after the wedding . . . *Kāma Sūtra* 3.2. KS: 78–82; for the male debates on women's pleasure, see 2.1; KS, 30–37.

the authorship . . . As discussed in the *Kāma Sūtra* (1.1) and its commentary; KS: 4–6. The chapter on courtesans is the Sixth Book.

"Because the things people" . . . *Kāma Sūtra* 2.4.24; KS: 47. See *anuraga* and *raga* on these points, and KS: xxi–xxv; and 2.1.33, KS: 36.

kama muta

Being Moved (*and* Being Moved by Sensual Desire) (Sanskrit and English)

We come to the curious case of *kama muta*. *Kama muta* is a modern construct developed quite recently to serve as a scientific term in the work of an American psychologist of emotion, Adam Page Fiske. Fiske has created a "Kama Muta Lab," and he and his collaborators have studied a cluster of experiences to which he has given the Sanskrit name *kama muta*. *Kama muta* is defined by Fiske as an experience felt in a variety of ways that may be most closely rendered in English as "being moved": it is the tears springing to one's eyes when hearing children sing, the lump in one's throat when one's beloved proposes marriage, the warmth in the heart while cuddling a baby, emitting an "Awwww!" when seeing a fluffy kitten, or putting one's palm on one's chest singing one's nation's anthem. It lasts just moments, but is often intense and usually quite positive. It feels deeply from cuteness to love to awe. Fiske suggests that it is an emotion of communal sharing and connection. His team has published its results on this experience as it is reported among 10,000 participants in fifteen languages in nineteen nations. They find that the experience is widely recognized, even if not all of these cultures have a term for it.

Fiske chose to use a lexeme from Sanskrit to name this experience in order to avoid the hazards of using a modern vernacular term that is unstable and context-dependent in its usage, and which means different things for different speakers and discourses. He notes a "lexical fallacy" of assuming that because we have a term for something, it must refer to an actual psychological entity—language does not track psychological entities very precisely or in any stable way, and emotion words are unreliable labels. Moreover, Fiske argues, English (and other languages Fiske and his team had ready to hand) does not quite do the construct of *kama muta* full justice even in the notion of "being moved." And even if it did, English terms rarely map one-to-one on to terms in other languages. It seemed easier to start from scratch with a new construct and then carefully stipulate what it could be. That is where Sanskrit came in. As a "dead language" (in Fiske's rendering) Sanskrit could furnish a term that could be filled in with such content as Fiske deemed necessary to stipulate in describing the emotion.

> Stipulating the meaning of this term using a dead language minimizes the hazard of denoting the construct with a vernacular lexeme that means different things in different discourse contexts, to different people, in different dialects and social classes, and at different points in history. (In Sanskrit, *kama muta* meant moved by love, which approximates what we mean—but our stipulation of the meaning of the scientific term does not depend in any way on whatever this lexeme once meant to Sanskrit speakers.)

Fiske disclaims "any intent to mean what Sanskrit speakers ever meant by the lexeme," as he creates a theoretical posit of an experience that can then be studied empirically with modern psychological studies. He's a psychologist looking for emotions, not a lexicographer trying to describe meanings of words. And his research has led him to suggest that *kama muta, as he defines it*, may be a "natural kind," an actual, perhaps universal, human psychological entity.

But is Sanskrit really a dead language? And what does *kama muta* (*kāmamūta*) actually mean in the texts? For his purposes, Fiske did well to choose something in Sanskrit that is scarcely known and thus apparently not already "filled in," but *kama muta* is not entirely unclaimed. *Kama*, of course, is sensual pleasure and erotic love; *muta* is the past participle of a verb for move, so "moved by love" can work as a definition. In a hauntingly beautiful Rig Veda hymn sung by the cosmic progenitors of creation, Yami and Yama are twins and yet Yami desires to lie with Yama. The myth is a Vedic version of the widely attested cosmogonic dilemma of primordial incest faced also by Adam and Eve, a couple created from the same body yet whose reunion is needed to start creation. Yami describes herself as "driven by *kama*" (*kamamuta*), but Yama resists his sister. This experience of incestuous lust suggests a rather different quality than what Fiske has in mind.

One point raised by Fiske's use of Sanskrit for his purposes centers on whether Sanskrit is dead or alive. Is Sanskrit really dead, forgotten, and inert, useful simply in the past tense for furnishing hoary-sounding but forgotten terminology that can be reinvented for modern constructs? Or is it still living, its texts like the *Rig Veda* still sounding, its meanings still reverberating as they continue, even in Fiske's usage, to share with us how humans can feel? Whatever his assumptions about the vital life-breath of Sanskrit, Fiske seems to have intuited something important about Sanskrit in its capacity to name reality and to do so with universal significance (readers may wish to see a discussion of this very point about language in the entry on *cakshuraga*).

My proclivities as a lexographer (of sorts) are to explore the rich conceptual connections and contextual nuance of words in their worlds. This makes me suspicious that Fiske can ever ascend up out of the culturally and contextually tenacious webs of meaning in which words live, to achieve a view from nowhere and identify natural kinds (*even* with a Sanskrit lexeme in hand). For all the empirical study of *kama muta* experiences his lab has produced, we still see a culturally conditioned and presentist clustering of experiences in his construct. *Kama muta* can't save him from that.

So what term in the Indian lexica might denote the moist eye and thickness in the throat prompted by your child's piano recital? I think that *mudita*, sympathetic joy, gets at something of this swelling sense of joyful sharing, but one would want to look at a range of terms for love as well—*prema*, *priti*, *sneha*, and *vatsalya*.

See also **cakshuraga; kama; mudita; prema; priti; sneha; vatsalya**

REFERENCES

Adam Page Fiske . . . See A. P. Fiske, "The Lexical Fallacy in Emotion Research: Mistaking Vernacular Words for Psychological Entities," *Psychological Review* (November 4, 2019); and kamamutalab.org.

"Stipulating the meaning" . . . Fiske 2019, 2.

"moved by love" . . . According to Monier-Williams, *mūta* in *kāmamūta* is the past passive participle from the verb *mīv*, "to move" (Sanskrit English Dictionary, 272, 818). I know of no instance of it outside the *Ṛgveda*. I wrote to Fiske to ask him how he came by this term, but he was not able to recall how he did so.

Yami and Yama . . . *Ṛgveda* X.10.11. See *The Rigveda, Vol. II*, trans. S. Jamison and J. Brereton, New York: Oxford University Press, 2014: 1381–1383, for this hymn.

kapha

A Phlegmatic Disposition (Sanskrit)

India's traditional medical science, Ayurveda (the "Science of Longevity"), suggests that human health depends on a balance of the three humors (*dosha*): *kapha*, *vata*, and *pitta*.

Principally, these are qualities of the body's fluids and tissues and are connected to certain specified diseases, but they have correlates with qualities we would consider emotions. *Kapha* are the "phlegmatic qualities" of "heavy, cool, soft, unctuous, sweet, stolid, and slimy." (See separate entries for *pitta* and *vata*). The languid qualities of *kapha* correlate with the torpor that is *tamas*, and together they produce a stolid disposition, impassive, indolent, and dull when found in excess. While different views prevail on whether health requires an equal balance of the three humors, or whether it can be obtained according to a person's natural predominance of one of the three, therapy for illness requires counteracting practices of balancing food, environment, activity, and medicine to avoid excesses and aggravations of the humors.

The Ayurveda humoral psychology may be compared with that of the second-century Galen, the Greek physician whose theory of human temperament and physiology cast a long shadow across Arabic and European thought through the modern period. In the nineteenth century, European authors still spoke of temperaments and emotions in these terms. In the Western theory, four bodily fluids, or humors—phlegm, blood, yellow bile (choler), and black bile—are produced by the spleen and spread through the body; imbalances in them affect mood, temperament, and health. A preponderance of one of them results in pathology: too much phlegm yields a phlegmatic disposition, too much blood corresponds to the sanguine personality, yellow bile to the choleric, and black bile to melancholy. While not an exact match, black bile may be similar to *kapha*. Still, the two humoral systems differ significantly with respect to the nature and number of the other humors, and how they create disposition and mood.

See also **matsara; pitta; tamas; vata/vayu**

REFERENCES

"heavy, cool, soft" . . . "heavy, cool, soft, unctuous, sweet, stolid, slimy; these phlegmatic qualities are relieved by opposite qualities" (*Caraka Saṃhitā* I.61, my translation, but see also CS: 43).

different views prevail . . . Dagmar Wujastyk, *Well-Mannered Medicine: Medical Ethics and Etiquette in Classical Ayurveda*, New York: Oxford University Press, 2012: 192–193 n. 77.

karuna

Sorrow; The Tragic; Compassion (Sanskrit and Pali)

Karuna (*karuṇā*) has two distinct meanings: sorrow and compassion, and it is important to keep them conceptually separate. We'll take sorrow and its aesthetic refinement into the tragic first. In literary texts, *karuna* is great sorrow, such as how Rama feels when Sita is kidnapped. In the *rasa* systems that theorize literature, grief (*shoka*) can be refined aesthetically into the *rasa karuna*, a deep appreciation for the tragic side of life. *Karunarasa* is the sweet sorrow we feel when we weep at sad movies. It is prompted by all the forms of loss and distress that people face as we lose those whom we love.

But how is it that we can find aesthetic pleasure—the tragic—in sadness? The literary theorist Anandavardhana suggests that two kinds of *rasas* are the sweetest, that is, the aesthetic erotic relish of love-in-separation (*vipralambha*) and *karuna*: "this is because in these cases the heart is softened to a greater degree." (The key difference between love-in-separation and *karuna* is that in the former the lovers will be reunited; with *karuna*, the loss is permanent. But both involve a similar sense of sorrow and loss.) In both instances, sorrow exposes our deep vulnerability, and vulnerability can soften the heart. Anandavardhana's commentator, Abhinavagupta, elaborates: "the meaning is that the heart of the sensitive audience hereby abandons its natural hardness, its imperviousness, its liability to the flame of anger and its passion for the marvelous and for laughter . . . in the relish of *karuna* the heart completely melts." This suggests an exquisite pleasure in setting aside our usual proclivities for desire and aversion, as the tragic levels our passions, makes us porous to the world, and melts down our rigidities.

In the religious and philosophical literature, *karuna* is compassion, and this meaning is to be held apart from sorrow or the savoring of the tragic, though the connective tissue between the two meanings must surely be the empathy involved in sharing others' distress. *Karuna* (and the related *karunya*) is a foundational ethical and religious virtue in Indian culture. It consists of "a disinterested desire for removing the pain of others," and is often used interchangeably with *anukampa*, *anrishamsya*, and *daya*. It is everywhere endorsed for gods, kings, noble persons, and ordinary folks. It appears, for example, on the famous early Sanskrit inscription of King Rudradaman, where both his compassion and martial valor are eulogized.

Karuna is one of the four *brahmaviharas*, "the sublime attitudes" celebrated across religious systems in India (the other three are lovingkindness, sympathetic joy, and equanimity). In Theravada Buddhist formulations, these sublime attitudes "break down barriers" between people, and expand our hearts in all directions as they free us from our own hate, cruelty, envy, and indifference. *Karuna* is defined as "not bearing another's suffering," and requires one to remove it.

In Theravada therapies of emotions, *karuna* is a matter of intensive emotional work as one practices compassion first toward completely wretched people (Buddhaghosa gives an example of a person with arms and legs cut off) and then toward condemned criminals. Notably, nowhere in the literature is compassion limited to feeling for the innocent, as Aristotle, and much subsequent Western thought, would have it. Anyone suffering, including hardened criminals, should prompt our compassion precisely because they are suffering. This is because the opposite feeling that would exult in or tolerate the punishment of criminals is a hardness of heart that is in fact quite bad for us, stymying our efforts to achieve freedom from negative emotions.

In the meditation practices of the sublime attitude of compassion, the meditator gradually expands the depth and the scope of this emotion and in doing so comes to be rid of two emotional "enemies" that destroy one's freedom and peace. The first is compassion's "far enemy," cruelty, in that cruelty is compassion's opposite. When cruelty is present, there can be no compassion at all, and compassion is the removal of this ruthless feeling that constricts the heart. Compassion also has a "near enemy," distress; in encountering suffering in the world, we often devolve into hopeless despair and depression, feelings that can hinder us in effectively alleviating others' pain. *Karuna* here is not to be mistaken for this sense of sorrow, which lies near to compassion, but rather it is to be clearly distinguished from it.

The *karuna* of a bodhisattva, the religious hero who resolves to someday become a buddha, is extolled with great exuberance in the Mahayana Buddhist traditions. As they developed it, compassion is the flip side of the awakened mind: "the act of generating the enlightenment mind is a natural outcome of compassion." As one recognizes the emptiness of a hard distinction between self and other—given how mutually interdependent we are—compassion becomes a natural disposition. The enlightenment mind is the wisdom of the interconnectedness of all things, and a fundamental rejection of the essentialist thinking that throws up barriers between us. Compassion is the wish that everyone be free of suffering, prompting the bodhisattva to work ceaselessly to relieve the suffering of all beings throughout all worlds. Shantideva's beautiful prayer, one that H.H. the Dalai Lama takes to be his own highest hope and aspiration, voices this powerful compassion:

> As long as space abides and as long as the world abides, so long may I abide, destroying the sufferings of the world.

See also **anrishamsya; anukampa; anukrosha; brahmaviharas; daya; domanassa; hridaya; rasa; shoka; vipralambha**

REFERENCES

such as how Rama feels . . . Bhavabhūti's *Uttararāmacarita* is explicitly centered both on Rāma's *karuṇā* and evoking the *rasa karuṇā*, as a paradigmatic example.

The literary theorist . . . See DL: 254; for *Abhinavagupta*, see p. 255; they translate *karuṇā* as compassion here, but I have swapped it out and left *karuna.* "Sweetest" is *mādhurya.*

"a disinterested desire" . . . This is the Vaiśeṣika text, the *Padārthadharmasangraha of Praśastipāda with the Nyāyakaṇḍalī of Śrīdhara*, trans. G. Jha, Allahabad: E. J. Lazarus and Co., 1916: 560–561. The word for desire here is *icchā.*

In Theravada Buddhist formulations . . . The next three paragraphs are drawn from Buddhahghosa's *Visuddhimagga*, chapter IX, especially IX.94, IX.99. See pp: 306–307, 310–312. "Distress" as the near enemy of compassion is *domanassa*; "cruelty" is *vihiṃsā.*

as Aristotle . . . Rhetoric II.8 on *eleos*, pity.

"the act of generating" . . . Bodhisattvabhūmi 1.2.2. BP: 23.

"As long as space abides" . . . Bodhicaryāvatāra 10.55, BCA: ix, 143.

kashaya

Passions (Sanskrit)

Kashaya (*kaṣāya*) functions chiefly in Jain psychology as an organizing term for the passions, though it is not unknown to the rest of India. *Kashaya* gets at basic feelings of either the attraction (*raga*) or aversion (*dvesha*) that set up the polarities of our emotional life. Four main *kashayas* drive the human being: anger, pride, deceitfulness, and greed. These passions are themselves caused by previous "conduct-deluding" karma and then further cause karma to adhere to our souls, trapping us in samsara. The stickiness or resinous quality of this word in its primary meaning captures Jain metaphysical theories of how the passions make karma stick to us like glue: without the passions, karma would bounce off the soul like a clod of dirt thrown against a wall.

In their grossest forms, the *kashayas* are "pursuers from the limitless past" manifesting now in overt acts of grasping and aggression. In their subtlest forms, they "smolder" away, producing apathy and inertia. The great twelfth-century Jain polymath Hemacandra says that the four *kashayas* can be further distinguished by varying degrees of intensity and duration, suggesting that they are both episodic and dispositional: flaring up for a fortnight, lasting four months, a year, or a whole life.

And he adds specifics on each of the four: anger (*krodha*) "burns at its own foundation," destroying oneself whether it harms others or not, and must be managed with forbearance (*kshama*). Pride (*mana*) makes us blind because it "robs the eye of discrimination," as we magnify our virtues and obscure those of others; it needs kindness (*mardava*) to keep it in check. The "poisonous snake" of deceitfulness (*maya*) is "the mother of nontruth," and needs straightforwardness to counter. And greed (*lobha*), which starts off small but grows and grows to become an ocean, should be contained with the dike of contentment (*samtosha*).

An additional nine subsidiary passions (*nokashaya*) are also given: laughter (*hasya*), attraction to pleasure (*rati*), displeasure (*arati*), sorrow (*shoka*), fear (*bhaya*), disgust (*jugupsa*), male libido, female libido, and intersex libido. These linger until the main four *kashayas* are driven out, and all are eliminated as one reaches the highest rungs of the ladder of spiritual attainment.

See also **dvesha; krodha; lobha; mana; raga**

References

not unknown to the rest of India . . . Buddhist Vasubandhu describes "stains" (*kaṣāya*) of body, speech, and mind at AKB 4.58; and Asaṅga sees them as "degeneracies" of human behavior and disposition at *Bodhisattvabhūmi* I.2.4. BP: 26 n. 157. Also, *Mahābhārata* XII.179.27.

cause karma to adhere . . . *Tattvārtha Sūtra* of Umāsvāti 6.5, 6.15, and 8.2. Trans. N. Tatia, San Francisco: HarperCollins Publishers, 1994: 152, 158, and 190.

stickiness . . . *clod of dirt* . . . Akalaṅka's *Tattvārthavarttika* as described in P. Dundas, *The Jains*, London: Routledge, 1992: 84.

"pursuers from the limitless past" . . . *"smolder"* . . . *Sarvārthasiddhi* 751, as quoted in P. S. Jaini, *The Jaina Path of Purification*, Delhi: Motilal Banarsidass, 1979: 119–120.

Hemacandra says . . . This paragraph is from Hemacandra's *Yogaśāstra* IV.6–22. YŚ: 77–80.

male libido, female libido, intersex libido . . . For a discussion of these in a Digambara text against the possibility of women and intersex people attaining *moksha*, see P. S. Jaini, *Gender and Salvation: Jaina Debates on the Spiritual Liberation of Women*, New Delhi: Munshiram Manoharlal, 1992: 11–12 and chapter VI.

kleshas/kilesas

Depravities; Afflictions (Sanskrit/Pali)

The Yoga system of Patanjali shares with the Buddhist sources the idea that repeated patterns of experience become laden with emotional baggage—that is, toxic impurities called the *kleshas* (*kleśa*) When we fall into patterns of thought and action, we create deep traces or grooves (*vasanas*) that add up to inclinations and dispositions of the personality. These deep impressions remain at a subliminal level, and we inherit them from time immemorial. When such patterns and inclinations erupt into experience, they are called *kleshas,* afflictions, so named because they torment and afflict us

In the Yoga system, there are five *kleshas*: ignorance, ego, attachment, hate, and clinging to life. These can lie dormant or be in various stages of manifestation and activation, and are the roots of karma. Yogis practice the stilling of these defiling afflictions by asceticism and meditation to interrupt and remove the patterns that keep us from liberation.

Buddhists also offer lists of *kilesas* (as they are known in Pali), such as the three roots of all our troubles in samsara: greed (*lobha*), hate (*dosa*), and delusion. Other lists count attachment, hostility, pride, wrong views, doubt, and ignorance among the *kleshas.* Often the term is synomymous with, or defined in terms of, *asavas,* the oozings.

See also **anushaya/anusaya; asava/ashrava; vasana; yoga**

References

ignorance, ego, attachment, hatred, and clinging to life . . . avidyā, asmitā, rāga, dveṣa, abhinirveśa . . . See *Yoga Sūtras* 2.3–13, YSU: 44–47. The *Mahābhārata* also recognizes *kleśas,* as at 12.174.24, where these afflictions crush us much as oil pressers crush sesame seeds.

three roots . . . Dhammasaṅgaṇi 982, 1007–1008.

attachment, hostility, pride, wrong views, doubt, ignorance . . . rāga, pratigha, māna, dṛṣṭi, vicikitsā, avidyā . . . Abhidharmakośabhāṣyam 5.22–23 and commentary. My translation, but see AKB, volume III: 804. Vasubandhu focuses on the *anuśayas,* latent defilements, which he identifies in places with the *kleśas* and *āśravas.*

kopa

The Rage of Ill Temper (Pali and Sanskrit)

There was once a wealthy woman who was known for being peaceful, gentle, and tender. But her clever maid wondered if she was truly free of *kopa* or if it lurked in an unmanifest form beneath her gentleness. So she tested her by sleeping in late for a few days and being negligent in her otherwise impeccable work. Her mistress exploded and struck the maid in the head with a rolling pin until she bled. The maid ran to the street denouncing her mistress to her neighbors, and a bad report spread from there of this harsh and rough woman. The story suggests that anger can lurk in even the gentlest among us. The Buddha used this parable to instruct his monks that it is not enough to be implacable as long as nothing disagreeable happens but then detonate at adversity. He goes on to give one of the most demanding of moral codes conceivable:

> Monks, even if savage bandits were to saw off your limbs with a two-handled saw, if your mind erupts in anger, you would not be carrying out my teaching.

And he urges them to keep this simile of the two-handled saw ever present in their minds to ward off *kopa*.

Kopa is often interchangeable with other words for anger, *krodha*, *rosha*, and *manyu*, but if it has a distinctive quality, it is an unstoppable rage whose presence may not be known until it erupts. It is the end of great *Mahabharata* war, and we've spent many pages with the great king Dhritarashtra submerged in grief. Yet his sorrow surrenders to rage when he confronts his nephew Bhima, who has killed Dhritarashtra's son in a terribly vengeful way, striking below the belt. Dhritarashtra is overcome with *kopa*. Fortunately, wise

Krishna has the foresight to replace Bhima with a metal statue just as Dhritarashtra embraces him, for Dhritarashtra squeezes the statue so hard and with such fury that it shatters against his chest, and Dhritarashtra himself falls to the ground, splattered with blood. He is gathered up in the arms of the kind Sanjaya who soothes him, and finally Dhritarashtra lets go of his *kopa*.

A specialized sense of *kopa* is gendered; women's jealous anger is considered an appealing affectation in the arts of love. In the asymmetrical geometry of love poetry, women can be jealous when their lovers philander; the inverse is never true, as an untrue woman cannot be an aesthetic object in these conventions. But when a man has strayed and his beloved is jealous, her *kopa* can make her all the more attractive to him because it indicates how fond she is of him: "here women's anger with their frowning brows, trembling lips, and their charming threatening fingers, makes their lovers long for return to favor."

See also **irshya; krodha; manyu; raudra; rosha; ushma**

References

There was once . . . Majjhima Nikāya i.125–26, MLD: 219–220.
"even if savage bandits" . . . Majjhima Nikāya i.129, MLD: 223.
sorrow surrenders to rage . . . Mahābhārata XI.12.14–24. Trans. K. Crosby, *Mahābhārata, Book Eleven, The Women,* New York: CSL, 2009: 240–243. A few pages later, we meet with Gāndhārī's *kopa,* again directed at Bhīma (XI.14.14, 14.21).
"here women's anger" . . . Kālidāsa's *Kumārasaṃbhava* 6.45, BK: 224–225.

kripa

Compassion; Pity (Sanskrit)

Kripa (*kṛpā*) often fills the eyes. Arjuna's eyes are distraught with the tears of compassion as he declares his unwillingness to fight the great war of the *Mahabharata*. Another source tells us that when Lord Krishna contemplates the sufferings of the great patriarch Bhishma at the end of the war, he is bathed in "compassion with tears from his quivering eyes." In fact, the eyes of the great gods and goddess often become suffused with *kripa* as they contemplate human suffering. The third eye of the great Devi can "in compassion, bathe even me, distant and wretched," sings a devotee.

Perhaps most extraordinarily, the Jina Mahavira looks upon even his enemies "with eyes moistened by tears and pupils wide with *kripa*." Compassion is an important exception when it comes to the lack of emotions of the great enlightened beings. Despite his having transcended the vicissitudes of all emotions, here Mahavira's eyes are wet with *kripa* and the pupils are dilated as they fully take in the human condition.

These are astute observations about the phenomenology of compassion. Its operations entail seeing the suffering of others, a matter of attention and careful looking. The same organs that see the suffering also hold the compassion. And the tears suggest deep feeling in even the most equanimous of beings.

See also **daya; karuna**

REFERENCES

Arjuna's eyes . . . Bhagavad Gītā 2.1.

Another source . . . BR: 156–157.

"in compassion, bathe even me" . . . Saundaryalaharī 57. Trans. W. N. Brown, *The Saundaryalaharī or Flood of Beauty*, Cambridge, MA: Harvard University Press, 1958: 70–71. Devī conveys *kripa* to Kāma through a side glance at verse 6 (pp. 50–51). Her eyes convey compassion of all sorts, including *karuṇā* and *dayā*.

"with eyes moistened by tears" . . . Hemacandra's *Yogaśāstra* 1.3. My translation, but see also YŚ: 19.

kritajna/katannu

Gratitude (Sanskrit/Pali)

Kritajna (*kṛtajñā*) is, literally, "knowing what was done." Gratitude remembers the good things others have done and keeps them in mind. To apprehend rightly about benefits received is to feel gratitude. Its opposite is a similar word—*kritaghna*—which means "destroying what was done": to forget or refuse to keep in mind kind services rendered, is to destroy them. The ingrate is everywhere despised.

Upon hearing an aged jackal howl at the break of dawn, the Buddha takes it to be the old fellow's gratitude (*kataññu*) for the new day. The jackal both *knew* and *felt* this gift. Jackals are usually rather craven in Indian lore, but this moment recalls a better side to their nature. Another story has it that once a farmer rescued a jackal from a python. When the python later seized the farmer, the jackal, out of gratitude, fetched the farmer's brothers to save him. Such considerations make the Buddha urge that his disciples train themselves in gratitude: we should never overlook even the least favor done for us. If jackals can do this, so can we.

See also **anumodana; audarya**

REFERENCE

both knew and felt . . . Kataññutā and katavedita in the Pali: *Saṃyutta Nikāya* II.272, CDB: 712. The story of the jackal and the python is supplied by the commentary, *Sāratthappakāsini* 2.231–232.

krodha

Anger (Sanskrit)

I blind the world, I deafen it.
    The mindful wise, I make mindless.
The learned see not what is to be done,
    nor hear advice from anyone,
    nor recall at all their learning.

Anger usually shouts, but here we catch it calmly giving a clear-eyed reckoning of itself. *Krodha*, the most common word for anger, is the powerful emotion that distorts even wise and careful persons, its sheer force bending perception, memory, and reason to its ends. It flares up from insult, abuse, quarrelling, disputing, and hostility, and, once arrived, all too readily takes over.

And when it does take over, *krodha* is the blazing up of rage, everywhere connected to fire and conflagration. While resentful wrath (*manyu*) stays on the low boil, the rage that is *krodha* flames up swiftly. Fortunately, it often dissipates sooner. When the epic hero Bhima is enraged at the disgrace of his wife Draupadi, fire exploding with sparks bursts from the openings of his body like flames from the hollows of a burning tree. More than any other word for anger, *krodha* fuels the eighteen-day war of the *Mahabharata*. Indeed, *krodha* is valorized as a martial virtue in the bardic traditions and savored in the *raudra rasa*; anger is so prevalent that it practically becomes a character in its own right, and everywhere drives plot.

Krodha, along with *kopa*, is also the anger of infuriated sages whose curses advance plot lines in the epics and legends. It is one of the curiosities of the many ascetics, yogins, and sages who populate the epic stories that, despite lives devoted to meditation, celibacy, and peaceful retreats in sylvan hermitages, they are forever flying off the handle at the slightest of slights. Consider Durvashas, a hot-tempered sage who regularly pops up as a guest at the most inconvenient times, ever ready to take offense if he is not received properly. In Kalidasa's epic poem, the unfortunate Shakuntala fails to greet Durvashas promptly. This results in his cursing her to lose the very beloved whom she had been absent-mindedly pondering when he happened to stop by. And no matter how carefully people tiptoe through the penance groves frequented by the sage Narada, someone invariably offends this prickly character. Once, enraged, he cursed a hero to a life as a beast in the Himalayas for accidentally dropping a flower garland in the Ganges river waters in which Narada happened to be bathing.

Anger expresses asceticism's antipathy to its opposite, love, as we see again in another of Kalidasa's dramas, the *Birth of the Prince*. The gods need Lord Shiva to bear a son to slay a demon, an unlikely possibility since Shiva is an ascetic. They send the mountain goddess Parvati to seduce him, aided by the love arrows of Kama, the god of love. When Shiva discovers this, he is beyond furious, and though the gods cry out "Lord, hold back your *krodha*, hold back!" fire shoots from Shiva's third eye and incinerates Kama. Kama—Love!—become bodiless, a personal tragedy for him and his wife, but also a cosmic disaster. Without love, colors fade and the world wilts. Of course, Parvati prevails, and their love regenerates the cosmos. But Shiva's fury captures asceticism's vulnerability to anger and ultimate capitulation to eros.

We ordinary mortals who are neither sages nor deities cannot usually permit ourselves to give way to such rage. Physicians treat anger as an urge to be suppressed, moralists everywhere deplore it, and religious thinkers catalogue its perils. Where Aristotle thought that anger could be a virtue, an appropriate response to insult and injustice when exercised in proportion and according to the circumstances, Indian thinkers developed therapies for dismantling it by cultivating lovingkindness and forbearance (though Draupadi's forceful defense of anger stands as an important exception—see *manyu*). There is simply no sense, the Buddhist thinker Shantideva insists, in which someone prone to anger is well off.

See also **kopa; kshama/kshanti; manyu; metta/maitra; raudra; rosha; sthayibhava**

REFERENCES

"I blind the world" . . . Kṛṣṇamiśra's allegorical play, *Prabodhacandrodaya*, trans. M. Kapstein, *The Rise of Wisdom Moon*, New York: CSL, 2009: 82–83.

insult, abuse, quarrelling . . . *Nāṭyaśāstra* 7.16.

fire, exploding with sparks bursts . . . *Mahābhārata* 2.63.15, 2.64.14.

unfortunate Shakuntalā . . . See *The Recognition of Shakuntala by Kalidasa*, trans. S. Vasudeva, New York: CSL, 2006: 179–180, where she is subjected to Durvashas's wrath (*kova*, in Prakrit).

frequented by the sage Narada . . . From the *Kathāsaritsāgara* 4.2.137–144. Trans. J. Mallinson, *The Ocean of the Rivers of Story*, volume II, New York: CSL, 2009: 116–119.

"Lord, hold back your krodha" . . . Kālidāsa's *Kumārasaṃbhava* 3.72, BK: 124–125. The Purāṇa accounts of the story emphasize the cosmic dimensions of this more than Kālidāsa does.

Shantideva insists . . . *Śāntideva: The Bodhicaryāvatāra* 6.5. BCA: 50; see ch. 6 for the cultivation of forbearance (see also the following entry) as an antidote to anger.

kshama/kshanti

Forbearance; Patience; Forgiveness (Sanskrit)

Here, we cluster emotions deriving from the verbal root, *ksham*, to be patient (and Prakrit, *khama*; Pali *khanti*). All refer to a feeling of patience, endurance, and forgiveness that allows one to forbear injury without anger or retaliation. This is a combination of forgiving one's enemies and forbearing suffering with patience, grace, and love. A Jain prayer reads: "I grant forgiveness to all living beings. May all living beings grant me forgiveness. My friendship is with all living beings. My enmity is totally nonexistent." Here, *khama* is the counter to hostility, anger, and hate; as we ask others to forgive our faults, we must in turn forgive theirs.

The Buddhist figure Asanga defines its essence: *kshanti* (*kṣānti*) is enduring every sort of abuse from others, and is made possible either by one's natural disposition or else by relying on a calm consideration of the matter. This endurance is not based on expectation of reward and it is the absolute compassion of a bodhisattva. *Kshanti* is made possible by a cognitive therapy considering and reconsidering the others whom one might blame, the injury itself, the workings of karma, the nature of impermanence, and one's own hopes to avoid inflicting further suffering on self and others. Above all, one should consider the happiness that *kshanti* brings because it renders impossible the painful afflictions that are anger and hate (see *krodha* and *dvesha*).

Kshanti, though widely admired in classical India, would likely not attract similar appreciation today among those social justice advocates who argue for the moral value of anger. In the face of systematic racist and sexist oppression, anger is perhaps both appropriate and necessary for effective resistance. In this view, *kshanti* would seem to deprive social justice movements of anger's energy and power because it is anger that often galvanizes recognition of injustice and action against it. Advocating forbearance of harm would seem to justify and support the status quo, perhaps even make one complicit in accepting one's own and others' oppression. (Supporters of this view will find an eloquent spokeswoman for anger in the heroine Draupadi—see *manyu*.)

Although this critique can feel anachronistic when applied to ancient sources that did not consider systemic oppression, considering how classical Indian moralists might respond to it is a worthwhile undertaking. The texts point out just how toxic and corrosive anger is to those who bear it and how it distorts vision and effective action; anger makes one repellent to others and only generates more suffering. *Kshanti* avoids all of this and makes clear-eyed compassion possible, and compassion is always about alleviating suffering, not submitting to persecution. Such texts do not, however, tend to consider structural injustice and the moral considerations involved in social reform and resistance.

But Mahatma Gandhi does consider all of these and then offers a sustained modern rebuttal to those who would champion anger. For Gandhi, the commitment to nonviolence (*ahimsa*), requires and is realized through forgiveness (*kṣama*) as an empowering restraint on one's own vengeance. Based on his readings of the ancient texts, particularly the *Bhagavad Gita*, Gandhi finds that courage and strength consist of forgiveness, while vengeance is always weakness and fear. "Nonviolence is a weapon of the strong," and "forgiveness is the virtue of the brave." But patience is not cooperation with one's oppressors. Satyagraha, self-rule, and noncooperation are achieved through forgiveness: "this refusal to speak, to participate in the evil, to assist one's own degradation, to cooperate with the wrongdoer, gives strength to oneself, and awakens and purifies the wrongdoer."

See also **dvesha; krodha; manyu; ushma**

REFERENCES

A Jain prayer . . . As cited in A. Hunter and A. Rigby, "Gandhi and the Virtue of Forgiveness," *Gandhi Marg* 30, no. 4: 432.

Buddhist figure Asanga . . . This is my paraphrase of *Bodhisattvabhūmi* I.11.1, but see all of chapter I.11 on *kṣānti* and BP: 313–329.

who argue for the moral value of anger . . . See, for example, b. hooks, *Killing Rage: Ending Racism*, New York: Henry Holt and Company, and L. Tessman, *Burdened Virtues: Virtue Ethics for Liberatory Struggles*, New York: Oxford University Press, 2006: especially her review of these views on pp. 116–125. I am grateful to Kristen Culbertson for drawing me to this debate.

"Nonviolence is a weapon" . . . *Collected Works of Mahatma Gandhi*, v. 25, p. 483, as cited in Hunter and Rigby, pp. 436–437.

"this refusal to speak" . . . *Young India*, June 22, 1921.

kukkucca

Worry; Regret; Remorse (Pali)

Kukkucca is the worried regret that keeps looking back at one's bad deeds. The English word "remorse" has the sense of "emotional gnawing at oneself over one's wrongdoing," and etymologically it means "to bite again" suggesting continual reopening of wounds as one rehearses again and again a vivid appreciation of one's wrongdoing. *Kukkucca* is a similar relentless scratching, "like a point of an awl on a metal bowl," which captures the anxious distress of it. In the Pali Buddhist tradition, it is often paired with *uddhacca*, agitation, where both together—"flurry and worry"—constitute one of the main hindrances to religious contemplation.

The texts recognize also the unfortunate condition of worrying about worrying, as in the case of the fastidious monk Bhaddali, who announces that he cannot undertake the monastic regulations of eating only one meal a day because he worries that he will have *kukkucca* and remorse (*vippatisara*) about possibly violating this. The Buddha scolds him for this foolishness.

But not all regret and remorse are unwise. In fact, they can be morally salutary when they are the repentance that confesses and makes amends. In these contexts, they signal a valuable sense of scruple, for surely it would be much worse to be blithely indifferent to, or worse, to take arrogant pleasure in, one's past failings. *Kukkucca*, along with *vippatisara*, appears frequently in the monastic rules when describing the bad conscience that sets in after a monk or nun has committed a transgression, communicating, even before the Buddha must do so, the wrongness of the act. The effects of such regret are palpable: one becomes "haggard, wretched, pallid, yellowed, emaciated with veins showing, downcast, mentally sluggish, miserable, depressed, remorseful, and disappointed." In the case of the worst offenses, these depredations themselves indicate that one is no longer a monastic.

See also **hiri/hri; pashcattapa; uddhacca; vippatisara**

REFERENCES

"emotional gnawing" . . . C. Card, "Rectification and Remainders," in *Routledge Encyclopedia of Philosophy*, ed. E. Craig, London: Routledge, 1998: 1.

worrying about worrying . . . *Majjhima Nikāya* i.437–438, MLD: 542.

"haggard, wretched, pallid" . . . As for example, in Vinaya iii.19 (Suttavibhaṅga).

L

lajja

Shame; Embarrassment; Bashfulness (Sanskrit)

Lajja (*lajjā*) can refer to many types of shame and is often a synonym of *vrida*, with both meaning the shame and humiliation following from recognizing and becoming aghast at one's misdeeds. But in the context of eros, *lajja* is a highly pleasing bashfulness about the body, and here we explore this territory. Male admiration of female beauty is much enhanced, the literary critics say, by a quality of female modesty and bashfulness they refer to as *lajja*. Abhinavagupta says that "bashfulness is the chief gem of ladies even if they are wearing jewels." But *lajja* is not modesty just for the sake of it, but rather a shyness that indicates hidden desire. He continues

> Bashfulness is that by which a luster is suggested in the form of that beauty of the heart which bursts forth from inner emotion, for bashfulness is a manifestation of emotion in the form of a desire to hide the workings of love which are bursting forth from within . . . [it] is a beauty the essence of which is concealment.

Lajja is an attempt to conceal the body or the emotions that yet shine forth in intimate gestures and movements of the eyes and limbs. The critics find it exemplified in this verse, uttered by a male lover speaking these words to himself:

Prompted by intimacy and by Love's command,
the soft-eyed damsel uses graceful gestures
which are indescribable and come forth ever new.
I must find some solitary spot to ponder them
with my whole thought in constant meditation.

The graceful modesty of the soft-eyed damsel is full of hidden purpose that the lover must ponder at great length. Anandavardhana asks, "what beauty is not given by the easy and endless suggested sense arising from this?" He sees a direct analogy between this feminine shyness and the arts of suggested meaning (*dhvani*) of the poet. As a fine verse only indirectly suggests its ineffable and endless potential for meaning, an attracted woman intimates her desire through her very gestures of concealing it.

To make the point by contrast, Abhinavagupta mentions the complete lack of bashfulness of ascetics "who are devoid of the emotions of love, even if their loincloth is taken away." The naked male ascetics wandering India have no embarrassment at their exposure precisely because they have no love and desire to conceal.

See also **hiri/hri; shringara; vrida/vridita**

REFERENCE

the literary critics . . . All examples and quotations in this entry are found in DL: 614–615.

lobha

Greed; Lust (Sanskrit and Pali)

Money is not the root of all evil, greed is. On this, all sources, from the practical wisdom of statecraft to religious tracts, find agreement. Greed is sticking fast to an object, and is not sated even upon acquiring it. And the texts agree in finding greed (and lust—*lobha* is both) pernicious not only in itself but also because it generates other problematic states like anger, desire, hatred, and delusion. The practical wisdom of the *Hitopadesha* asserts: "From greed comes anger, from greed arises desire, from greed there is delusion and ruin: greed is the cause of evil." In religious texts, *lobha* (or variants of it like *raga*, *kama*, or *trishna*) always occurs on lists of toxic states that cause our suffering. For Buddhists, *lobha* is one-third of a triad of toxic roots—greed, hatred, and delusion—generating all our suffering.

Part of what makes them so toxic is how they interact and reinforce one another. When greed or lust is doing the driving, we are more likely to be hateful and deluded. This is because when we want something badly, we hate anything that prevents us from acquiring it. And aversion and greed each blinds us to a wider perception that would let more facts in, especially facts that are inconvenient for our getting what we want; we rearrange our perceptions and understanding around our grasping what we desire. The result is a vicious feedback loop between greed, hatred, and delusion, each amplifying the other, and unless at least one of them is interrupted, we are battered along through samsara, ultimately wretched and unhappy, always craving things, none of which finally satisfies us (see *trishna*).

The phenomenology of *lobha* is given characteristic metaphoric precision by Buddhaghosa, a Buddhist commentator. *Lobha* generates delusion, which is a kind of blindness. It is characterized by grasping its object much like the lime used to trap birds or monkeys. It makes one stick to an object like meat slapped on a hot pan. And it doesn't give up, just as lampblack adheres to fabric. And then it only swells with more craving (*trishna*), ultimately carrying us along to hell much like a swift river flows to the ocean.

See also **abhijjha; dvesha; iccha; kama; kleshas/kilesas; trishna**

REFERENCES

"From greed comes anger". . . *Hitopadeśa* 1.27, 1.142.

The phenomenology of lobha . . . *Visuddhimagga* XIV.161–162. PP: 472. For a long list of ninety-nine synonyms, modes, and types of *lobha*, see *Vibhaṅga* 361–362, *The Book of Analysis*, trans. P. A. Thittila, London: Pali Text Society, 1969: 470–471. See also *anuraga* for a similar style of such listings in a different genre.

M

mada

Vanity; Intoxication (Sanskrit and Pali)

Mada is both drunkenness and exorbitant pride or vanity. The cutting satirist Kshemendra and the modern translator Somadeva Vasudeva give us this verse showing how the two meanings converge in the various forms of *mada*:

> The mania of valor,
> The giddiness of vanity,
> The dizziness of infatuation
> And the delirium of nobility,
> —these are mankind's trees of intoxication
> sprung from one root: pomposity.

Mania, giddiness, dizziness, delirium, intoxication, pomposity—all are *mada*. We get drunk on our own vanities.

Buddhist philosopher Vasubandhu describes *mada* as "the snatching away of the mind by one enamoured of their own qualities." In a curious way, the more one becomes "inflamed and intoxicated" with the self, the more the mind retreats. Other authorities, he says, liken the intoxication of *mada* to that of wine that can so excite the mind as to erase it. Closely linked to but distinguished from pride (*mana*), *mada* is not so much an arrogance born of comparison to others, but rather an obsessive self-adoration.

Hindu masters treat *mada* along similar lines, with some suggesting that the inflation of the mind owing to *mada* is based on a deluded sense of one's own fine qualities. Others see it as a "haughtiness that comes from much repudiating" of others' qualities, and would distinguish it from conceit (*abhimana*), which is instead the "wrong attribution of one's own eminence." In the aesthetic literature of Bharata, *mada* is represented on stage variously ranging from slightly tipsy to the foibles and stumbling of a drunk.

See also **abhimana; atimana; darpa; garva; mana**

REFERENCES

"The mania of valor" . . . Kṣemendra's "Grace of Guile," in *Three Satires: Nīlakaṇṭha, Kṣemendra, and Ballaṭa*, trans. S. Vasudeva, New York: CSL, 2005: 228–229, verse 6.4.

Buddhist philosopher Vasubandhu . . . *Abhidharmakośabhāṣyam* 2.33. My translation, but see also AKB, volume 1: 204–205.

Hindu masters treat . . . Specifically, Advaita commentators Madhusūdana, who suggests that *mada* is owing to a deluded sense of one's qualities, and Ānandagiri, who distinguishes between *mada* and *abhimāna*. Both are quoted and cited in IP: 121 (with my translation of text in n. 84).

aesthetic literature of Bharata . . . *Nāṭyaśāstra* 7.38–46.

madana

Passion; Lovesickness (Sanskrit)

Madana is passionate, romantic, and erotic love. Our deities of erotic love, Krishna and Kama, are both at times called Madana. There are springtime Madana festivals of passion where everywhere love is celebrated with birds chirping and bees buzzing. Everyone revels in the blooming, blossoming, bursting of spring.

But *madana* is most acute when it is lovesickness. In court poetry, heroes and heroines fall in love at first sight and are left in a "condition of *madana*" where they pine for their sweethearts, languish, grow wan, and worry their friends. The lovely heroine Ratnavali, the Lady of the Jewel Necklace, catches sight of the king at one such Madana festival and is intoxicated, smitten, enamored, and obsessed thereafter. The condition is traced to the flower arrows of Kama, the Indian Cupid, who goes around shooting innocent victims with his bow.

See also **abhilasha/ahilasa; autsukya; kama; vihara; vipralambha**

REFERENCE

Ratnavali . . . The references in this entry are to the eponymous drama, trans. W. Doniger, *"The Lady of the Jewel Necklace" and "The Lady Who Shows Her Love,"* New York University Press: CSL, 2006. The Madana festival is described in act I, the heroine's *madanāvastha*, condition of lovesickness, opens act II (pp. 124–145), and we see the exertions of Kāma.

madava/mardava/maddava

Kindness; Softness (Prakrit/Sanskrit/Pali)

Throughout his inscriptions on pillar and stone across India, the Mauryan emperor Ashoka (who called himself "Beloved of Gods," Devamampiya), urged *madava* (*mādava*), kindness and softness. The kindness he endorses is something he himself practices and urges for his successors. He preaches vegetarianism and nonviolence to animals, softens his punishments, and pledges to desist from state violence (at least whenever possible). He supports Buddhism and counsels "conquest by righteousness," rather than conquest by military might.

To be sure, Ashoka's policy was two-pronged, urging kindness by all, but also letting the "forest people" know that he has not foresworn military might altogether.

> And even the forest people who live within the dominion of Devanampiya, even them he conciliates and urges to reflect. And they are told of the power that Devanampiya has in spite of his remorse [because of

> the Kalinga war] so that they may turn away from their crimes and may not be killed. For Devanampiya desires for all beings freedom from injury, self-restraint, impartiality, and kindness.

Here, inviting all beings—particularly former enemies—to feel kindness helps make possible his own disavowal of violence.

In Jain teachings, Sanskrit *mardava* (*mārdava*) is the antidote to pride, as it softens it and takes it down. Buddhists gloss Pali *maddava* as "softness, gentleness, smoothness, malleability, and humility." The idea of a mind that is soft and pliable and thus easily changed and developed is widely valued in Buddhist therapies of emotions since they aim to fundamentally reconstruct its workings. The Buddha once announced that he could perceive nothing "so unwieldy as an undeveloped mind": a mind rigid, hard, or brittle is almost impossible to change or develop. Hence the value of being soft and malleable, at least when in the right hands.

See also **anrishamsya; anukampa; anushaya/anusaya; daya; dovacassata**

REFERENCES

policy was two-pronged . . . This is U. Singh's formulation of Ashoka's policy of nonviolence, and it is her translation of Rock Edict 13 here (lines 7–8) on page 388 of PV. See also her n. 48 on page 542 noting that *mādava* is mentioned on the Girnar, Yerragudi, and Kalsi inscriptions too.

In Jain teachings . . . Hemacandra's *Yogaśāstra* IV.14. YŚ: 79; note that Quarnström translates *mārdava* in this context as "modesty."

Pali maddava *as "softness"* . . . *Dhammasaṅgini* 230.

"so unwieldy as an undeveloped mind" . . . *Aṅguttara Nikāya* i.5. BW: 267.

mahura/madhurya

The Quality of Sweetness or Charm Evoked by Love, Poetry, and Music (Prakrit/Sanskrit)

Sweetness is the charm of the taste (*rasa*) of love. It is thought that all creatures have the capacity to find delight in the emotion of attraction (*rati*). This is owing to an underlying proclivity (*vasana*) toward erotic love that is thought to be universal; even those who would shun it in this life, such as ascetics, have partaken in the delights of love in previous lives. And so, like sugar on the tongue to which all respond with pleasure, the sweetness of the erotic can be savored by all.

Sweetness is also a quality of poetry that can deliver this relish. The Prakrit treasury of poems called *Seven Centuries* inaugurates a sophisticated culture of pleasure, in which the connoisseurship of love was explored in both courtly poetry and scholarly reflection that theorized how poetry produces its charm. One of its poems asserts:

> Prakrit poetry is nectar.
> Those who don't know how to recite it or listen to it
> make love into a science.
> How are they not ashamed?

Against those who would subject the art of lovemaking to the schematization and systematization of the *Kama Sutra*, the poem contrasts the beautiful evocations of Prakrit poetry as the very nectar in which the beauty of love may be tasted. The poem makes clear that poetry can make us savor the sweetness of its subject in a way no didactic literature ever can. (Note too that the *shastric* authors are to be ashamed not for their *graphic* rendering of lovemaking but for their clinical treatment of it.)

The quality of sweetness that the Prakrit tradition first identified as a literary quality refers specifically to the way in which a poem or a poetic line can be heard over and over again without losing its charm. (This specification would contrast most sharply this Indian quality of "sweetness" with that of the clichéd commercial greeting card, which can't be heard even once without provoking annoyance.) The idea was already known to King Ashoka, who publicly aspired to the quality of sweetness (*madhuliya*) in his diplomatic efforts in his rock edicts, hoping that his propaganda would not grow wearisome with repetition. Andrew Ollett suggests that Prakrit poetry has qualities of musicality in how it is pronounced (a softness from having more vowels than consonants, at least compared with Sanskrit), as well as its qualities of indeterminacy in semantic possibility. These give Prakrit poetry a special potential to be savored time and time again.

The idea of literary art producing sweetness was further developed in the Sanskrit tradition in poems like this one:

> Music and poetry,
> Saraswati has two breasts
> One's sweet at first sip–
> the other, well, you need to
> chew it a while.

The goddess of learning and the arts, Saraswati, gives us the instantaneous sweetness of music as well as the less immediate nectar of poetry that may require rumination. One should keep a poem in one's mouth for a while to relish fully its sweetness, a sweetness that depends on the taster as much as the tasted.

See also **kama; preyas; rasa; shringara**

REFERENCES

It is thought that . . . Abhinavagupta says that there is no one who is not inclined to the sweetness of love owing to the "unbroken proclivity" (*vasanā*) for it in all creatures. See DL: 252.

"Prakrit poetry is nectar" . . . Seven Centuries, W2. Trans. and discussed by A. Ollett in *Language of the Snakes: Prakrit, Sanskrit, and the Language Order of Premodern India,* Oakland: University of California Press, 2017: 59–60, 118–119, 228 n. 43. See also P. Khoroche and H. Tieken, *Poems of Life and Love in Ancient India,* Albany: State University of New York Press, 2009: 2–6.

King Ashoka . . . H. Tieken discusses Rock Edict XIV, which mentions how Ashoka describes himself as raising topics repeatedly in order that their sweetness (*mādhuliya*) may arise; as Tieken notes, the earliest text on aesthetics, the *Nāṭyaśāstra,* mentions this quality (*guṇa*) in very similar terms: "When a sentence has been heard many times or has been said again and again and (nevertheless) this does not cause annoyance, we speak of (the *guṇa* of) *mādhurya*" (*Nāṭyaśāstra* XVI 104). This verse is translated and the issue discussed by Tieken in "Aśoka's Fourteenth Rock Edict and the Guṇa *mādhurya* of the Kāvya Poetical Tradition," *Zeitschrift der Deutschen Morgenländischen Gesellschaft* 156, no. 1 (2006): 95–115.

Andrew Ollett . . . Language of the Snakes, 88–93.

"Music and poetry" . . . BAM: 38–39.

mana

Conceit; Pride (Sanskrit and Pali)

Mana (*māna*) is perhaps the most common word for pride, but see *mada, garva,* and *darpa* for similar territory. Like the English word conceit, *mana* can mean both "pride" and "a fanciful notion," and both senses are intertwined in its usages. At its most basic operation, *mana* is the conceit that is embedded in language and thought when one says or thinks "I am." Buddhist sources speak of the processes of "I-making, mine-making, and the underlying tendency to conceit," as a rudimentary sense of ego and self-construction that skews our experience of the world. This subtle and ubiquitous conceit is to be "cut off at the root like a palm stump" for those seeking selflessness and freedom. Practices to do so involve meditations on impermanence, often impermanence of the body such as contemplations of corpses.

The sources give various lists of conceit, such as one list of three: conceit as such, the conceit of self-loathing (see *omana*), and the conceit of vainglory (see *atimana*). Even when one thinks one is the worst—*omana*—there is preoccupation with and inflation of "I." *Mana* is glossed as "haughtiness, loftiness, bearing a flag, presumption, and a desire for recognition." Other lists add superlative conceit, where one thinks "I am the best of the best," baseless conceit, where the pride leads one to overestimate one's qualities, and mistaken conceit, where one takes pride in things that are low and vile.

Mana is often conceived as relational in an important way. One variety of it, described by a Hindu authority, involves the imputing of inferiority to others who in fact are full of virtues. An Advaitan thinker speaks of the yogin who has achieved an "awakened impartiality" toward self and others. Yogis in this highly developed state "do not see another person as different from themselves," and so "pride and contempt are difficult to experience." The flipside of the self-love that is *mana* is *avamana*, contempt for others, and both dissolve when the distinction between self and other dissolve.

Conceit is often a matter of social class, wealth, or clan. Puffed up with *mana*, one becomes "stiff with pride, swollen like a full bellows, and does not bend to anyone." On a cautionary note, the Buddhist commentaries mention the case of the haughty Shakyas, the Buddha's own clan. The Shakya royalty despised and insulted their kinsman, Vidudabha, the son of King Pasenadi and a slave woman, for his low birth. Furious at this, when he came to power he massacred the whole lot of them.

As often, religious authorities deprecate emotions that aesthetic experts admire. For the latter, *mana* is a kind of wounded pride and anger evidenced in romantic scenes when a woman puts on a jealous sulk. One poet cites the "playful sulks of lustful ladies" as a device of protracted love play that infuriatingly postpones the exhilarations of the lovemaking that is the making-up. But sometimes it is not a performance: women get jilted and cheated on in this literature, and *mana* becomes one of the many causes of frustrated love (see *vipralambha*).

See also **abhimana; ahamkara; atimana; avamana; darpa; garva; kashaya; mada; omana; vipralambha**

REFERENCES

"I-making, mine-making" . . . Such as at *Aṅguttara Nikāya* i.132–133 in NDB: 228–230.

"cut off at the root" . . . *contemplations of corpses* . . . *Aṅguttara Nikāya* ii.217, iii.324–325. NDB: 590, 891.

Such as one list of three . . . *Dhammasaṅgaṇi* 1116.

Other lists . . . *Vibhaṅga* 353–356. AKB, volume III, 1989: 784–785. Superlative conceit is *mānātimāna*, baseless conceit is *adhimāna* (but *mithyāmāna* in Vasubandhu), and mistaken conceit is *micchāmāna* in the *Vibhaṅga*.

described by a Hindu authority . . . Viśvanātha's *Nyāyasūtravṛtti* as cited in IP: 94 n. 33.

"do not see another person" . . . Vidyāraṇya's *Jīvanmuktiviveka* 5.2.5. Trans. J. Madaio, "Transparent Smoke in the Pure Sky of Consciousness: Emotions and Liberation-While-Living in the *Jīvanmuktiviveka*," *BRH*: 163, 171 n. 57).

"stiff with pride, swollen" . . . *Paramatthajotikā* i.171–172. Trans. Bhikkhu Bodhi, *The Suttanipāta*, Somerville, MA: Wisdom Publications, 2017: 542. The commentary mentions Viḍūḍabha, but the full story is in the Dhammapada commentary, 345–360, trans. E. W. Burlingame, *Buddhist Legends*, volume II, Cambridge, MA: Harvard University Press, 1921: 36–46.

"playful sulks of lustful ladies" . . . *Pavanadūta* of Dhoyi. Trans. J. Mallinson, *Messenger Poems*, New York: CSL, 2006: 118–119.

manoratha

The Mind's Desire (Sanskrit and Pali)

> How can the mind's desire, that the mind will never abandon, ever be expressed? What girl is it who will shamelessly own up to wanting to catch the moon, that king of the twice-born, with her own hands?

Damayanti, the young woman who utters these words, has fallen deeply in love—on the strength of a description by a messenger gander—with King Nala long before she meets him in person (see *vihara*). While their love is eventually culminated (and most richly described by Shri Harsha), in its early stages it is pure fantasy. In her open confession of desire here, the bold Damayanti tosses away all expectations of maidenly modesty: in asking what girl will own up to her fantasies, she declares her own.

In another case of fantasy, Kalidasa has a hero, upon falling in love-at-first-sight with a goddess, note that this thing called fantasy, *manoratha*, has no limits. Pururavas's fantasy is "a longing hard to get," as this divine woman pulls his heart from his body. But in the fantasy world of these dramas, the mind's desire will always be fulfilled, for the mind so compelled is always something real.

See also **abhilasha/ahilasa; bahumana; rati; vihara; vipralambha**

REFERENCES

"How can the mind's desire" . . . *Naiṣadhīyacarita* of Śrī Harṣa III.59. HB: 150.

Pururavas's manoratha . . . *Vikramorvaśīya* 1.118–119, 2.109, 2.118. See V. Narayana Rao and D. Shulman, trans., *How Urvashi Was Won*, New York: CSL, 2009: 28–29, 58–61.

manyu

Simmering Wrath (Sanskrit)

> When Drupada's daughter heard that their enemies were flourishing, she could no longer hold back the resentment they had provoked. She spoke words designed to arouse the king's *manyu*, to stir him to action.

Manyu is the simmering wrath of resentment rather than the explosion of fury that is *krodha*. Where *krodha* is the fury of battle, *manyu* is the deep rage that causes and sustains wars to begin with. Often *manyu* is the impotent rage of the powerless, particularly women, who have been humiliated and abused, and it sharpens their acuity and rational power. Draupadi, the feisty heroine of the *Mahabharata*, whose disgrace by the Kauravas leads inexorably to the tragic war in the first place, is a master of *manyu* and she wields it like a sword (though, to be sure, she is often full of *krodha* as well). Her penetrating interrogation of the patriarch Bhisma on the circumstances in which the Pandavas gambled away themselves, their property, and her very self, wins his respect even as it shames everyone in the hall. And her rage never goes off the low boil during the thirteen years of the Pandavas' exile.

Catching her in such a moment, the court poet Bharavi gives Draupadi voice to express her wrath and to urge her husband, the gentle and righteous Yudhishthira, to himself nurture *manyu*, reject peace, and take up manly force against their enemies: "How can *manyu* not inflame you?" "Why are you not stirred to *manyu*?" (Elsewhere, wise heads counsel self-control and urge that Yudhishthira appease and contain his *manyu*.)

In the bardic traditions, women's anger is righteous and deeply sympathetic. It may not always lead to the best course of action—Draupadi's thirst for revenge leads to tragedy—but her anger fuels a sharp and unrelenting assault of words that is not easily dismissed. Her anger may be compared with the righteous anger of the long-suffering heroine Kannaki in the ancient Tamil epic *The Anklet.* Kannaki is so enraged by a false accusation against her husband leading to his execution that she tears off her left breast and hurls it at the city of Madurai, where it incinerates the entire kingdom.

See also **kopa; krodha; kshama/kshanti; rosha**

REFERENCES

"She spoke words" . . . *Kirātārjunīya* 1.27, and *"how can manyu not inflame you,"* 1.32, 35. Trans. I. Peterson, *Arjuna and the Hunter of Bharavi*, Cambridge, MA: MCLI, 2016: 11–17. See also *Mahābhārata* 3.28.25–35. In the *Mahābhārata*, Yudhishthira counters her arguments but discusses not *manyu*, but *krodha*, thereby evading the sense of injustice sustaining her wrath by dismissing it as merely hotheaded anger (3.30.1–30). I am grateful to C. Ram-Prasad for helping me see this point (personal communication).

simmering wrath of resentment . . . This distinction between explosive but quickly dissipating *krodha* and deeply seated impotent *manyu* is drawn in the Vaiśeṣika text, the *Padārthadharmasangraha of Praśastipāda with the Nyāyakaṇḍalī of Śrīdhara*, trans. G. Jha, Allahabad: E. J. Lazarus and Co., 1916: 561–562.

that causes and sustains wars . . . Grandfather Bhisma, lying on his bed of arrows having been felled by the Pandavas while fighting on Duryodhana's side, beseeches Duryodhana to give up the *manyu* that has caused this war. *Mahābhārata Book Six: Bhīṣma*, volume II, trans. A. Cherniak, New York: New York University Press, 2009, 518–521.

marsha

Forgiveness and Indulgence (Sanskrit)

Marsha (*marṣa*) is the patience, forgiveness, and forbearance that allows one to put up with annoying things and people, much like the more commonly used *kshama* or *kshanti*. Doubtless, we should be more patient and forgiving with others, but then of course, much depends upon what one is being asked to forgive. Bhima tells his brother Yudhishthira that one wishing to prosper can "easily put up with the growing ascendency of his enemies" only if one knows they will fall eventually. Otherwise, indulging rivals is misplaced, at least in the warrior ethic espoused here (see *amarsha*, *marsha*'s opposite).

In a different context, Vasubandhu, a Buddhist commentator, finds no value in having *marsha* for wrong views because it involves taking something vile as excellent. Sometimes, the gloves just have to come off, perhaps especially when dealing with bad ideas.

See also **amarsha; kshama/kshanti**

REFERENCES

"easily put up with" . . . *Kirātārjunīya* 2.8. Trans. I. Peterson, *Arjuna and the Hunter of Bharavi*, Cambridge, MA: MCLI, 2016: 11–17.

Vasubandhu, a Buddhist commentator . . . AKB 5.15–16, volume III, 1989: 793–794.

matsara

Spite (Sanskrit)

Matsara and *matsarya* are closely related, and both can mean a rancorous jealousy, envy, and spite. In the next entry, I consider a more specialized meaning of *matsarya* in Buddhist sources, while here we consider the qualities of *matsara*, a kind of exhilarating and spiteful bitterness, resentment, and acrimony. This is the spite that would prevent others from having what they need even at no cost to oneself, such as begrudging people drawing water from a public well. The Nyaya tradition makes a psychologically astute distinction about shades of envy and resentment when it puts *matsara* on the side of passion and desire, and assigns *amarsha, asuya,* and *irshya* to varieties of aversion and hatred. This makes *matsara* an envy or a bitterness that is more about attachment than hatred. It has elements of desire, self-regard, and exhilaration in it, a rancor not entirely unpleasant in the one fostering it, no matter how much it may be censured by moral authorities.

Shankara identifies *matsara* as a type of enmity (*vaira*). In its exhilarating qualities, the acrimony of *matsara* may share some features of that "unruly spleen" of Shakespeare's usage. Its connections to pride—Yajnavalkya urges that a good person set aside vanity and *matsara*—recall Shakespeare's account of a heart "cramm'd with arrogancy, spleen, and pride." In Western humoral psychology, the spleen is the seat of the humors and thus emotions; for Shakespeare, spleen can be the strength of martial fury ("inspire us with the spleen of fiery dragons") and the turbulence of the uncivil ("unto a mad-brain rudesby full of spleen").

See also **amarsha; asuya; irshya; matsarya; vaira**

REFERENCES

The Nyaya tradition . . . Vātsyāyana's *Nyāyabhāṣya* 4.1.3. *Matsara* is a kind of *rāga*, and *amarṣa, asūyā,* and *īrṣyā* are types of *dveṣa*. The public well example is given at *Nyāyasūtravṛtti* as cited in Sinha 1961: 92.

Shankara identifies matsara . . . *Gītābhāṣya* on *Bhagavad Gītā* 4.22.

"unruly spleen" . . . *Romeo and Juliet*, act III, scene 1; "crammed with arrogancy, spleen, and pride," *Henry VIII*, act II, scene 4; "inspire us with the spleen," *Richard III*, act V, scene 3; and "unto a mad-brain," *The*

Taming of the Shrew, act III, scene 2. See "Spleen" by J. Marinas in *Dictionary of Untranslatables: A Philosophical Lexicon,* ed. B. Cassin, trans. from the original French by S. Rendall et al., Princeton, NJ: Princeton University Press, 2004: 1047–1048.

matsarya

Meanness (Sanskrit)

Perhaps the most despised vice in all of Indian tradition is the feeling of stinginess and spitefulness captured by the term *matsarya* (*mātsarya*). In English, both meanings of the adjective "mean"—miserly and malicious—get at it. Civilized norms across all religious and traditions in India prize the virtues of open-handed generosity, neighborly kindness, and hospitality to the stranger, especially if the stranger happens to be a wandering monk or almsman of any sort.

Close-fistedness comes in for special condemnation, for example, in the Sanskrit Buddhist literary tradition of earthy folk stories called the *Avadanashataka.* As Andy Rotman shows, tales of *matsarya* in this collection are everywhere scatological, associating meanness with a pathological preoccupation with holding on to one's stuff; one becomes "anal retentive" (as the modern parlance would put it). *Matsarya* earns one an afterlife as a "hungry ghost," devoted to, quite literally, excrement.

In one tale illustrative of the genre, we encounter a hungry ghost, "with a stomach like an ocean, a mouth like the eye of a needle, and who was totally covered with hair. He was ablaze, completely aflame, a single fiery mass, a perpetual cremation. Racked with sensations that were searing, piercing, distressing, agonizing, and acute, he was crying out in pain. Wherever he wandered, the ground turned to excrement and urine, and so he made his way with difficulty."

What did this unfortunate wretch do to deserve this fate? He had been a workman at a sugarcane factory who refused to offer a solitary buddha a drink of sugarcane juice. Instead, "this wicked and cruel-hearted man" pissed urine into his almsbowl and offered it to this great enlightened being.

In Rotman's analysis, the karmic consequences that yield this unfortunate rebirth are not just recompense for such meanness but are fully congruent with it: in an important sense, one is already a hungry ghost when one's mind is so maliciously grasping and venal toward others.

See also **amarsha; matsara**

REFERENCE

As Andy Rotman shows . . . See Rotman's translation of the story discussed here and his introduction in *Hungry Ghosts*, Boston: Wisdom Publications, 2021: 76–78.

metta/maitra

Friendliness; Lovingkindness (Pali/Sanskrit)

In India, friendship can be an emotion. *Metta* (*mettā*) and *maitra* are the strong sense of love and kindness we have toward our friends. In more specialized religious contexts, *metta* has a specific aspirational content, which is the hope that others be happy, and it is a religious sentiment to be cultivated and expanded by disciplinary training (we'll consider the Pali formulations here). Just as we hope that our friends are happy and can flourish, so too should we flood ourselves with this warm and soothing hope for all others, even our enemies. Doing so counters the corrosive hatred and anger that otherwise narrow our vision and constrict our freedom. The resulting "freedom of the loving-heart" is conceived as a much more capacious way of being, one that is not distorted or hemmed in by one's usual prejudices, resentments, hatreds, and aversions.

In teaching how to cultivate *metta* as one of the "divine abidings" that dismantle the toxic emotions that obstruct freedom and happiness, Pali commentator Buddhaghosa insists, against possible objections, that you should start by directing lovingkindness toward yourself (see *brahmaviharas*). He quotes the Buddha to the effect that those who love themselves can never harm another. You should realize that at bottom you want to be happy, for such a thought comes very naturally to all of us. From here, you should realize that just as you want to be happy, so do all creatures. And as you flood yourself with hopes for your happiness, you can begin to hope too for theirs, gradually extending this feeling to loved ones, neutrals, and then enemies. A loving embrace of one's wish to be happy can then become the foundation of generous love to others that ideally becomes immeasurable in scope and extent.

For Buddhaghosa, it is not enough simply to decree that one love one's enemies. Concrete and specific strategies must be offered to show people how to do so. One is to try to shame yourself out of your hatred by considering the Buddha's extraordinary model of patience with wrongdoing and constant disavowal of hatred and anger. Another is to scold yourself for nurturing petty resentments that only bind your mind, sap your energy, and make you ugly (because anger distorts the face). Another technique is to break down your fixed conception of your enemy into the complex parts and history that comprise a human being to ask what part, exactly, you are angry with. When you see that your enemy is a continuous process of ever-changing phenomena and, like you, is a work-in-progress, it becomes harder to hold on to a single fixed and frozen identity of the person you are angry with. Or you might do a meditation practice that requires you to see your enemy as, in a previous life, your mother or father, who in that life cared for you most tenderly. Given that previous care, it is unseemly to continue to nurture hostility toward them now. If nothing else works to reorient you to a friendly disposition, you should give a gift to your enemy. Almost magically, giving a gift to someone you resent dissipates the hostility and frees up your mind and heart.

See also **brahmaviharas; dosa; patigha; sauharda**

REFERENCE

the Pali formulations . . . The content of this entry is taken from chapter IX of Buddhaghosa's *Visuddhimagga* (PP) See also M. Heim, "Buddhaghosa on the Phenomenology of Love and Compassion," *The Oxford Handbook of Indian Philosophy*, ed. J. Ganeri, New York: Oxford University Press, 171–189.

moksha

Perfect Freedom; Liberation (Sanskrit)

Well done! You have conquered anger!
Well done! You have vanquished pride!
Well done! You have banished delusion!
Well done! You have put down craving!
Hurrah for your firmness!
Hurrah for your gentleness!
Hurrah for your perfect forbearance!
Hurrah for your perfect freedom!

For millennia, Indian religious thinkers have wished to know what it feels to be free. This Jain celebration of perfect freedom hints at what it might be. *Moksha* (*mokṣa*) is not so much a matter of liberty in a public and political sense, but rather the deeper and even more elusive kind of freedom that is the release from all suffering, contingency, and human frailty. The renunciatory systems—Yoga, Jainism, Buddhism, and the various Hindu schools of theology based on the Upanishads—seek *moksha*, complete liberation from suffering in this life and forever (though Buddhists usually call this nirvana). *Moksha* is the "freedom from samsara" that liberates us from the otherwise endless cycle of rebirth and redeath; all schools agree that *moksha* is the end of karma, the causal actions and results that bind us to samsara.

There are, of course, as many conceptions of what this freedom is as there are schools of thought and philosophers pondering it. Our concern here is with what may be said of it in relation to emotion: *What does perfect freedom feel like?* Because emotions and feelings are transient states tied up with the body and mind, they are always implicated in suffering; even happy and pleasant experience is contingent on variables we cannot control, and so will end (see *sukha*). This basic insight suggested to many that whatever *moksha* might be, it cannot be the episodic and conditioned experiences of pleasure, happiness, and heaven. As the Mimamsa thinker Kumarila puts it: if you conceive of *moksha* as "the enjoyment of happiness, then it would be synonymous with heaven, and therefore perishable." The Nyaya pundits agree: for *moksha* to be the permanent end of suffering, it cannot rest on changing conditions; it is an absence of suffering "not pervaded by happiness," understood as the utter absence of delusion. It is a decisive and radical shift away from all attraction and aversion.

But others insisted that *moksha* must be supreme happiness, a kind of unconditioned bliss beyond all worldly conceptions of what happiness might be. Advaita Vedanta, the school of Hinduism started by Shankara, takes happiness to be the aim of human life; *moksha* then is not just the absence of suffering, but rather ultimate bliss (see *ananda*).

This freedom is a radical epistemic shift, where the scales of delusion fall away and one stops seeing the world through the veil of subject-object dualism. With the end of all ignorance, one stops superimposing self on the world and stops appropriating everything into the greedy organism of one's being. *Moksha* is the pure, blissful, and unobscured consciousness that remains.

As the *bhakti* traditions gained preeminence in Hinduism, *moksha* became achievable by devotion to God and through the gracious agency of God. Ramanuja states that God—the "Supreme Brahman"—is the "sole cause of the cessation of samsara" and is the "goal of those who seek *moksha*." And Brahman's essential nature is "infinite knowledge and bliss." According to Ramanuja, the *Bhagavad Gita* teaches the discipline of *bhakti* directed to God as "a means of attaining the supreme goal of human life, *moksha*."

Jains also see *moksha* as a blissful state, and posit a soul that achieves it. When the soul has shed all karma, all conditions of cause and effect, and all moral stains that bind it to the transient and painful world of samsara, it floats up to the highest realm of the cosmos, *perfectly free*, to abide in everlasting and sublime bliss. *Hurrah for perfect freedom!*

See also **ananda; bhakti; duhkha/dukkha/duha; nirvana/nibbana; shama; sukha; yoga**

References

"Well done! You have conquered anger"... This is a Jain text, *Uttarādhyayana Sūtra* 9. Trans. A. Embree, *Sources of Indian Tradition*, volume 1, New York: Columbia University Press, 1988: 70.

wished to know what it feels to be free... To borrow from Nina Simone, of course.

"freedom from samsara"... We begin to see this kind of language in the Upaniṣads, at Śvetāśvatara 6.16, EU: 432–433.

Mimamsa thinker Kumarila... *Ślokavārttika* v.16.105. Trans. C. Ram-Prasad, *Knowledge and Liberation in Classical Indian Thought*, New York: Palgrave, 2001: 48.

the Nyaya . . . According to Udayana, *Ātmatattvaviveka,* 429. Ram-Prasad 2001: 79.

Advaita Vedanta . . . The conception of *mokṣa* in this paragraph relies heavily on Ram-Prasad's discussion and translations of Advaita texts (Ram-Prasad 2001: chapter 4).

Ramanuja states . . . Vedārthasaṁgraha, paragraphs 6, 42, and *Gītābhāṣya* 3 and introduction. Trans. J. Carman, *The Theology of Rāmānuja,* New Haven, CT: Yale University Press, 1974: 70, 78. The "discipline of *bhakti*" is *bhaktiyoga.* It is notable that the *Gītā* itself refers more frequently to *brahmanirvāṇa* than *mokṣa.*

muda

Elation; Rejoicing (Sanskrit)

In an ancient Vedic rendering of the gods' creation of humans, we learn how sleep, conversation, prosperity, poverty, ignorance, and knowledge, and so many other qualities of our being "entered the body as a home." Among these qualities, we see that "bliss, joy, delight, gladness, elation, laughing, joking, and dancing entered into the body as a home." Already in these ancient sources, fine grades and varieties of joy and happiness are recognized and come in their various ways to inhabit our bodies. Several of these terms come from the verbal root *mud,* to rejoice, that gives us *muda,* elation, and several other gems (*mudita, pamojja/pramodya*).

Muda is pure elation and exhilarating joy. A gorgeous verse in a much later poem celebrating the texture of the celebrated lovemaking of Nala and Damayanti gives us this instance:

> Looking at her and looking at her, he looked at her once more and yet more in *muda.* Holding her and holding her again, he yet held her more; he kissed her but eager, kissed her again. But they never found it enough.

We have deep beholding of the beloved that brings this elation, a joy that breaks forth anew with each additional moment of gaze, embrace, and kiss. Yet it is never enough.

See also **ananda; harsha; hasa; mudita; pamojja/pramodya; piti; priti; rati; sukha**

REFERENCES

"bliss, joy, delight" . . . *Atharvaveda* 11.8.24: *ānandā́ mó́dāḥ pramúdo 'bhīmodamúdaś ca yé / hasó narí́ṣṭā nṛttā́ni śárīram ánu prā́viśan.*

"Looking at her" . . . Śrī Harṣa's *Naiṣadhīyacarita* VII.106. Trans. and discussed by C. Ram-Prasad, HB: 173.

mudita

Sympathetic Joy (Sanskrit and Pali)

Mudita (*muditā*) is the unalloyed delight we feel when sharing another's success, happiness, and good fortune. One Buddhist commentator describes it as the tender joy parents, for example, feel as they see their children grow up and thrive: the parents' "minds become tender, like a hundred fluffy balls of cotton soaked in the finest clarified butter." But sympathetic joy is by no means limited to parents. Our capacity to find happiness in others' happiness is an expansiveness of emotion highly sought in the therapeutic practices of Buddhist meditation. The aim is to "break down barriers" so that one will come to share in the joyfulness of anyone and everyone. It makes for a happy state of being.

Mudita bears comparison with the fellow feeling Adam Smith extols in *The Theory of Moral Sentiments*. He acknowledges that "sympathy" is usually taken to refer to our feeling with those in sorrow, but in fact, he argues, our sympathy with joy is far more pervasive, and we enter into it far more readily: "it is agreeable to sympathize with joy; and wherever envy does not oppose it, our heart abandons itself with satisfaction to the highest transports of that delightful sentiment." We seem by nature inclined to seek out the joy of happy companions and we spontaneously and instantaneously share in it; we are not, contrary to the Hobbesian view he argued against, entirely self-interested and competitive beings. Indeed, our sympathies with both the joy and the sorrow of others are strong and sincere.

Unfortunately, it is not always easy to feel sympathetic joy. For both Buddhaghosa and Smith, the chief obstacle thwarting this delightful sentiment is envy. Buddhaghosa considers envy the "enemy" of sympathetic joy because it makes us feel displeasure at the success of others and it blocks how we might share in their happiness. In this way, it constricts and confines us, and so the earnest practitioner should engage in disciplinary contemplative practices to dismantle the envious mind's envy and malice toward the good fortune and achievements of our enemies. With the other three "sublime attitudes"—lovingkindness, compassion, and equanimity—*mudita* is both the practice and the goal of achieving freedom from the aversions, hatreds, resentments, and cruelties that narrow and distort our vision and understanding of other beings.

See also **amarsha; brahmaviharas; irshya; karuna; muda**

References

"minds become tender" . . . *Manorathapūraṇī* 2.204. Trans. H. Aronson, *Love and Sympathy in Theravada Buddhism*, Delhi: Motilal Banarsidass, 1980: 70.

"it is agreeable to sympathize" . . . A. Smith, *The Theory of Moral Sentiments*. London: Harrison and Sons, 1853: 63. See my comparison of Buddhaghosa and Smith in "Toward a 'Wider and Juster Initiative': Recent Comparative Work in Buddhist Ethics," *Religion Compass* 1 (2006): 1–13. "Envy" here is *issā*, Pali for *īrṣyā*.

N

nanda

Rejoicing (Sanskrit and Pali)

Nanda means rejoicing, gladness, joy. Buddhists tell a tale of the Buddha's half-brother who was named Nanda because of "the constant joy he gave to his family." Yet, as developed by Ashvaghosa, the earliest of the Sanskrit court dramatists, Nanda's story raises profound questions about what joy and happiness might consist of, and the poet playfully evokes his name throughout. We first find Nanda lost in love with his beautiful wife—she "the loveliest of women and he the happiest (*nanda*) of men"—where together they are a "home to joy and rapture (*nandi*)." But their sweet and tender love-play, though most sympathetically rendered by Ashvaghosha, is not to last, as the Buddha contrives to pull Nanda away from his wife and coerce him into joining, most reluctantly, a life of celibacy in the monastic order. At this eventuality, "Nanda knew no gladness"—*na nananda Nandah*, as the Sanskrit delightfully states it—and languishes in utter misery hating life as a monk and the loss of his darling wife. Various attempts by his monastic brethren to help him renounce the pleasures of wife and family leave him unmoved, and he remains "the unhappy Nanda" (*Nandam niranandam*).

Determined to help break Nanda's ties of attachment, the Buddha takes him on a trip to heaven to see the gorgeous damsels with whom he will eventually enjoy dalliances owing to the merit made by his current renunciation. This ploy works, and Nanda forgets his wife as he commits to the monastic regime out of longing for the heavenly damsels. But he faces another blow when he learns that should he win such heavenly rewards, they too, like all pleasures on earth, will end, and he will eventually face the sorrow of losing them as well. At this, the poem's Buddhist didacticism begins to work as he listens to and puts into practice the techniques for conquering passion and achieving peace. At this point, his joy becomes the lasting and secure kind, the peace (*shanti*) and bliss (*sukha*) of religious liberation.

But we hear no more of his *nanda*.

See also **ananda; nirvana/nibbana; piti; priti; shanti; sukha**

REFERENCES

"the constant joy he gave to his family" . . . *Saundarananda of Aśvaghoṣa*, HN: 58–59.

"the loveliest of women . . . home to joy and rapture" . . . HN: 80–81. There are puns on both their names here—Sundarī, his beloved wife's name, means Lovely. He too is most handsome, and so is sometimes called Sundara; hence the title of the text, *Handsome Nanda* (*Saundarananda*), which might also echo their two names together.

"Nanda knew no gladness" . . . HN: 132–133.

"the unhappy Nanda" . . . HN: 193.

nirvana/nibbana

Liberation; Awakening; Enlightenment (Sanskrit/Pali)

"Nirvana is stopping."
"Nirvana is highest happiness."

These two claims uttered in the Buddhist texts suggest something of how we might imagine the felt quality of nirvana (*nirvāṇa*), the sublime liberation and awakening at the heart of the Buddhist tradition and the ultimate aim of its practice. (Where Jains and Hindus usually refer to this perfect freedom as *moksha*, Buddhists tend to use the term *nirvana*.)

The first claim conceives of nirvana as "stopping:" It is the "end of suffering" that occurs when one stops all craving, attachment, and desire. The third noble truth speaks of nirvana as "the complete cessation of craving, giving it up, renouncing it, freedom from it, and doing away with it." Nirvana is ceasing the restless craving and attachment with which we grasp each moment of existence. When that craving ends, "there is the stopping of birth, and when birth is stopped, the grief, lamentation, suffering, distress, and trouble that are old age and death end." With the ceasing of all negative and transient emotion one is utterly and irreversibly "free": "free of passion, free of hatred, free of delusion, free of pride, and free of views, one crosses over samsara and reaches nirvana," where nirvana is "stainless, dustless, pure, fair, birthless, ageless, deathless, happy, cooled, and without fear." Nirvana is the ultimate freedom from emotion, a complete release from the pulls and pushes that knock us about and that keep us scrabbling after the scraps of pleasure that come our way. When we fully let go of all desire, we achieve freedom from emotionality altogether.

Yet at the same time, the Buddha consistently identifies nirvana with *sukha*, happiness or bliss. In the Pali sources, *nibbana* (*nibbāna*) is the "highest happiness," the most exalted *sukha*. In one discussion of this, a student quite naturally asks: "What kind of happiness could there be when nothing is felt there?" The sublime response: "Just this, friend, is the happiness here, that nothing is felt here." Nirvana is not, at least according to these sources, a sterile or barren annihilation; one is not an automaton. But then how can it be understood? "It is to be understood as safe, secure, free of fear, tranquil, peaceful, happy, agreeable, excellent, pure, and cooled." Like the person pulled away from a blazing fire is cool and happy, so too is the one who has achieved nirvana. Nirvana is "entirely happy."

Among Sanskrit poets, Ashvaghosa's account of Nanda, the Buddha's brother, suggests a nirvana of blissful happiness. Nanda must forsake the rejoicing of sexual love to achieve the peace and calm of nirvana, and when he does so, he celebrates: "The arrow of lust that was lodged in my heart was pulled out under the direction of the compassionate teacher. Immense bliss (*sukha*) is mine right now, and oh! my peace in the annihilation of it all." In the absence of pleasure and pain, "I am straightaway joyful (*sukha*) like one who is spared extremes of cold and heat."

In contrast, the Buddhist philosophical schools treat nirvana in relation not so much to emotions, but to conceptual thought. Mahayana texts emphasize that attachment occurs in the very ways we conceptualize experience in the first place. By its very nature, conceptualization—that is, cognition itself with its dualistic construction of subject and object and its constant naming, essentializing, and reifying—distorts "the way things are." And thus, it is only with the ceasing of all cognition that one attains nirvana. Of course, this idea makes it very difficult for those of us on this side of nirvana's far shore, still mired in conceptual thought, to cognize what it might be. All our thoughts about nirvana, as about all things, are inescapably mired in conceptualization. While for centuries, Buddhist philosophers engaged in vigorous debate about how to understand nirvana, and how their own highly conceptual philosophical thought could itself relate to the project, others, perhaps wisely, remained silent.

See also **duhkha/dukkha/duha; moksha; nanda; parideva; sukha**

References

"Nirvana is stopping" . . . *Nirodho nibbāna. Milindapañha* 69; see also *bhava-nirodho nibbānaṃ* (nirvana is the stopping of existence) at *Aṅguttara Nikāya* v.9 in NDB: 1345.

"Nirvana is highest happiness" . . . *Nibbānaṃ paramaṃ sukhaṃ* at *Majjhima Nikāya* i.508; see MLD: 613.

third noble truth . . . *Saṃyutta Nikāya* v.421. For a translation of the passage on the noble truths, see BW: 75–78.

"stopping of birth" . . . The remaining quotations in this paragraph are from *Milindapañha* 69 and 332–333.

"what kind of happiness" . . . *Aṅguttara* iv.414–418. NDB: 1292–1294.

"safe, secure, free of fear" . . . *"entirely happy"* . . . *Milindapañha* 323–324 and 313.

"The arrow of lust" . . . HN: 336–339.

Mahayana texts . . . See, for example, Sthiramati's *Madhyantavibhāga-bhāṣyaṭīkā*, trans. C. Ram-Prasad, *Knowledge and Liberation in Classical Indian Thought*, New York: Palgrave, 2001: 115. See his chapter 3 on this matter.

nirveda

Despair and World-Weariness (Sanskrit)

> In the beginning, there is certainly nothing; and afterward, nothing. In between, suddenly, for no apparent reason, one occupies oneself, running after good fortune or bad:
>
> Like some kind of dancing creature with no head and no feet, a person leaps about for a time, but when the curtain falls on his existence, we have no idea where he goes.

Such is the bleak assessment of the twelfth-century historian Kalhana as he concludes his account of a Kashmiri king, Harsha, whose reign began with great optimism but fell into corruption and misrule. Harsha's "distasteful" downfall came when he fled the capital and was captured and decapitated by his enemies; in the end, he was unmourned by his people. For Kalhana, the lesson of Harsha's life, indeed that of all of us when we reflect on our own pointless leaping about on the stage, is a poignant sense of despair that should prompt us to throw it all up and take to the quiet life secluded in the forest: "It's a great shame that people, when they see this, do not give in to *nirveda* and develop a taste for forest life, which does end well."

Nirveda features variously in *rasa* theory. In Bharata's system, *nirveda* is a transitory emotion that consists of the despair one feels from poverty, being abused, insulted, or reviled, and losing loved ones. Perhaps more darkly, it can also be the despair one feels when one grasps the true nature of reality. Bhanudatta adds that *nirveda* can be the despair issuing from self-reproach or from the idea that life in samsara should be abandoned.

The more existential dimensions of the experience make *nirveda* a candidate for the underlying emotion savored in the *rasa shanta*. Those theorists who championed the idea that drama and literature can generate the ninth *rasa*, peacefulness (*shanta*), sometimes took *nirveda* to be the emotion that gets aestheticized in *shanta*. In this capacity, *nirveda* becomes a fundamental disenchantment with life in the world; it is "revelatory of a knowledge of truth" that can be savored religiously and aesthetically in peaceful equanimity. With knowledge of the true ephemerality of worldly desires, desire dries up and one becomes indifferent to worldly things. It is in this way that the term *nirveda* comes to convey both despair at the horrors of the world and the cool indifference such despair can lead to.

But others would draw a distinction between *nirveda* as "a flow of sadness," and *vairagya*, dispassion, as a higher form of detachment. And they would further distinguish both of these from the dispassion (*shama*) that must surely be the enduring emotion savored by *shanta*. That is, for them, *shanta* does not savor existential despair, but rather calmness.

See also **rasa; shama; shanta; vairagya; vyabhicaribhava; yoga**

REFERENCES

"In the beginning . . . It's a great shame" . . . Kalhaṇa's *Rājataraṅgiṇī* 7.1731, 1730. Trans. and discussed by L. McCrea, "*Śāntarasa* in the *Rājataraṅgiṇī*: History, Epic, and Moral Decay," *Indian Economic and Social History Review* 50, no. 2 (2013): 198. McCrea points out that the ending of Harṣa's life is compared by Kalhaṇa to the "distasteful" (*virasa*) ending of the *Mahābhārata*, and that he deliberately aligned his own history to the epic's overall *rasa* of the peacefulness (*śānta*) prompted by world-weariness and despair.

Nirveda features variously . . . Nāṭyaśāstra 7.28; *Rasataraṅgiṇī* 5.8. BRRR: 204–205). Bhānudatta's element of "self reproach" seems also to have been picked up on by religious thinkers: Vedānta Deśika defines *nirveda* as "self-contempt" (*svāvajñā*), as cited in IP: 131.

the ninth rasa . . . Abhinavagupta suggests that the *sthayibhāva* of *śāntarasa* is *nirveda*. (DL: 143, 479, 521).

"revelatory of a knowledge of truth" . . . In Abhinavagupta's words. DL: 514; *nirveda* as indifference is on page 521.

others would draw a distinction . . . Abhinavabhāratī. ŚR: 127–128. See *shanta* for more on the debates about it.

nrishamsa

Cruelty (Sanskrit)

Kaikeyi, King Dasaratha's second wife, is persuaded by her malevolent maidservant to call in a promise of two boons the king had made to her long ago, and she makes a shocking demand: the king must deny succession to the rightful heir apparent, the eldest brother Rama, and instead crown her own son, Bharata. Though it desolates him (see *dina*), King Dasaratha consents, and Rama is exiled. Everyone is anguished, and Kaikeyi comes to be reviled throughout the kingdom.

What began as selfish anxiety in a vain woman about what would happen to her when her co-wife's son is crowned, hardens into the malice, misanthropy, and cruelty that is *nirshamsa* (*nṛśaṁsa*). Her crooked and ruthless maidservant who conceived the hideous plan is also *nirshamsa*, and has been so all along. But Kaikeyi grows into her malevolence. Though her husband, the mighty king, falls to her feet begging her for mercy until he falls unconscious, her heart is unmoved. And the deeper and wider the despair around her grows and the more hated she becomes, the crueler she gets.

See also **anrishamsya; dina**

REFERENCE

Kaikeyi . . . *Rāmāyaṇa* II.11.14, 72.8, 86.25. The maidservant Mantharā is described as full of *nṛśaṃsa* at II.72.7, 10, for example, and she is ruthlessly beaten up by one of Rāma's brothers, Śatrughna, for it.

O

omana

The Conceit of Self-Loathing (Pali)

Among the varieties of conceit (*mana*) listed in Buddhist sources, we find the curious conceit of self-loathing. *Omana* (*omāna*) entails deriding and debasing oneself in one's own eyes, chastising oneself for being low and vile. Having "contrived" such a conceit—for all conceits are manufactured products of an obsession with self—one rouses a malicious scold and turns it inward, berating oneself: "you have birth, but your birth is like a crow's birth; you have a clan, but your clan is like that of an outcaste; you have a voice, but your voice is like that of a crow." *Omana* is a *conceit*, rather than a variety of hatred, because it involves a subtle form of preoccupation with the self. This inferiority complex is not a matter of depression or dejection but of pride and self-promotion. *I am the worst, truly despicable. No really, I am. I must insist. I am the very worst. Ever.*

As much as conceit involves a relationship with self, it is yet everywhere infused with social convention. In one account, there are nine types of conceit: three varieties (the conceits of finding oneself superior, equal, and inferior) times three kinds of people (those *actually* superior, middling, and inferior). For example, superior persons like kings can have all three types of conceit, as when a king compares himself with other kings, and deems himself superior, equal, or inferior to them based on the size of his treasury, the prosperity of his kingdom, and the size of his army. The king coming up short in this estimation laments that "only the pleasure of being labeled a king is mine, for what kind of king am I?" A slave born into a proud family of slaves compares himself smugly to other slaves who have fallen into slavery by destitution, while the truly inferior slave complains in despair: "I have come to slavery because of my belly. On neither my mother's nor my father's side is there slavery. What kind of slave am I?"

We notice several intriguing features of these valuations. First, they promote the tendency to eye oneself in relation to others, and among others, the others nearby. One looks to one's betters located just a rung or two up from one's own position, and sneers at those just a rung or two below. But the slave does not presume to compare himself to the king, nor does the king disdain to notice the slave. Comparing oneself to those entirely out of one's class is simply not thinkable, and so these conceits and modes of self-address subtly reaffirm the fixities of the social order.

A further feature is that the texts insist that some of these conceits are "real" and some are simply baseless. Some kings do enjoy more prosperous and successful reigns than others, and only these kings can *truly* feel the conceit of superiority. There is always a pecking order of slaves, and they will only ever feel, correctly, the conceit corresponding with their status. The superior slave who fancies himself below other slaves is simply being perverse. In these considerations, conceits aren't entirely fancies, but are instead affects tightly indexed to social status. Despite the Buddhist idea that all conceit involves contrived constructions of self (which in turn are to be subjected to the religious project of dismantling such obsessions), the hard stamp of social class proves trickier to escape.

See also **mana**

REFERENCE

"you have birth". . . All references in the entry are to the *Vibhaṅga and the Samohavinodanī*, cited and discussed in M. Heim, "The Conceit of Self-Loathing," *Journal of Indian Philosophy* 37 (2009): 61–74.

ottappa

Apprehension; Fear of Getting Caught (Pali)

In Buddhism, this distinctive kind of fear, the fear of one's own potential for wrongdoing and the consequences that can follow, is paired with the moral sentiment of shame, *hiri/hri*. *Ottappa* is the visceral fear of the exposure and retribution one will face if caught committing evil. Knowing that "human society is large" and the eyes of others are ever upon one, a fastidious monk should imagine their gaze and avoid falling into disrepute. Similarly, in the psychoanalytic literature "apprehension" names the fear of getting caught.

A commentary gives a graphic analogy to distinguish between *hiri* and *ottappa*:

> If there were two iron balls, one cool but smeared with excrement and the other hot and on fire, the wise would not touch the cool one because of being disgusted by the smearing of excrement, and the hot one because of fear of being burned. Desisting from evil owing to shame (*hiri*) is like not touching the cool one out of disgust for the smearing of excrement, and desisting from evil out of fear (*ottappa*) of hell is like not touching the hot one out of fear of being burnt.

Hiri has elements of disgust: one would feel revolted doing something wrong. *Ottappa* is fear of the consequences: one would face the disapprobation of others and perhaps go to hell. But *ottappa* can also refer to the dread of one's own self-reproach: "If I were to engage in bodily, verbal, or mental misconduct, wouldn't I reprove myself because of my behavior?" How would I appear in my own eyes having done such a thing?

Together, *hiri* and *ottappa* are considered our internal "guardians of the world," those useful checks on our tendencies to disgrace ourselves and commit evils. Like *hiri*, *ottappa* is forward-looking. This is not the territory of remorse or guilt after the fact, but rather the capacity to imagine beforehand how it will be for oneself if one behaves badly. Properly ordered humans come with these internal audits whereby we are acutely sensitive to the opinion of others and seek to avoid their censure. Such sentiments are to be cultivated and enhanced, of course, in Buddhist monastic training.

See also **hiri/hri**

REFERENCES

"human society is large" . . . *Atthasālinī* 126, as cited in M. Heim, "Shame and Apprehension: Notes on the Moral Value of Hiri and Ottappa," in *Embedded Languages: Studies of Sri Lankan and Buddhist Cultures*, ed. C. Anderson, S. Mrozik, R.M.W. Rajapakse, and W. M. Wijeratne, Colombo: Godage International Publishers, 2012: 240. In Sanskrit, *ottappa* is *atrapa* and discussed in similar terms as the Pali sources by Vasubandhu (AKB: ch. 2).

"If there were two iron balls" . . . *Atthasālinī* 126–127. Heim 2012: 242.

"If I were to engage" . . . *Aṅguttara Nikāya* ii.122. NDB: 501.

P

pamojja/pramodya

The Delight of Being Free of Regrets

(Pali/Sanskrit)

Pamojja—we'll start with its occurrence in the Pali sources—is the pleasure of the free and easy conscience (if we may be forgiven for using such a heavily Christian notion of "conscience"). It's the ease brought about by the absence of the remorse and worry that otherwise nip away at our contentment. The Buddha outlined a sequence of practices starting with morality and ending with religious liberation that sees this joy as a crucial step on the path: when one refrains from wrongdoing, one becomes, naturally, free of remorse (*avippatisara*); with no remorse, there naturally arises *pamojja*; when there is *pamojja*, there naturally arises joy (*piti*); when there is joy, one comes to have a calm body; when one has a calm body, one comes to feel happiness (*sukha*); when there is happiness, one can concentrate; when one can concentrate, one can come to know and see things as they really are; when one knows and sees things as they really are, one naturally becomes disenchanted and dispassionate; and one who is disenchanted and dispassionate realizes the knowledge and vision of liberation. It all begins with morality—that is, stopping wrongdoing, which delivers, among other advantages, the freedom from remorse that can allow the distinctive delight of *pamojja* to set in. From there, the other experiences of increasing refinement can emerge naturally.

This idea is reinforced in the Sanskrit Buddhist sources, where avoiding remorse's "scratches on the heart" is the secret to *pramodya*, which in turn leads to joy, calmness, and the rest. Heart scratches, those painful impressions made on the vital organ from regretting wrongdoing, are the agitation that keeps us from the delight that would otherwise arise.

Pramoda, a variant of the term, features in Jainism and is defined by Hemacandra as a "predilection for the virtuous by those whose defects have been removed and who see reality as it is." This is suggestive of semantic continuity with the Buddhist ideas of *pramodya*, where the lack of wrongdoing leads not just to delight but also clear vision. It is to be cultivated by equanimity, meditation, friendliness, compassion, and balance.

See also **kukkucca; muda; piti; sukha; vippatisara**

REFERENCES

The Buddha outlined . . . The following is a paraphrasing of *Aṅguttara Nikāya* v.2, see also NDB: 1340–1341, for slightly different translational choices.

"scratches on the heart" . . . HN: 246–247. Note that "scratches on the heart" is my translation of *hṛllekhaḥ*; this accords with ideas about regret (*kukkucca*) that we see elsewhere.

"predilection for the virtuous" . . . Hemacandra's *Yogaśāstra* IV.97. YŚ: 97.

parideva

Mourning (Sanskrit and Pali)

I measure every Grief I meet
With narrow, probing, eyes—
I wonder if it weighs like Mine—
Or has an Easier size.

Like Emily Dickinson with her measuring eye, the Buddha closely examined the varieties and dimensions of grief.

Parideva is one of the many kinds of suffering mentioned in the first of the Buddhist Four Noble Truths. This Truth states that "birth is suffering, aging is suffering, death is suffering, sorrow, mourning, pain, depression, and despair are suffering; association with what is disliked is suffering, separation from what is liked is suffering, not getting what one wants is suffering." This global assessment of the underlying and recurrent painfulness of life in all its forms is the starting place of Buddhist soteriology, which then seeks final release from it.

In even this general assessement, we get shades and types of pain, including *parideva*, which is the mourning that involves weeping, wailing, lamenting, and crying. With its characteristic precision, the Abhidhamma further describes *parideva*: "to one afflicted by loss of relatives, wealth, health, virtue, or worldview, or any other kind of misfortune or any other kind of pain, there is crying, mourning, deploring, weeping, the state of having cried, the state of having mourned, blubbering, babbling, wailing, prattle, prattling, and the state of having prattled." Other forms of pain are treated with similar exactitude.

Despite the Buddha's ultimate achievement of freedom from pain, Buddhist texts speak the hard truth of the costs of his journey paid by others in his life. No one was more cruelly affected than Yashodhara, his faultless wife, who was left behind with their newborn baby when the young Siddhartha slipped away under cover of darkness to renounce the world. Her piercing lament of bitter reproach and devastation is given full development in the texts, as she demands of his charioteer, Chandaka, who helped him flee the household:

> Leaving me helpless and alone in the dark of night
> as I slept, o Chandaka, tell me, where did he go,
> my heart's
> sweet joy?

She collapses in pain and then "slowly began to murmur over and over again under her breath confused fevered laments in a voice choked back by incessant endless sobbing." Yashodhara speaks the cruel irony of the Buddhist path—the ultimate freedom from suffering is achieved only by inflicting grievous pain of its own, a pain often imposed particularly on the women left behind.

See also **domanassa; duhkha/dukkha/duha; nanda; shoka; upayasa; vilapa**

References

"I measure every grief I meet" . . . *The Poems of Emily Dickinson*, ed. R. Franklin, Cambridge, MA: Belknap Press of Harvard University Press, 1998: 248–249.

"birth is suffering" . . . This is the classic statement of the First Noble Truth, found everywhere in the Pali canonical sources, but said to have been announced first at the Buddha's first sermon. See BW: 75–78.

"to one afflicted by loss" . . . *Vibhaṅga* 99. This is my translation, but for a different translation and to see the whole discussion in one Abhidhammic formulation, see *The Book of Analysis* (*Vibhaṅga*) trans. P. A. Thiṭṭila, London: Pali Text Society, 1969: 130–131.

"Leaving me helpless" . . . *she slowly began to murmur* . . . *Buddhacarita* 8:32, 8:60. Adapted by S. Hopkins from P. Olivelle's translation, *The Life of the Buddha*, New York: CSL, 2009: 222–223, 232–233 (S. Hopkins, "Lament and the Work of Tears: Andromache, Sītā, Yaśodharā," BRH: 120). On Yashodhara's lament, see also "Bimba's Lament," trans. D. Swearer in *Buddhism in Practice*, ed. D. Lopez, Princeton, NJ: Princeton University Press, 1995: 541–552, and on her story, see V. Sasson, *Yashodhara and the Buddha*, Bloomsbury 2020.

pashcattapa

The "Afterburn" of Remorse (Sanskrit)

Pashcattapa (*paścāttāpa*) is the burning anguish that sinks in as one realizes one's evil deeds. Perhaps the most arresting display of the afterburn of remorse is that of King

Yudhishthira at the end of the great epic's war that has resulted in the catastrophic destruction of the kingdom and his family. Though victorious, Yudhishthira is so devastated by the bloodshed at the hands of his own side that he seeks to renounce it all and retreat to the forests in contemplation. Recalling how as a child he played on his Grandfather Bhishma's lap, but then saw him fall on the blood-soaked earth in battle, Yudhishthira is seized by a "terrible fever." He had grieved even when his own side's victory was assured: "if one were to win but yet burn afterward, afflicted and sick at heart, how can he consider it victory? For he is more vanquished than his enemies." His remorse becomes something of a problem for his family, kingdom, and the martial values he is supposed to represent, and his wife and brothers labor to talk him out of it.

In a more religious vein, the great Mahayana Buddhist thinker Shantideva raises afterburning to a high art form in his celebrated *Bodhicaryavatara,* where it is expressed in a ritualized mode of self-presentation, though no less poignant or anguished for that. As Shantideva readies himself to take the extraordinary bodhisattva vow—an aspiration to work tirelessly over countless lifetimes to help all beings attain spiritual awakening—he prostrates before buddhas past and present in highest reverence and abject self-effacement. This requires a turn inward to examine his worthiness, or lack of it, before such august beings. He finds that he doesn't like what he sees, and so he begins a doleful confession:

> To the perfect Buddhas arrayed in all directions, and also to the Bodhisattvas of great compassion, holding my hands together in reverence, I declare:
>
> Throughout the beginningless cycle of existence, and again in this very birth, whatever evil I, a brute, have done or caused,

> Or anything I, deluded, have rejoiced in to my own detriment, I confess that transgression, tormented by remorse (*pashcattapa*).
> The harm I have done, in arrogance, to the Three Jewels, or to my mothers or fathers, or to others worthy of respect, with body, speech, and mind;
> The cruel evil I have wickedly done, corrupted by many faults; O Leaders, I confess it all.

Shantideva's ritualized act of contrition is an expression of bad conscience about acts of evil he does not even remember. In a world of infinite previous lives wandering through samsara, of which our memories are innocent even if our actions in those lives were not, we have doubtless committed countless brutalities as we marched in war as soldiers, slayed animals as predators, disrespected parents, and slandered good people. Shantideva arrives at last at his moment of reckoning. Though his fear and alarm will only heighten as he expunges all previous evil acts and their afterburn, his confession clears the ground for regeneration as he takes up the "awakening mind" that seeks only wisdom and compassion for all beings henceforth.

See also **abhaya; anutapa; hridayakrosha; kukkucca; samvega; vippatisara**

REFERENCES

"terrible fever" . . . *Mahābhārata* XII.27.12. The reader is encouraged to read G. Das's chapter, "Yudhishtira's Remorse," in his *The Difficulty of Being Good*, New York: Oxford University Press, 2009.

"if one were to win but yet burn afterward" . . . *Mahābhārata* X.10.13.

"To the perfect" . . . *Śāntideva: The Bodhicaryāvatāra* 2.26–31, BCA: 16.

patigha

Hostility (Pali/Sanskrit)

In Buddhist psychology, *patigha* (*paṭigha*) is an underlying tendency of hostility that blocks and repulses. An "underlying tendency" (*anusaya*) is so deeply buried that one might not even be aware of its operations though it drives one's responses to the world, and to remove it will take some digging out. *Patigha* is a hostility that occurs when one is distressed (*domanassa*) and thereby disaffected by the world; it is a "mind depraved by hate or contemptible by having base feeling." It is oppositional to its object, and any contact with its object is marked by antipathy. When developed into malice (*byapada*), it can be the basis of a violent action. *Patigha* is the word used for hate and aversion in Buddhaghosa's therapies of lovingkindness, where hard work can replace it with a friendly feeling.

See also **anushaya/anusaya; brahmaviharas; byapada/vyapada; metta/maitra**

REFERENCE

"mind depraved by hate" . . . *Atthasālinī* 256. EX: 341. *Pratigha* is the Sanskrit equivalent.

pidita

Crushed (Sanskrit)

Pidita (*pīḍita*) from the verb *pid*, to squeeze or crush, is often used with other emotions. One can be *hard pressed* by fear or *stricken* by grief for example. But sometimes, *pidita* is used alone to indicate that one is simply crushed, tormented, trounced. When the Pandava brothers learn after they have killed him that Karna, their arch enemy in the war, was in fact their eldest brother, they are *pidita*, crushed. "A hundred times more devastating" than all of the other losses they faced in war, is this new revelation, and they turn their fury on their mother, Kunti, who, in shame over this out-of-wedlock baby, had sent Karna up a river at birth and hid his true identity until now.

See also **dina; vyatha**

REFERENCES

they are pidita . . . Mahābhārata 11.27.22.

"A hundred times more devastating" . . . These are Yudhiṣṭhira's words, trans. K. Crosby, *Mahābhārata, Book Eleven, The Women,* New York: CSL, 2009: 340–341.

piti

Joy (Pali)

Joy is different from happiness in that it seems to come from outside and hit us unawares; unlike happiness, it is a short-term episode and strikes unexpectedly. As one modern commentator has observed, "a moment of joy can blast you right out of the life to which it makes you all the more lovingly and tenaciously attached." We have an example of a blast of joy sweeping up a heavily pregnant young woman in ancient Sri Lanka. She'd been left at home at the full moon festival when everyone else went to the great mountaintop shrine in the evening. From her doorway, she looked up at the moonlit mountain shrine and thinking of the Buddha became so transported that she "soared through the air" and arrived at the shrine ahead of everyone. When her family arrived, they were astonished to see her, and she could only report that the rapture of joy had propelled her there.

The Pali sources everywhere note *piti*'s buoyancy and expansiveness. When there is *piti* (*pīti*), there is "delight, rejoicing, jubilation, mirth, laughing, felicity, elation, exultation." There are said to be five kinds of it: "lesser joy, momentary joy, recurrent joy, transporting joy, and all-pervading joy." "Lesser joy" is when one's hairs stand upright on the body, "momentary joy" is like a strike of lightning, and "recurrent joy" breaks upon the body over and over, like waves crashing on the shore. "Transporting joy" is so strong that it lifts the body and launches it into the air, as it did with the young woman. Last, "all-pervading joy" is a complete suffusion of jubilation "like a full bladder bursting or a mountain cave waterfall gushing a great rush of water."

These five kinds of joy have special significance in Buddhist meditation; one need not wait until joy happens to strike, but instead can learn to invite it in. Joy is encouraged and developed because the sheer expansiveness of it crowds out all negativity, especially hate and anger. It is closely affiliated with love (see *priti*). Above all, *piti* is generative of calm meditative states. When any of the five types of joy "become pregnant and then fully mature," they generate a calmness (*passaddhi*) of both mind and body; calmness in turn becomes pregnant and then fully matures to generate mental and bodily pleasure; pleasure in turn becomes pregnant and then fully matures to generate advanced stages of concentration.

See also **ananda; pamojja/pramodya; priti; somanassa; sukha**

REFERENCES

"a moment of joy can blast" . . . C. Wiman, *Joy: 100 Poems*, New Haven, CT: Yale University Press, 2017: xii.

"delight, rejoicing" . . . *Dhammasaṅgaṇi* 10. My translation, but see C.A.F. Rhys Davids, *A Buddhist Manual of Psychological Ethics*, London: Royal Asiatic Society (1900) 1975: 11–12.

"lesser joy" . . . *Atthasālinī* 115. The remaining entry is from *Atthasālinī* 115–117 (see also EX: 153–154).

pitta

A Choleric or Bilious Disposition (Sanskrit)

A disposition afflicted by a preponderance of *pitta,* the humor (*dosha*) in classical Ayurveda described as "oily, hot, pungent, fluid, acidic, flowing, and acrid," is subject to certain diseases and maladies associated with heat. A chronically bilious or choleric person is a fiery and acidic sort and should seek cooling and calming remedies. (See *kapha* for a discussion of the Sanskrit humoral system and how it compares to that of the Western humors.)

While the Ayurveda humors are not usually mapped directly onto the ancient system of the three *gunas* (modal qualities), the medical texts discuss the *gunas* and sometimes articulate their understanding of the human organism within a larger cosmic interpretation of primordial nature (*prakriti*), or lived reality as it is experienced in the dynamic and shifting interactions of its three modes: *rajas, tamas,* and *sattva.* The physician Caraka says that "*kapha, vayu* (that is, *vata*), and *pitta* are said to be the collection of humors relating to the body, while *rajas* and *tamas* are described as related to the mind." Hot and sharp *pitta* partakes of the passionate and restless qualities of *rajas.* Ayurveda also describes five elements that comprise the human organism: fire, water, earth, space, and wind. Not surprisingly, *pitta* is connected to the fire, heat, and energy (*tejas*) animating human biology and psychology.

See also **guna; kapha; rajas; vata/vayu**

References

"oily, hot, pungent" . . . Caraka Saṃhitā I.60, see also CS: 43.

three gunas . . . See, for example, *Suśruta Saṁhitā,* Śārira Sthāna I.1–23, where the Sāṃkhya system is elaborated. The medieval commentator on this text, Ḍalhaṇa, suggests that the *doṣas* correspond neatly with the *guṇas* (A. Cerulli, *Somatic Lessons*, Albany: State University of New York Press, 2012: 28). See G. Larson's discussion of the two systems, "Āyurveda and the Hindu Philosophical Systems," *Philosophy East and West* 37, no. 3 (1987): 245–259.

"kapha, vayu, and pitta are said to be" . . . *Caraka Saṃhitā* I.57, see also translation at CS: 41–43. *Sattva* is not mentioned here because it is not related to pathologies of body or mind.

prasada

Clarity; Serenity; Delight (Sanskrit)

Perhaps even more than many of the other terms here, *prasada* (*prasāda*) is an "untranslatable." English stumbles and misdirects; paragraphs of explanation are required. The term refers to a clarity or calmness prompted in one entity from contact with another, with the other being a king, a god, a saint, or religious place, relic, or monument. The calmness is augmented with delight because in religious texts, serenity is joyful. *Prasada* is the calm and happy religious feeling that keeps the faithful coming; they receive, often via a visual conduit and rather automatically, a feeling of lucid calmness from the object of their trust.

As with the faith that is *shraddha*, there are transactional elements in this relation that serve ideological and hierarchical purposes, though the pleasurable aspects of the encounter can obscure these. People go to temples to see gods, saints, relics, *jinas*, and buddhas, and are suffused with *prasada*. In addition to its immediate pleasures, this purity of heart secures them a heavenly rebirth. For their part, the objects of this worship gain a steady stream of the pious honoring them with their presence and their gifts. Completing the circle while denying the circle, the *prasada* bestowed by the worshipped is configured as grace, blessings, or divine favor.

The sensual and bodily contact of being present is essential to the experience: one *sees* the image or relic or saint. Or, according to one devotee of Krishna, one sees God's grace and or hears it in stories and song; and one can feel it in one's heart. In Hindu temples, *prasada* becomes very tangible and material: "prasad" is the offerings from the offerings—one gives food to the image, and then enjoys the leavings in return. Another circle.

As in the temple, so too at court. A king confers his favors—*prasada*—to secure the loyalty of his subjects. *Prasada* becomes a chief mechanism to distribute wealth and advancement to the king's subordinates, while also securing their fidelity and service. Manu notes that "in *prasada* lies the lotus-like Goddess of Prosperity."

Last, *prasada* is one of the ways to indicate begging for and conferring forgiveness. Bharata, Rama's honorable younger brother, horrified at his mother's mischief in forcing the king to exile Rama and install himself instead, seeks Rama's forgiveness—*prasada*—and Rama, righteous prince that he is, readily grants it.

See also **shraddha**

References

secures them a heavenly rebirth . . . As at *Dīgha Nikāya* ii.141, as cited and discussed by A. Rotman, *Thus Have I Seen*, New York: Oxford University Press, 2009: 125; he also offers Sanskrit sources to this point. My discussion of *prasāda* in the Buddhist sources here draws on his work.

according to one devotee of Krishna . . . Rūpa Goswāmin in BR: 100–103.

"in prasada lies the lotus-like" . . . Manu's *Dharmaśāstra* 7.11 This quotation is cited in a discussion by D. Ali, where he draws also on epigraphical evidence; I am indebted to this discussion for these observations on the court (D. Ali, *Courtly Culture and Political Life in Early Medieval India*, Cambridge: Cambridge University Press, 2004: 106–108).

forgiveness . . . At *Rāmāyaṇa* II.97.9, for example.

prema

Love (Sanskrit)

Prema is deep love, ranging from erotic love to affection. *Prema* is the "inscrutable bond" of love that attaches Parvati to even the fierce and frightening aspect of Lord Shiva. He may wear a necklace of heads and an antelope hide, but she adores him. We cannot always understand the deepest bonds of love between two people, or for that matter, gods.

The poets are hopeless romantics in a world of arranged marriages that must, at least for elite persons, conform to all manner of social convention. But love is foremost in poets' hearts as they consider erotic relationships. As here, with Bhoja—

> All a woman's adornment—her lovely form, good family, youth, beauty, firm devotion, affability, character, sophistication, modesty, breeding—all counts for nothing if she does not have deep *prema* for her lover.

To find love present in the other is the deepest attraction of all.

Like all love, *prema* makes us vulnerable to pain, and because it lies so deep in our core, *prema* makes us *very* vulnerable to it. We find a poignant instance of this when we switch registers from the erotic to the affectionate. When the Buddha returns to his family after his nirvana and tries to ordain his young son as a monk, his father reprimands him. Having lost his own son to the monastic life, the king has no wish to lose his grandson as well. When a young person leaves parents to renounce the world, he says, it causes them "not a little sorrow," for "*prema* for children pierces the skin, cuts the flesh, pierces the sinews, pierces the bones, and stays there pressing into the marrow." At this, the Buddha backs off and institutes a new rule that young children may only be ordained with their family's permission.

Prema is picked up by the aesthetic theorists, most interestingly, by Bhoja, who interprets *rasa* in terms of love. Bhoja sees *shringara* as the ultimate *rasa* underlying all aesthetic feeling. About *prema,* he says that "all forms of emotion, erotic desire and the rest, once they reach their full development, ultimately turn out to be nothing but this." For him, *prema* is the basis of our emotional and aesthetic engagement with the world. When we say that people "love sex" and "love quarreling," we are getting at this idea: underneath even negative experience like quarreling and anger is *prema,* a love that draws us to these things. To extrapolate, *prema* is fundamental to all human experience, as it is the very desire and love connecting us to the world through our emotions.

Last, *prema* gets sacralized in *bhakti* thought. For Rupa Goswami, *prema* is a *rasa,* and at the same time is the ultimate state of love between God and his devotees. However one approaches Krishna, in whatever form the *bhakti* relationship takes, *prema* is present. And when emotion "softens the heart completely and becomes very intense, and when it is marked by a high degree of 'myness,' it is called *prema.*" ("Myness," in this case, refers to a sense of singularity in one's love for God, as one's individual self merging with love of God.) *Prema* becomes this supreme love present in all emotions related to God.

See also **bhakti; kama; preyas; priti; rati; sneha; vatsalya**

REFERENCES

"inscrutable bond" . . . Bhānudatta's *Rasataraṅgiṇī* 8.34. BRRR: 326–327.

"All a woman's adornment" . . . *Śṛṅgāraprakāśa* as translated by S. Pollock, "Bhoja's *Śṛṅgāraprakāśa* and the Problem of Rasa: An Historical Introduction and Annotated Translation," *Asiatische Studien/Études*

Asiatiques 70, no. 1 (1998): 152. Used in this discussion is also *priya*, an adjectival form of the substantive *prema*.

"not a little sorrow" . . . Vinaya i.82. The Pali of *prema* is *pema*, which is used here.

"all forms of emotion" . . . Pollock 1998: 153.

in whatever form . . . BR: 78–79, verse 281; 116–117, verse 1. "Myness" is *mamatvā*.

preyas

An Affectionate Utterance (Sanskrit)

We take up here a specialized sense of *preyas* in literary theory, as articulated by the great literary critic Dandin. Indian literary theory evinces a fascination with how emotion lives in literary language. Dandin says, "A poem is defined as 'sweet' when it has *rasa*. *Rasa* is found in both the language and the subject matter, and insightful people become intoxicated by it like bees by honey." This invites us to consider, perhaps using our ecological paradigm where defined boundaries between "inside" and "outside" are softened, how emotion exists not only "inside" people, but also in language, spoken and on the page, and in certain subject matters.

An "affectionate utterance" is an expression of "heightened affection." Dandin's commentator suggests that emotions are "internal" to people, but when greatly intensified or heightened they can become manifest in *rasa* in an utterance or another register of acting, like a gesture. Certain poetic utterances are the manifestation of this high emotion. It is not so much that they *convey* emotion (though they do), but rather, that they are the manifestation of it. An example of *preyas*, an affectionate utterance, is Vidura's exclamation, upon receiving Krishna into his home: "The joy I experience today by your coming to my house, Govinda, I will have in the future only if you return." The speaker feels such affection that his utterance is saturated with it. These ideas provide another example of a long strand of Indian thought that finds powerful emotion in the words we utter (see *shoka*, *udana*, and *urjasvi*).

See also **daruna; mahura/madhurya; prema; priti; rasa; shoka; udana; urjasvi**

Reference

"A poem is defined as 'sweet'" . . . Daṇḍin's *Kāvyādarśa* 1.51; "heightened affection" is at 2.273, and his commentator on this is Ratnaśrījñāna. Translated and discussed by S. Pollock, RR: 60–65. See the discussion of *preyas* by Bhamaha, Daṇḍin, and Bhoja, and Pollock's discussion of them (pp. 56–65; and the chapter on Bhoja). I am able only to gesture toward the complexity here.

priti

Joy and Love (Sanskrit)

Priti (*prīti*) is the Sanskrit of the Pali *piti*. In the Pali sources, *piti* means a kind of bursting joy that strikes unbidden. *Priti* can mean joy too, but it often means love and affection, suggesting perhaps how closely love lies next to joy. *Priti* is what is agreeable to us and the pleasure we take in it, so it can also be the love that we feel toward someone appealing to us. We see both meanings in the *Bhagavad Gita*, which mentions the pleasures we take in things and the love for God, the latter a *priti* that Shankara glosses as affection (*sneha*). The great Kalidasa has the skin of proud brahmans "prickle with *priti*," when they find Lord Shiva noticing them. He probably meant joy, but it is fun to consider that these learned Vedic ritualists horripilated with love too.

In erotic contexts, *priti* is love and sexual attraction, and can work as a synonym for a range of words in this sphere.

Vatsyayana, India's chief authority on sexual love, names four types of such *priti*: the love arising from habit, sexual arousal arising from imagination (erotic fantasy), the passion arising from transference (transposing attraction from a previous encounter to the present situation), and the arousal that comes from enjoying the objects of the senses (the ancient Indian equivalents to candlelight and sunset walks on the beach). *Priti* is the word for the finer feelings of love in sexual contexts: when lovers behave in their flirtations and secret intimacies "with modesty and concern for one another's feelings, their love will never wane, not even in a hundred years." The mutual *priti* between partners can be enhanced and refreshed by the passionate arts of *kama*.

Priti gets valorized as a special kind of love for God in the *bhakti* traditions, which increasingly distinguish, in fine grain, the different types of devotional love. Ramanuja defines *bhakti* as a happy, blissful, and intense *priti* for God (see *bhakti*). As theorists try to systematize *bhakti* theology in terms of *rasa* theory, sacralized love of God becomes a *rasa*. In this context, one of the foundational kinds of love is *priti*, which for Rupa Goswami means a kind of "respect." This kind of love looks up to its object, and a commentator glosses it as "servitude." But another north Indian Vaishnava figure sees *priti* a bit differently, as a kind of platonic affection possible between men and women who are not married to each other, such as the love between Draupadi and Krishna.

Buddhist psychology sees *priti* as joy, and most technically, a kind of joy present in several of the higher stages of meditations called *dhyana*, although this exuberant joy, which Vasubandhu treats as delight, gets left behind in the most advanced contemplations, which favor equanimity.

See also **bhakti; guna; kama; piti; prema; rati; romaharsha; sneha; somanassa**

REFERENCES

Bhagavad Gita . . . *Bhagavad Gītā* 1.36, 5.21, and 10.10, with Śaṅkara's *Gītābhāṣya* on 10.10, see BGC: 164. Ideally, one should take joy in the Self (*ātman*), according to Śaṅkara's commentary on 5.21.

"prickle with priti" . . . *Kumārasaṃbhava* 6.15; see also 6.22. BK: 212–213, 216–217.

In erotic contexts . . . *Kāma Sūtra* 2.1.32, 2.1.39–45, 2.5.40–43, 2.10.10–13. Synonyms for *rati*, sexual love, are given as *rasa* (sexual feeling), *prīti* (love or ecstasy), *bhāva* (climax), *rāga* (passion), *vega* (sexual energy), *samāpti* (satisfaction). KS: 36–39, 51, 71.

a kind of "respect" . . . Rūpa Gosvāmin in BR: 354–361, 388 n. 4, 389 n. 17.

another north Indian Vaishnava figure . . . That is, Kavikarṇapūra, a sixteenth-century Caitanya Vaiṣṇava. See R. Lutjeharms, *A Vaiṣṇava Poet in Early Modern Bengal*, Oxford: Oxford University Press, 2018: 164.

several of the higher stages of meditation . . . *Abhidharmakośabhāṣya* 8.1, 8.9, AKV, volume IV: 1218–1219, 1237–1238. Delight is *saumanasya*, the Sanskrit variant of *somanassa*. Both joy and delight drop out at the third *dhyāna*, though happiness (*sukha*) remains. See *somanassa* for a brief account of the *jhānas* (Pali for *dhyāna*).

R

raga

Attraction; Passion (Sanskrit)

One of the charming qualities of the *Kama Sutra*, India's *ars erotica*, is its readiness to undermine its own *shastric* orientation. Why do we need a manual for sexual passion? it asks. And how could it possibly help to fumble with a textbook while in the throes of sexual passion?

> This is no matter for numerical lists
> Or textbook tables of contents.
> For people joined in sexual ecstasy,
> Passion is what makes things happen.

To be sure, the *Kama Sutra* is full of lists of methods, procedures, rules, and techniques. But perhaps the most important of these is to know when to fling it aside and let *raga* (*rāga*) take over. "For just as a horse in full gallop, blinded by the energy of its own speed, pays no attention to any post or hole or ditch on the path, so too lovers blinded by *raga* in the friction of sexual battle are caught up in their fierce energy and pay no attention to danger." Best to know the text in advance, and apply it, as passion dictates, to the lovers' unique circumstances. At its height and by its nature, passion will elude rulebooks.

Raga has a sense of sexual passion, but it can be wider than this to refer to any sort of attraction. For philosophers, *raga* is the elemental force of passion or attraction often discussed along with its opposite, aversion or hatred (*dvesha*). We are pulled and pushed by these two primary forces throughout our lives as we constantly react to this or that stimulus. But where do they come from? Some thinkers suggest that babies have attraction and aversion from the start. Passion is not something one perceives in its object; it isn't like blue that is picked up from a blue object. Rather, attraction doesn't have a necessary or invariable connection to its object: the person you are attracted to may be repellent to me. Its presence in the cradle means that the proclivities of passion are carried over from previous lives and not known empirically. Where we might suggest that attraction is innate or instinctual, classical India takes recourse in past lives: dispositions present from birth in this life clearly came from a past life. Thus, it seems that from time immemorial, attraction and aversion—passion and hatred—have been doing much of the driving.

See also **dvesha; kama; priti; ranj/rajjati; rati**

References

the Kama Sutra . . . Vātsyāyana's *Kāma Sūtra* 2.7.31, 2.7.33; to the same point, see 2.2.31. KS: 59–60, 42.

Some thinkers suggest . . . Namely, Śāntarakṣita in the *Tattvasaṃgraha,* along with Kamalaśīla's commentary, as discussed by J. Tuske, "The Concept of Emotion in Classical Indian Philosophy," *The Stanford Encyclopedia of Philosophy*, ed. E. Zalta (Fall 2021 edition).

rajas

Passion; Restlessness (Sanskrit)

In the ancient metaphysics of Samkhya and Yoga philosophy, *rajas* is one of the three *gunas*, or modes of reality that characterize all known experience. *Rajas* is passion, agitation, activity, and stimulation, and contrasts to the light and buoyancy of *sattva* and the dull and indifferent heaviness of *tamas*. These qualities go far beyond psychology, but they also constitute how we feel and behave. In the estimation of the physician Sushruta, a person with a preponderance of *rajas* is "given to much suffering, inclines to wandering, and is inconstant, egotistical, untruthful, without compassion, proud, deceitful, happy, passionate, and angry."

In the *Mahabharata*, *rajas* is "dissatisfaction, torment, grief, greed, and impatience." The *gunas* are elaborated in the *Bhagavad Gita*, which defines *rajas* as "having the nature of passion" and "arising from clinging to craving." Both desire and anger emerge from it; and it is owing to *rajas* that one clings to karma.

See also **guna; pitta; raga; sattva; tamas**

References

"given to much suffering"... "The rājasic disposition is given to much suffering, inclines to wandering, and is inconstant, egotistical (*ahaṃkāra*), untruthful, without compassion, proud (*māna*), deceitful, happy (*harṣa*), passionate (*kāma*), and angry (*krodha*)." *Suśruta Saṁhitā* III.1.18.

In the Mahabharata... *Mahābhārata* XII.194.35.

in the Bhagavad Gita... *Gītā* 3.37, 14.7, 14.9; passion is *rāga*, craving is *tṛṣṇā*, anger is *krodha*.

ranj/rajjati

To Grow Red Hot and Become Enamored

(Sanskrit/Pali)

It is high time for a verb, emotions being, of course, actions and undergoings. The Sanskrit verbal root, *ranj* (*rañj*), from which we get *raga* (passion), *anuraga* (attraction), and words for loving, being enamored with, and falling in love (*ranjana*, *rakta*, and *anurakta*), means to redden or be dyed with color. Red is the color of sexual and sensual passion, and we become reddened and hot in its throes.

The Pali texts are not the usual place to look for erotic phenomenology, but an extraordinary passage in the Buddha's teachings illustrates an important feature of the Buddha—he was said to have fully known and understood pleasure and happiness in all their forms before he renounced them (see *sukha*). Here he gives a clinical analysis of what occurs in sexual feeling:

> Monks, a woman attends internally to her feminine faculty, her feminine comportment, her feminine appearance, her feminine aspect, her feminine desire, her feminine voice, her feminine ornamentation. She enjoys (*abhiramati*) these and becomes enamored (*rajjati*) with them. Enjoying them, enamored with them, she attends externally to a [man's] masculine faculty, his masculine comportment, his masculine appearance, his masculine aspect, his masculine desire, his masculine voice, his masculine ornamentation. She enjoys these and is enamored with them. Enjoying them, enamored with them, she desires union externally, and she also desires the pleasure (*sukha*) and delight (*somanassa*) that arise on account of such union. Creatures delighted with their femininity enter into union with men. It is in this way that a woman does not transcend her femininity.

The next passage describes exactly the same processes for a man—he becomes enamored with his own masculinity and then attends to the woman's femininity; it happens the same way for both men and women. Taking pleasure in gender, both one's own and the other's, makes one desire sexual union, and there is pleasure and delight to be found in this. But then of course (this being a Buddhist text addressed to monks), the next passages describe in the same clinical tone the processes of disengaging one's attention on these features, stepping back from these attractions, and "transcending" one's gender. The religious path involves transcending gender and its enticements.

In its equally frank and clinical way but without such religious scruples, the *Kama Sutra* describes the ins and outs of growing hot. Its players seek to make their partners enamored with them, or when passion cools, to fall out of love. A young woman seeks to make a man fall for her before she accepts his advances. A man seduces a woman by becoming aware of her feelings. A courtesan works to make a man enamored with her while keeping her feelings detached. Later when she wishes to be rid of him, she labors to make his passion wane.

See also **anuraga; kama; raga; rati; somanassa; sukha**

REFERENCES

"Monks, a woman attends" . . . *Aṅguttara Nikāya,* sutta 51. My translation, but see also NDB: 1039–1041. These are fascinating observations, not least because they suggest that transcending gender is a possibility.

the Kama Sutra . . . Vātsyāyana's *Kāma Sūtra* 3.2.30, 3.4.46, 6.1.33, 6.2.1, 6.3.45. See KS: 81, 89, 136–137, 147.

rasa

Taste; The Aesthetic Savoring of Emotions (Sanskrit)

Rasa is the main idea in Sanskrit aesthetic theory. At its most literal, *rasa* means juice, essence, or sap, and from here it becomes the taste, savor, or relish of the juices or the essence of something. In aesthetics, *rasa* is this sense of savoring the emotional experience yielded by artistic production. India offers more than a millennium and a half of sophisticated and probing reflection on the phenomenology of this experience and the formal properties in artistic production that bring it about.

It all begins with the sage Bharata (perhaps third or fourth century CE) in his compendium on dramaturgy, the *Natyashastra*. Bharata disaggregates, in classic *shastric* fashion, the components of performance art to understand how they can be mastered. Along with the other elements of stagecraft, Bharata gives his attention to *rasa*, the aesthetic relish that is the aim of drama. He lists eight *rasas*: the erotic, comic, tragic, violent, heroic, horrific, macabre, and fantastic (*shringara, hasya, karuna, raudra, vira, bhayanaka, bibhatsa, adbhuta*). These correspond to eight stable emotions (*sthayibhavas*): attraction, amusement, grief, anger, determination, fear, disgust, and amazement (*rati, hasa, shoka, krodha, utsaha, bhaya, jugupsa, vismaya*). Each *rasa* is the *savoring* of its corresponding emotion (the erotic is the savoring of passion and so on), and it occurs through the skillful mixture of the elements of dramatic production. As Bharata puts it: "*rasa* arises from the conjunction of factors, reactions, and transitory emotions"—that is to say, it emerges from the totality of the characters, setting, techniques of acting, and the emotions conveyed by the actors, staging, and the play itself. He offers a metaphor:

> Just as connoisseurs eat and savor their fare when prepared with many condiments and substances, so the learned fully savor in their heart the stable emotions when conjoined with the factors, transitory emotions, and reactions.

To underscore the metaphor, a later commentator suggests that a properly mixed drink is more than its parts, and its taste cannot be located in any one of its ingredients; it is the mixture that matters. *Rasa* is savoring a cocktail of emotions.

Bharata also suggests that the underlying stable emotions are what generate *rasa*, but that there is also a sense that emotions and *rasas* bring each other into being, much as condiments and food make each other savory. A later commentator, Abhinavagupta, puts it this way: "emotions 'bring *rasas* into being,' that is, produce them, and *rasas* 'bring the emotions into being,' that is, make them 'emotions' in the first place—in other words, make them identifiable as aesthetic elements."

Exactly how all of this works became the subject of penetrating reflection and vigorous argumentation in the centuries following Bharata, especially as the theory comes to be extended beyond drama to literary art. At first, *rasa* appears to be something inherent to or emergent in the play or poem itself, either the poet's own effusive emotional and aesthetic sense or that of the characters. Over time, however, theorists come to see *rasa* as something savored by the audience or the reader. Later theorists made many modifications to Bharata's basic model, and in some cases added a ninth *rasa*, the peaceful (*shanta*), though this was controversial. Bhoja floats other *rasas* as well, specifically the affectionate (*prema*), the vainglorious, and the noble; others added parental love (*vatsalya*). Later theorists took *rasa* in fascinating philosophical directions (in some cases, these were metaphysical and religious, while others stayed resolutely on aesthetic terms) as they tried to figure out how our capacity to savor our deepest, most enduring emotions is so pleasurable, and even blissful and rapturous (see *camatkara*).

For all its *shastric* specificity and its lists, *rasa* theory is meant to convey a very fluid, and "ecological" paradigm that can explain how it is that we enjoy a huge range of diverse aesthetic experience. There are these specific *rasas*, to be sure, and they correspond to specific emotions, but the myriad of combinations suggests that the nuances of emotion and aesthetic relish can take myriad forms. This idea is captured by the poet Bhavabhuti in discussion of how a play may have a single dominant *rasa*. In discussing his own play, *Rama's Last Act*, he specifies that the tragic dominates:

> There is only a single *rasa*—
> the tragic—but it takes different forms
> since it changes in response
> to circumstances that are changing,
> just the way that water forms
> into whirlpool, bubble, or wave
> though in the end it all remains
> the same: nothing but water.

We can use the same term and feel roughly the "same" experience even as it changes form, texture, and quality depending on context. In this conception, the pleasure of a play or a poem is not the single generic experience of the *rasa* (whatever that would be) but its vicissitudes, how the poet creates its ever-changing nuances.

See also **adbhuta/abbhuta; bhava; bhayanaka; bibhatsa; camatkara; hasya; karuna; raudra; shanta; shringara; sthayibhava; vira**

REFERENCES

He lists eight rasas . . . *Nāṭyaśāstra* 6.15; the stable emotions are listed at 6.17; RR: 50.

"Just as connoisseurs eat" . . . *Nāṭyaśāstra* 6.32–33. S. Pollock's translation (RR: 51). I rely heavily on his translation and discussion of *rasa*. *The Rasa Reader* is essential reading for anyone interested in Indian aesthetic theory and the long textual tradition exploring it.

A later commentator . . . Abhinavagupta (*Abhinavabhāratī* 1.279; RR: 203).

Abhinavagupta, puts it this way . . . *Abhinavabhāratī* 1.287 (RR: 211–212); Bharata's metaphor of condiments and food is at *Nāṭyaśāstra* 6.36–37.

Later theorists . . . The peaceful (*śānta*) was mentioned by Bhoja (RR: 132–133) as well as the affectionate, noble, and vainglorious. The addition of the peaceful was critiqued on many points by Dhanika (RR: 165).

Motherly love or parental love (*vātsalya*) was first added by Rudraṭa Kāvyālaṅkāra (RR: 359 n. 65).
"There is only a single rasa" . . . *Uttararāmacarita,* RLA: 228–229. I replaced his "pity" for "the tragic" for *karuṇā.*

rati

Sexual Attraction and Feeling (Sanskrit)

Rati is used mostly in the sphere of sexual attraction and excitement, and even where it is elevated or extended beyond this, it carries its passion. *Rati* is unapologetically affirmed as essential to the good life, at least for married people in the prime of life—for example, the jurist Yajnavalkya requires male householders to feel *rati* toward their wives.

Rati is the name of one of Kama's wives, the Goddess of Sex, and together, the couple is the epitome of sexual pleasure and desire. (His other wife is Priti, and their union is based more on the affectionate love indicated by her name). For its part, while the *Kama Sutra* often entangles sexual attraction (*rati*) and love (*priti*) (and in many contexts these terms mean both), it also sometimes separates them, at least to make a certain point. But perhaps the heights of both can best be reached when they occur together:

Even at the end, love (*priti*)
enhanced by thoughtful acts
and words and deeds exchanged in confidence
gives rise to the highest ecstasy (*rati*).

To be sure, the *Kama Sutra* often takes a clinical view of sexual practice and documents its many vicissitudes, including the most primitive lusts and the coldest calculations that can reign in this arena. But throughout, it carries a romantic strain as it locates the highest forms of sexual feeling in contexts of tender mutual love (see *kama*).

Given that *shringara*, the relish of *rati*, is the quintessential *rasa* for so many of the *rasa* theorists, there is no shortage of the savor of *rati*, always configured as the *mutual* love of a couple, in the literature. But it is almost always suggestive rather than graphic, since suggestion in poetry is more emotionally saturated than description. A beautifully suggestive conceit concerns how quickly a night of passionate lovemaking flies by. Lovers in the throes of eros plead, "grow long, blessed night, so that tomorrow just won't be." On this theme, the poet-philosopher Shri Harsha, whose lovemaking scenes are rather more explicit than those of other poets, suggests that the night is cruel to grow so short when the *rati* is so good. We may savor first a few verses from his long poetic sequence evoking the *rati* of the lovers Nala and Damayanti, and then end with the shortness of the night.

> When she arched her eyebrow as they made love (*rati*), it was as if the love god had bent his bow. And then when she moaned, it was the hum of his discharged arrows . . .
>
> In the joyful frenzy of climax, their fingernails dug into each other. It was piquant and sweet, like molasses juice with a sprinkling of red pepper . . .
>
> They held each other, put their lips together; thighs entwined, as if seeing in their dreams what they had done to each other, enfolded in their embrace, holding on tight. And they slept . . .

But damn that fleeting night!

> Their love for each other an elixir, they sought to love each other again. But their wish remained unfulfilled, for short-lived was that malicious night.

See also **anuraga; kama; muda; priti; ratyabhasa; sambhoga; shringara; sneha**

REFERENCES

the jurist Yajnavalkya . . . *Yājñavalkya Dharmaśāstra* I.120. Trans. P. Olivelle, *A Treatise on Dharma*, Cambridge, MA: Harvard University Press, MCLI, 2019: 38–39.

his other wife is Priti . . . Her story is told in the *Skanda Purāṇa* VI.127.1–19; she was a woman who had grown beyond the typical marrying age and did asceticism to attract the notice of the Devi, the Goddess, who was pleased and helped her restore her youthful beauty and marry Kāma, who marries her out of *prīti*. Cited and discussed by C. Benton, *God of Desire: Tales of Kāmadeva in Sanskrit Story Literature*, Albany: State University of New York Press, 2006: 34–38.

"Even at the end" . . . Vātsyāyana's *Kāma Sūtra* 2.10.10. See KS: 71.

"grow long, blessed night" . . . This becomes the title of M. Selby's gorgeous collection of Sanskrit, Prakrit, and Tamil translated poems: *Grow Long, Blessed Night: Love Poems from Classical India*, New York: Oxford University Press, 2000: 181. This poem is a line from the Prakrit *Gāthāsaptaśatī* 1.46.

"When she arched" . . . *Naiṣadhīyacarita of Śrī Harṣa* XVIII.93, 118, 152, 141. HB: 168 and 178.

ratyabhasa

False Love (Sanskrit)

True love is to be distinguished from the appearance of it (*ratyābhāsa*). When Ravana kidnapped Sita, he thought he was in love with her. But his supposed *rati* was meaningless and transient, not only because it was not reciprocated, but also because it was spurious in this important sense: "it never occurred to the heart of Ravana that Sita might be indifferent to him or even hostile," and if it had, his desire would have disappeared. Ravana's infatuation was with passion itself, not with Sita, because to love her would be to notice and care about how she feels.

For *rasa* theorists, *rati* is always mutual love. It is not fleeting attraction, nor is it ever one-sided. It is the stable emotion between two lovers "that perdures from the beginning of their relationship to the attainment of the final goal, i.e., the plenitude of pleasure." It is a "mutual interpenetration" that endures. This stable mutuality is what gets aestheticized in the *shringara rasa*: "the very life breath of the erotic *rasa* is awareness of inseparability." The underlying emotion that is true love must never be confused with a pale and false imitation of it.

See also **rati; shringara**

REFERENCES

his supposed rati was meaningless and transient . . . This is the observation of Abhinavagupta in DL: 217.

"that perdures from the beginning" . . . *Abhinavabhāratī*. RR: 217.

raudra

Rage; Savoring Anger (Sanskrit)

Raudra evokes the deity Rudra, the howler storm god in the Vedas. Hymns to him plead for mercy from his destructive fury. Lord Shiva is also called Rudra, and has a fierce side to him renowned for its rage as he destroys his father-in-law's sacrifice, burns up Love God Kama's body, and destroys the Triple City taken over by a demon. A commonly cited account of Shiva's link to fearsome Rudra says that "he is called Rudra because he burns, and is fiery, fierce and flaming, consuming flesh, blood and marrow."

In aesthetic theory, *raudra* is the relishing (*rasa*) of anger and its violence, the thrill of sharing the rage of a character in a story. The *Venisamhara*, a courtly drama celebrating the heroism of the *Mahabharata*, depicts the Pandava brother Bhima's vengeance against Duryodhana for dishonoring their wife Draupadi (see *krodha* and *manyu*). This play perfects the literary artistry that generates the savor of *raudra*. Consider this verse of Bhima's terrible vow to do the very unwarrior-like thing of eventually slaying Duryodhana by striking below the belt:

> The brutal war-club whirling in my arm
> will crush both thighs of this Suyodhana,
> so that he whose name is truly Bhima
> may deck your hair, my lady, with his hands
> new-reddened in that fresh-congealing blood.

In this vow, which is ultimately fulfilled, the full truth of the name Bhima ("The Terrible") becomes shockingly clear. The literary critics see this verse as demonstrating the literary quality of "strength" (*ojas*) in its deployment of a very long compound that culminates in the horrible crushing of the thighs of Duryodhana (here called Suyodhana) revealing the whole hideous scene all at once. But his strength can also be conveyed in a more clipped arrangement:

> Whatever man proud of his strong arm
> bears weapons in the Pancala clan: dotards,
> children, down to babes in the very womb;
> and whoever saw that deed:
> I will slay them all when I come onto the field,
> every man who fights me, though he be Death himself;
> in blind fury I will be the death of Death!

This verse is more staccato, short words bearing down relentlessly to manifest finally the clear and calculating fury that is Bhima's vengeance. As the great Sanskritist Daniel Ingalls suggests, even when trying to peer through the English to the Sanskrit underneath, reading with the critics helps us to partake of the excitement of the poet's effect.

See also **krodha; manyu; vira**

REFERENCES

"he is called Rudra" . . . *Mahābhārata* VII.173.98, where Drona praises Shiva's fierce aspect. We can suggest that this account is "commonly cited" because we find it also in a Buddhist text, where it appears as a reason *not* to worship gods (*Abhidharmakośabhāṣya* 2.64. AKB, volume I: 307).

"The brutal war-club" . . . This verse and the next are quoted and discussed by the literary critic Ānandavardhana and his commentator Abhinavagupta. See DL: 34–35, 255–257. To be sure, not all critics approved of *raudra*: given their emphasis on nonviolence, Jain aesthetic theorists questioned whether violence is a matter to be savored (RR: 191).

romaharsha

Horripilation (Sanskrit)

Classical India has paid more attention to the hair-raising, skin prickling, and goosebumps induced by great pleasure, fear, or excitement than any other tradition, and beginning Sanskrit students everywhere come to incorporate the slightly obscure English "horripilation" into their translating toolkits. We have a number of words for hair standing on end—*romaharsha* (*romaharṣa*), *romaharshana*, *romanca*, *romodgama*—and everywhere we find people afflicted by it. Kalidasa very charmingly covers the Great Goddess Parvati with this condition when she takes the sweaty hand of Lord Shiva at the moment they marry: these two may be the highest deities in the cosmos, but their love is both nervous and electric.

Horripilation is not reserved solely for erotic excitement. In another context entirely, the Bactrian Greek king Milinda, who had been complaining loudly and bitterly for years that India is devoid of any good philosophers, finally meets an interlocutor worthy of his questions, the Buddhist monk Nagasena. The moment he sees Nagasena, Milinda becomes "afraid and stupefied, with hair standing on end": like a frog chased by a snake, a deer fleeing a leopard, and a fish thrashing in a net, he is "frightened, anxious, terrified, agitated, horripilating, distressed, confused, with his mind in turmoil and his thoughts awhirl" as he considers the large audience of five hundred Greeks and eighty thousand monks who have gathered to see their debate. He has but one thought: "May all these people not come to despise me."

The most sublime instance of horripilation must surely be Arjuna's in the terrifying theophany revealed in the *Bhagavad Gita*. God discloses his full reality, including his dark and destructive aspect. To Arjuna, who had only ever known Krishna as his dear friend, this vision of God as Time incarnate swallowing up the hosts of all creatures fills him with fear and trembling and he begs for mercy. His hair stands on end. But much later, in the *Gita*'s closing verses, we find Arjuna horripilating again, though now it is in joy and wonder.

See also **adbhuta/abbhuta; bhaya; bhayanaka; harsha; priti; vismaya**

REFERENCES

Kalidasa very charmingly . . . Kumārasaṃbhava 7.77. BK: 286–287. The word here is *romodgama*.

the Bactrian Greek king . . . Milindapañha 24.

must surely be Arjuna's . . . Bhagavad Gītā 11.14, 18.74–77.

rosha

Rage (Sanskrit)

This anger is rash and injurious to its object. Fine distinctions are not drawn between *krodha*, *kopa*, and *rosha* (*roṣa*): all involve fiery rage. *Rosha* is used less frequently, however. We often see this rash anger get fired up in Rama's dear and faithful brother, Lakshmana, who accompanies him into exile. Lakshmana's anger acts as foil to Rama's composure.

While devoted, brave, and "tender by nature," Lakshmana is also a bit of a hothead. When Rama is sent into exile, Lakshmana is furious (*roshita*), and he rages against Rama's calm acceptance of this shocking turn of events. When Lakshmana gets like this, we see his eyes redden, his breath come hard, his lips tremble, and a frown knit between his brows: his face is like that of a raging lion, and his heavy sighs are like those of a huge snake angry in its lair. He grows huge and frightening to all who cross in his path.

We find him raging again much later in the epic, when the brothers have lost Sita, and their monkey ally, Sugriva, tarries in helping them find her, breaking (at least it seems at first) their alliance. While Rama counsels calmness and friendship in nudging Sugriva to his pledge, Lakshmana cannot hold back, and in his fury advances upon Sugriva. In this case, it is only the wise Tara, Sugriva's wife, who manages to talk him down. She urges that he "not rashly succumb to *rosha* like a common man, without knowing the true state of affairs." As a noble prince, he should reflect and get the facts before flying off the handle, and surely, one must always consider the consequences of rash action.

Another hothead in the epics is Karna. He too is long-suffering and a victim of considerable injustice, and his *rosha* endures. At his death, as this noble warrior lies on the ground, he is recalled as a man of "long *rosha*," his fury a steady companion throughout his tragic life.

See also **kopa; krodha; manyu; pidita**

REFERENCES

Lakshmana . . . Rāmāyaṇa II.20.1–5, IV.30.7, IV.30.33, IV.34.10. Tara's words are translated by R. Lefeber, *Rāmāyaṇa, Book Four, Kiṣkindhā*, New York: CSL, 2005: 223; "tender by nature" is at IV.35.1 (Lefeber, 226–227).

Karna . . . Mahābhārata 11.21.3; Karna is remembered also as *amarṣi*, "unforgiving" or "full of resentment," here and at 11.26.36.

S

sambhoga

Love-in-Union (Sanskrit)

A woman said this when asked by her friend, "How was your lover in bed?"

When my lovcr came to bed,
the knot came untied
all by itself.
My dress,
Held up by the strings of a loosened belt
barely stayed on my hips.
Friend,
That's as much as I know now.
When he touched my body,
I couldn't at all remember
who he was,
who I was,
or how It was.

This poem, highly suggestive but at no points graphic, is the savoring of the pleasures of desire that lovers enjoy when they are together. The aesthetic pleasure, or *rasa*, that we experience in the poem is *sambhoga* (*saṃbhoga*), one of the two types of erotic sentiment (in contrast to love-in-separation, *vipralambha*, the savor of anguished desire when lovers are torn from one another). *Sambhoga* is a celebration of desire and its achievement in merging two human beings.

Another bedroom scene from the same collection flirts with love-in-separation only to dissolve it into *sambhoga*. We begin with a lover's quarrel:

They lay upon the bed each turned aside
and suffering in silence;
though love still dwelt within their hearts
each feared a loss of pride.
But then from out the corner of their eyes
the sidelong glances met
and the quarrel broke in laughter as they turned
and clasped each other's neck.

This intimate vignette has the lovers divided by pride until laughter at their own foolishness erupts and they embrace again.

Last, we might suggest for *sambhoga* another exquisite moment, well caught in David Shulman's translation, speaking of Rama and Sita:

Whispering wonderful whatevers
in any which order,
cheek touching cheek,
arms totally enmeshed
from so much loving,
we never knew the hours passing
when suddenly—night itself
was over.

Their union is all the more poignant because much as the night suddenly ends, so too, before they know it and forevermore, will their togetherness.

See also **rasa; rati; shringara; vipralambha**

REFERENCES

A woman said this . . . Amaruśataka 101. Trans. M. Selby, *Grow Long, Blessed Night*, New York: Oxford University Press, 2000: 29.

"They lay upon the bed" . . . *Amaruśataka* 667. Trans. D. Ingalls, *Sanskrit Poetry from Vidyākara's "Treasury,"* Cambridge, MA: Harvard University Press, 1965: 170.

"Whispering wonderful whatevers" . . . Bhavabhūti's *Uttararāmacarita* 1.112–113. Trans. D. Shulman in "The Arrow and the Poem," *New Republic,* August 13, 2008.

samskara/sankhara

Subliminal Impressions and Conditions (Sanskrit/Pali)

Emotions, thoughts, and actions don't just spring out of nowhere. All of the main religious systems advance various terms for the psychological conditioning—the traces (*vasana*), underlying tendencies (*anushaya*), and patterned dispositions (*kleshas*)—that shape our flow of experience. *Samskara* (*saṃskāra*) is one such term, indicating the impressions that stay residually in the mind from past experience, including past lives. These lurking impressions are active, as indicated by the verbal root of the term which means "to fashion or construct," and *samskaras* construct and shape every moment of experience to become some of the main drivers of emotional life. In this, they are sometimes conceived to be more dynamic than the *vasanas* that may lie dormant or at most color experience. Much like addictions, *samskaras* are pernicious in that whether they are good or bad karmic traces, they reinforce through habit and disposition the actions that keep beings trapped in samsara. The Yoga authority Patanjali says they are held together by cause and effect, the interdependent actions, reactions, motives, and responses that drive our experience until yogic cessation and peace can interrupt them.

Buddhists also identify *samskaras* (and in Pali, *sankhāras*) as central dynamic activities in human psychology, identifying them as one of the five clusters of phenomena that comprise a person and as one link in the chain of dependent origination. In the latter analysis, *samskaras* are conditioned by ignorance and they in turn condition every moment of awareness we have of the world. When ignorance is cut off, these conditioned and constructive patterns are cut off as well, and one attains spiritual awakening.

In pointed contrast, the aesthetic theorists have a more positive valuation of the *samskaras*, for it is these unconscious impressions that are the source of emotion (*bhava*) in the heart of wise persons of focused intelligence. It is owing to subliminal impressions that poets can stir our emotions the way they do (see *vasana* for more on this point).

See also **asava/ashrava; kleshas/kilesas; vasana**

REFERENCES

The Yoga authority Patañjali . . . See *Yoga Sūtras* 4.9–11, YSU: 76–77.

Buddhists also identify . . . Saṃyutta Nikāya ii.1–2; iii.58–61, CDB: 533–534, 895–897, the translator translates *sankhāra* as “volitional formations.”

the aesthetic theorists . . . Rūpa Goswāmin in BR: 384–385 (verse 133).

samtosha

Contentment (Sanskrit)

Samtosha (*saṃtoṣa*) is the contentment one feels when one resists the pull of acquisitiveness. Such contentment is itself happiness. For Jains, *samtosha*’s opposite, discontent, is the cause of suffering. And when developed, *samtosha* becomes a bulwark against greed (*lobha*), which is a passion (*kashaya*) that otherwise threatens to overwhelm us. Hindu Yoga treatises treat *samtosha* much the same way, finding it an observance to be put into practice for achieving highest happiness.

But in the more worldly contexts of *niti*—that is, the genre of political advice to young princes—*samtosha* swings both ways. It is the secret of happiness to be much celebrated: "one with a contented mind possesses all riches." But this same quality can also lead to the complacency that stifles ambition: contentment is listed as an impediment to greatness. "If you feel well-off even with little money, then I think fate has done its duty and does not increase it for you." The maxims guiding one through messy political reality frequently contravene one another: emotions and dispositions appropriate for a young prince in one context fail him in another.

See also **kashaya; lobha; tushti**

REFERENCES

the contentment one feels . . . Hemacandra's *Yogaśāstra* II.106, 114; IV.22. YŚ: 48–49, 80.

Hindu Yoga treatises treat samtosha . . . Patañjali's *Yogasūtra* 2.32, 42, YSU: 53, 55. Saṃtoṣa is also an important theme of the Laghu Yogavāsiṣṭha.

"one with a contented mind . . . If you feel well-off" . . . *Hitopadeśa* 1.326, 2.11–15. FA: 162–163, 214–215.

samvega

Angst; Apprehension; Urgency (Pali and Sanskrit)

When the lion's roar fills the forest, the uneasy and anxious feeling of *samvega* (*saṃvega*) penetrates all creatures and they flee to their dens. *Samvega* is the feeling of dread and anxiety that one should be doing *something* to secure one's safety, but can't quite make out just what that is even as danger closes in. The steed who sees the shadow of the goad falling on the wall is given to *samvega* wondering what his master has in store for him: what should he be doing right now? The king who looks in a mirror one day and sees his first gray hair is struck with *samvega* realizing that time is fleeting and his own expiration may be pending. Above all, realizing the horrors of the round of rebirth leads, according to the religious texts, to the most acute *samvega* of all, an ill-boding about the world that is highly expedient for those would teach a path of freedom from it.

Religious authorities the world over attempt to whip up *samvega* to turn the angst of the guilty or the complacency of the contented into an urgency for transformation. The Buddha was not above fire-and-brimstone preaching to startle people into changing their wicked ways. Once he demanded of his monks to know whether it would be better to have a "strong man force open one's mouth with a hot iron spike—burning, blazing, and glowing—and insert a hot copper ball—burning, blazing, and glowing—which burns one's lips, mouth, tongue, throat, and stomach, and comes out from below taking along one's entrails," or for a pretender monk to accept almsfood given with esteem by the faithful? The monks tend to think that accepting almsfood is far preferable to the business with the hot iron spike and ball, but are sadly misguided. Far better to have this torture now than for a wicked monk to accept alms from good people under false pretenses. So too, it is far better for a monk to submit to other fiery tortures (most vividly described) than to embrace tender maidens or to wear the robe or to accept homage while being wicked, for the torments of hell awaiting him for these violations of monastic practice are far worse. Upon hearing this sermon, sixty monks were said to have vomited hot blood and sixty others left the monastic life altogether decrying its difficulty. But a further sixty achieved liberation.

See also **ottappa; romaharsha; vismaya**

REFERENCES

lion's roar . . . *Aṅguttara Nikāya* ii.34, NDB: 420.

steed who sees the shadow . . . *Aṅguttara Nikāya* ii.114, NDB: 494.

first gray hair . . . "Makhādeva Jātaka," trans. R. Chalmers, *The Jātaka*, volume 1, New Delhi: Munshiram Manoharlal Publishers, 1990: 31.

"strong man force" . . . The Aggikkhandhupāma Sutta of the *Aṅguttara Nikāya* iv.128–136, NDB: 1092.

sattva

Brightness; Wisdom; Lucidity (Sanskrit)

Sattva is one of the three *gunas* or qualities of Samkhya and Yoga metaphysics, typically construed as the mode of being light, in both senses of the word as bright and not heavy. While the world of experience is a constantly interacting flux of *sattva*, *rajas*, and *tamas* and none of them is to be found in isolation, a preponderance of *sattva* is preferred, as it is the luminous mode of reality. Emotionally and temperamentally, a *sattva* disposition is "kind, disposed to sharing, bright, patient, truthful, *dharmic*, believing, knowledgeable, intelligent, wise, possessing good memory, constant, and undisturbed." In the *Mahabharata*, *sattva* is "rapture, joy, bliss, happiness, and a calmed mind." *Sattva* is always described in quite positive terms—the *Bhagavad Gita* describes it as "untainted, luminous, healthy"—yet even it ensnares us by causing us to cling to happiness and knowledge. The philosopher Shankara identifies the absence of *all* three *gunas* as the transcendence of desire necessary for spiritual liberation.

See also **guna; rajas; tamas**

REFERENCES

"kind, disposed to sharing" . . . According to the medical text *Suśruta Saṃhitā* III.1.18.

In the Mahabharata . . . *Mahābhārata* 12.194.35.
the Bhagavad Gita . . . *Bhagavad Gītā* 14.6.
philosopher Shankara . . . IP: 153.

sattvikabhava

Psychophysical Responses (Sanskrit)

Sattvikabhavas (*sāttvikabhāvas*) are a class of *bhavas* in Bharata's aesthetic system, specifically eight states, conditions, or "sensitivities" (one hesitates to call them emotions) that consist of a physical presentation: paralysis, perspiration, horripilation, a broken voice, trembling, pallor, tears, and fainting. These can be felt and performed by actors to convey and evoke emotion, and when artfully combined with the other elements of stagecraft, they help evoke aesthetic experience—that is, *rasa*. Bharata is quite aware that these physical experiences can have other causes than psychosomatic ones and so these are called *sattvika* to indicate a psychological aspect. (Tears can flow from smoke in the eyes, not just grief or joy. We sweat not just from fear, but also from summer's heat.) He limits *sattvikabhavas* to those experiences that "originate in the mind," when the actors concentrate their minds and feel the emotions.

Bhanudatta, a later theorist, develops further what *sattvika* must mean here. For him, the salient point is that *sattva* refers to a "living being," and thus "the enlivened body." These *bhavas* are bodily reactions in ways not as evident in the other *bhavas*.

These responses help with realism in the theater, capturing, Bharata says, "the nature of the world" in imitating how people actually feel. In discussing them, Bharata gives stage directions and actor's tips. Perspiration is presumably hard to see from the back, so the actors should take up a fan, wipe off sweat, and look for a breeze. Still, no matter how they are represented on the stage, these responses fundamentally arise from *sattva*, the quality of luminosity and pureness that in this context manifests as a seat of emotion. A broken or faltering voice may have many causes, but if it is to be considered a *sattvikabhava*, it occurs from sorrow, amazement, anger, joy, or fear.

See also **ashru; bhava; rasa; romaharsha; sattva**

REFERENCES

"sensitivities" . . . Sensitivities and psychophysical responses are Pollock's translations, and this discussion follows his translation of *Nāṭyaśāstra* 7.93. RR: 55.

when the actors . . . feel the emotions . . . Some manuscripts and other translations indicate that the actors feel pleasure or pain (*duḥkhitena sukhitena*) to produce these experiences, while Pollock, as he puts it, "in desperation reads *aduḥkhitena asukhitena*" (343 n. 53), leading to the idea that actors can produce these "even when not feeling pleasure or pain" (55), which is different from what I have suggested here.

Bhanudatta . . . Bhānudatta's *Rasataraṅgiṇī* 4.1–4. BRRR: 188–189.

take up a fan . . . *Nāṭyaśāstra* 7.102.

fundamentally arise from sattva . . . Rūpa Goswāmin in BR: 258–259 (verse 61); for the claims about the broken voice, see 252–253 (verse 37–42).

sauharda

Fondness (Sanskrit)

Sauharda (*sauhārda*) is affection between friends. Rama and Lakshmana are brothers, but their relationship is both leavened and fortified by this genuine fondness, which literally means "good-heartedness." The strength of their affection is pointedly contrasted to the tragic relationship between the monkey brothers Sugriva and Valin, where the "*sauharda* that should join brothers turned out quite otherwise."

Sauharda is also the friendship between allies, and in such contexts its sense of genuine good feeling can be in tension with the strategic considerations underlying political and mercantile allegiances (also called *sauharda*). Calling an alliance a friendship strengthens it tactically, and can obscure the political calculations involved. In the *niti* literature—that is, the wise strategy of rulers—*sauharda* is carefully scrutinized because when it is genuine, it brings loyalty, comfort, riches, and success in an arena that is otherwise treacherous. The *Hitopadesha* considers the treaty between Rama and Sugriva, his monkey ally, to be based on mutual benefit rather than pure friendly affection and admiration. But in the *Ramayana* itself, their *sauharda* is forged with both reciprocity and true feeling, despite the ways both will come to be tested.

Last, *sauharda* is the deep fondness binding lovers together in a friendship connecting them from previous lives. It is this fondness "deep in the heart" that Kalidasa tells us is recalled by the beautiful music and art that can make even a happy person edgy with longing for a forgotten lover.

See also **metta/maitra; rosha**

References

"good-heartedness" . . . There are many variants of this word: *sauhārdya, suhṛdya, sauhṛdaya,* and so on. Instances of this affection between Rāma and Lakṣmana are ubiquitous. Vālin laments the lack of *sauhārda* with Sugrīva at *Rāmāyaṇa* IV.22.5. Rāma and Sugrīva's *sauhārda* is forged at IV.5.10–15.

Hitopadesha . . . *Hitopadeśa* 4.306, 311. This text describes the various kinds of treaties and finds that the alliance between Rāma and Sugrīva is based on "requital," which is not the same as one based on friendship (here using *maitrī*); but in this text even friendly alliances are based on exchange of gifts and, for kings, daughters in marriage. The *Pañcatantra,* a *nīti* text full of stories, is obsessed with *sauhārda.*

Kalidasa tells us . . . *Abhijñānaśākuntala* 5.24. See *vasana* for reference and discussion of this verse.

shama

Tranquility (Sanskrit)

> Tranquility leads to everything good, tranquility is the highest state, tranquility is auspicious, tranquility is peace, tranquility ends confusion.

In a religious reading of Rama in the *Yoga Vashishta*, Rama has grown world-weary and desolate, and has come to a sage called Vasishtha for advice. The sage's fables and wise instruction everywhere urge Rama to acquire *shama (śama)*, the tranquility or peace that comes with the ending of desire and aversion. From the same word as *shanti*, *shama* is the peace one achieves when one is dispassionate and learns to transcend the dualities of love and hate, desire and aversion. And while this text articulates key ideas of Yoga and Advaita Vedanta, its emphasis on the peace found when the mind stops fluttering around with its endless desires and hatreds is shared by all early Indian religion.

See also **moksha; nirveda; shanta; shanti; upeksha/upekkha; vairagya; yoga**

REFERENCE

"Tranquility leads to everything good" . . . *Yogavāsiṣṭha* 2.13.52.

shanka

Disquiet; Apprehension; Suspicion (Sanskrit)

Like *cinta*, *shanka* (*śaṅkā*) is worry and anxiety, but it also can mean doubt, suspicion, and apprehension. The *rasa* authority Bhanudatta defines it as the "expectation of something extremely bad, or anxiety about the loss of something good." He sees it at work in this verse uttered by a woman, who, we come to suspect, has an adulterous lover:

> "My elders can see into my mind, and these villains
> have slurs on the tips of their tongues.
> The townsfolk are real experts in spreading slander,
> and my mother-in-law is a snake.
> What will happen?" She sighed as she thought over
> the seeds of her misfortune,
> and then she laid upon her breast a garland
> Of flame-red *kinshuka* flowers.

The flame-red flowers are carefully chosen, we must infer, to hide the red nail marks her lover has left on her bosom. She is an object of suspicion, but she is also filled with the dread and apprehension of getting caught. *Shanka*'s conditioning factors, Bhanudatta says, include the "poor advice and the cruelty of others" that get us into such predicaments.

See also **cinta; kukkucca; ottappa; samvega**

REFERENCE

rasa authority Bhanudatta . . . This entire entry is from *Rasataraṅgiṇī* 5.11–12. BRRR: 206–207.

shanta

The Aesthetic Experience of Peacefulness (Sanskrit)

Bharata's system of eight *rasas* does not list *shanta* (*śānta*), the aesthetic experience of peacefulness or dispassion. It seems to have been the Jains who first added it to the list of *rasas* as they pondered how literary art could be conducive to spiritual development. While Jain stories explore all corners of human emotion, they aim in the end at the composure of the sage who has renounced all desire. One example is their epic version of the *Ramayana* story, called the *Padmapurana*, which deploys sorrow (*shoka*) to arrive at world-weariness (*nirveda*). Through his many losses, the hero Rama comes to realize that all worldly pursuits are "as worthless as a cow's footstep in mud." This in turn leads to tranquility (*shama*) to be savored aesthetically in *shanta*.

Centuries later, Kashmiri theorists also added this ninth *rasa* to Bharata's eight, with some arguing that *shanta* is the predominate aesthetic experience overall of the *Mahabharata*. Its harrowing story of civil war and destruction of the family leaves one disenchanted with the world, argues Anandavardhana, and seeking the solace that comes from being free of wishing that things be otherwise. He says that *shanta* is "the full development of the happiness that comes from the dying off of desire," and quotes the *Mahabharata* on this point:

> The happiness of worldly pleasure
> and the greater happiness of heavenly pleasures
> are not worth a sixteenth of the happiness
> that comes from the dying of desire.

In this conception, we perceive once again the central Indian idea of a kind of happiness (*ananda* or *sukha*) that cannot be delivered through desire and sensual pleasure but comes only from the stilling of these.

King Bhoja also takes *shanta* as a *rasa*, and cites the following verse is a good example of the aesthetic relish that is *shanta*:

> He possesses all treasures who has a contented heart,
> To the man wearing soft leather shoes, the whole earth
> is covered in suede.

Not able to fix the world, enjoying balanced composure in the face of its ups and downs is true peace; and one does one's bit by treading softly on the world. The underlying emotion of which this *rasa* is the refinement is alternatively given as *nirveda* (world-weariness), *dhriti* (contentment), or *shama* (tranquility). Abhinavagupta suggests that the happiness of being free of desire can be known by the everyday example of the disinterest one enjoys when one's craving for a particular food has stopped. *Shanta* comes to be central to his thinking and he goes so far as to suggest that the peaceful is the chief of the *rasas* and basic to all of them.

These ideas met with controversy, as is evident from Abhinavagupta's own account. Some object that the *Mahabharata* does not have an overall *rasa* or that if it does, *shanta* is not it. Others insist that *shringara* is the chief and most basic *rasa*, not *shanta*. Others argue that dispassion cannot be depicted in a play, since it is the quieting of all activity and feeling, so how can it be performed and relished aesthetically? Still others doubt that the stilling of all desire and aversion is even possible in human life.

See also **nirveda; rasa; shama; shanti**

REFERENCES

the Jains who first added it . . . The *Anuyogadvarasūtra* speaks of the bright composure of the sage owing to the absence of mental turbulence, and lists nine *rasas*, though this may be a later interpolation (ŚR: 37–38).

"as worthless as a cow's footstep in mud" . . . Raviṣeṇa's *Padmapūraṇa* as cited, translated, and discussed in Gregory Clines, "Grief, Tranquility, and *Śānta Rasa* in Raviṣeṇa's *Padmapurāṇa*," in BRH: 34.

"the full development of the happiness" . . . Ānandavardana's *Dhvanyāloka* 4.5, DL: 692. The "happiness that comes from the dying off of desire" is *tṛṣṇākṣayasukha*, 695 n. 16, which is an echo of the *Mahābhārata* verse he goes on to quote here.

"The happiness of worldly pleasure" . . . *Mahābhārata* 12.168.36. My translation. This is quoted by Ānandavardhana in discussing the *rasa* of *śānti*, DL: 18, 520.

"He possesses all treasures"... Bhoja's *Śṛṅgāraprakāśa*, quoted in RR: 133, 363 n. 163, where Bhoja is quoting *Pañcatantra* v.75.

alternatively given as nirveda... Abhinavagupta suggests *nirveda* and gives the example of food at *Locana* 3.26, DL: 521. Rūpa Goswāmi says that contentment (*dhriti*) is sometimes said to be the *sthāyibhāva*, BR: 408–409.

met with controversy... Abhinavagupta raises some of it, DL: 522–526. Dhanaṃjaya, Dhanika, and Bahurūpa Miśra variously object to *śānta* as a *rasa*, since it cannot be represented or because it is an actual impossibility, RR: 165.

shanti

Peace (Sanskrit)

Om shanti, shanti, shanti

Shanti (*śānti*) the peace and tranquility toward which all of Indian religion aims, is a mantra—a powerful spell or prayer—in the Upanishads, uttered three times with the sacred sound of *om*. *Om* is the ultimate mantra said to encompass all the vowels in the Veda and thus, when voiced, recites the entire Vedic revelation (the consonants being just interruptions of the primordial sonic reality that is the Veda). There is no more powerful way to invoke peace.

Om shanti, shanti, shanti is the invocation, evocation, and realization of the ultimate peace underlying all of the phenomenal activity that we overlay onto this basic tranquility. To utter *shanti* is to bring it into being.

Lead us from the unreal to the real
Lead us from darkness to light
Lead us from death to immortality
Om, shanti, shanti, shanti.

See also **moksha; nirvana/nibbana; shama; shanta; sukha; yoga**

REFERENCE

"Lead us from the unreal to the real" . . . *Bṛhadāraṇyaka Upaniṣad* 1.3.28, EU: 44–45. This beautiful prayer actually does not mention the last line, though it often gets added to it when it is recited today. We do find *oṃ śāntiḥ śāntiḥ śāntiḥ* at *Taittirīya Upaniṣad* 1.1.1, EU: 290–291. For a discussion of *oṃ*, see *Mārkaṇḍeyapurāṇa* 39.1–14, trans. J. Mallinson and M. Singleton, *Roots of Yoga*, U.K. Penguin Classics, 2017: 267–268.

shoka

Grief; Sorrow (Sanskrit)

The world's first poetry begins with sorrow. One day, the sage Valmiki happens to see a hunter kill a male crane in the act of mating, whose mate dies also from grief and shock. Valmiki is stricken with *shoka* (*śoka*) and curses the hunter in a new form of metered language in a couplet called a *shloka*, the world's first poetic form:

> Oh, hunter, may you never find rest in ages to come,
> For you killed one from a pairing of cranes preoccupied with love.

Shoka has produced a shock, and Valmiki is astonished by the verse he has invented. He is instructed by the gods to take the story of Prince Rama's exile that he has recently heard and turn it into this metered verse. The result? The great epic poem *Ramayana*, which constitutes, in the Sanskrit historical memory at least, the world's first literature. The *Ramayana* is an adventure tale of divine descent, noble heroism, romantic love, and, throughout, great tragedy and sorrow.

This invention of verse by sorrow launches centuries of aesthetic reflection on how emotion, perhaps especially sorrow, gives rise to literary art. The episode is frequently referred to by later theorists who come to emphasize that it is the poet's feeling that infuses their poems with *rasa*. Anandavardhana insists that "if the poet is filled with passion, the whole world of his poem will consist of *rasa*; if not, it will be completely devoid of it." Whatever anguish grief involves, at least it can give us great literature.

Shoka also presents a powerful affront to the religious therapies of emotion. We see this in the *Mahabharata* at the apocalyptic end of the war. Dhritarashtra, the feckless king whose indecision and indulgence of his resentful sons make him bear no small responsibility for the war, is sunk in misery at the losses. Still, we pity him in his grief as the blood-caked battlefields with the body parts of his sons and kinsmen are described in relentless detail. To soothe him, Vidura, his wise advisor, offers the most reasoned and eloquent religious teachings of the time, suggesting ways of transcending grief and replacing it with equanimity by surrendering all desire and attachment; he speaks of heaven, fate, God. All to no avail: Dhritarashtra sinks to the ground in a faint.

And if we think Dhritarashtra's grief is unassailable, it pales next to that of the mothers and widows pouring out of their houses toward the battlefield. With her divine eye, Queen Gandhari studies each woman in her particular loss, as each one in turn cradles the dismembered remains of her husband, brother, or son, with hair loosened, dress disheveled, weeping and screaming, publicly and unrelentingly stunned by grief. None can be comforted, and the *shoka* does not relent. The *Mahabharata*, this "inauspicious text" (from the standpoint of so many religious teachings), allows grief to have the last word.

See also **dina; parideva; sthayibhava; upayasa; vyatha**

REFERENCES

"Oh, hunter" . . . *Rāmāyaṇa* I.2.15.

by later theorists . . . As for example Ānandavardhana: *Dhvanyāloka*, 83–88. RR: 90.

"if the poet is filled with passion" . . . *Dhvanyāloka* 497, RR: 97.

in the Mahabharata . . . See the Strī Parvan for the events described in this paragraph, trans. K. Crosby, *Book XI, The Women*, New York: CSL, 2009, sections 16–25. Gāndhārī, herself blindfolded to share her husband's blindness, sees these women with her divine eye: these two blind people can now see with faultless clarity the horrible state of things. I am grateful to conversations with C. Ram-Prasad about his forthcoming book chapter on grief, for the observations about the Strī Parvan's position on *shoka* and the gendered aspects of it.

shraddha

Trust; Faith (Sanskrit)

The *Rig Veda* often deifies virtues like trust and sings praises to them. In one such hymn, Shraddha (*śraddhā*) is praised for its role in the fire sacrifice. For without this trust, who would kindle the fire and offer oblations? The hymn implores Shraddha to make itself dear to those who give, especially for those who give lavishly, since without faith or trust, why would anyone give to the brahman priests who perform the sacrifice (and who are, of course, singing this hymn praising such faith)? Gods honor *shraddha*, the hymn asserts unapologetically, for it is through it that they find wealth. We must then call to Shraddha three times a day asking that Shraddha establish faith in us.

The trust that is *shraddha* is less a cognitive assent to a proposition, and more a sense of confidence. It has an affective dimension toward its object, and its object is usually God or an admired personage. As Indian religions develop, *shraddha*'s emotional elements make it less overtly transactional. It comes to involve not just belief or trust in something or someone, but attention to them and esteem toward them. It is an investment and commitment to the extent that, as the *Bhagavad Gita* puts it, "you are what you trust in." Ramanuja goes on to suggest that *shraddha* is "an eagerness to put into practice what one already has confidence in."

Buddhists see faith as vital to the religious project and define it as operating to "clarify" the mind. In Indian lore, there is a fabulous type of gemstone that when put in murky water, instantly clarifies it. *Shraddha* is like this, suddenly chasing away the muck of doubt and confusion and making clear the truth and value of the teachings. Another definition has it that faith is "leaping across," and likens its function to that of the brave fellow who girds up his loins and leaps across a rushing tributary when a village is struck by flooding. *Shraddha* is recognizing one's strength, power, and confidence to leap into the unknown.

A final parsing brings together the elements we've seen here: *shraddha* is "trusting in what is real, clear serenity (*prasada*) toward that which has virtuous qualities, and longing (*abhilasha*) for what is possible."

See also **prasada**

REFERENCES

Shraddha is praised . . . *Ṛg Veda* 10.151. See *The Rigveda, Volume III*, trans. S. Jamison and J. Brereton, New York: Oxford University Press, 2014: 1636.

"you are what you trust in" . . . *Bhagavad Gītā* 17.3. The commentary by Ramanuja is given in R. C. Zaehner, trans. *The Bhagavad Gītā with a Commentary Based on the Original Sources*, London: Oxford University Press, 1969: 376. David Shulman argues that *śraddhā* is a word for attention and translates this verse as "you are what you pay attention to" (*More Than Real*, Cambridge, MA: Harvard University Press, 2012: 138–139).

"clarify" the mind . . . *Abhidharmakośabhāṣya* 2.25. Trans. AKB, volume I: 191. Sthiramati also defines it as clarifying the turbidity of the mind and refers to the gem (A. Engle, trans., *The Inner Science of Buddhist Practice*, Ithaca, NY: Snow Lion Publications, 2009: 284). The gem-clearing simile and the alternative definition "leaping across" with its simile is found in *Milindapañha* 34–36.

"trusting in what is real" . . . *Asaṅga's Abhidharmasamuccaya* 16.7–8, as quoted in A. Rotman, *Thus Have I Seen*, New York: Oxford University Press, 2009: 145, 261 n. 46. This is my translation, but my interpretation has been informed by Rotman's discussion.

shringara

The Erotic (Sanskrit)

In order to illustrate *shringara* (*śṛṅgāra*), the *rasa* of sexual attraction and romantic love, the great literary critic Anandavardhana gives the following verse about a tender moment between newlyweds:

> Seeing that the attendant had left the bedroom,
> the young wife rose half upright from the bed
> and, gazing long upon her husband's face
> as he lay there feigning sleep, at last took courage
> and kissed him lightly, only to discover
> his feint from the rising flesh upon his cheek.
> When then she hung her head in shame, her dear one
> seized her, laughing, and kissed her in good earnest.

The poem captures the playful eroticism of the couple, where the young wife is still bashful, and the lovemaking is full of discovery. Abhinavagupta, commenting further, says of these lovers that they have "achieved the ultimate bliss which consists in regarding one's partner as the all-in-all of life."

We can use the example to analyze the elements contributing to the aesthetic feeling that is *shringara*. The underlying stable emotion is of course *rati*, sexual love and desire, and we have the transient emotion of shame or bashfulness inflecting the nature of it in this instance. "Rising flesh," suggests horripilation as a psychophysical response, further characterizing the erotic phenomenology here. These elements work in combination to get us to the particular texture of this couple's love. Since *shringara* can take such diverse forms, other poems will deploy different transient and psychophysical conditions to bring out the qualities of each instance. Abhinavagupta emphasizes the myriad possibibilities for the erotic, and claims that "the path of poetry may extend to infinity."

Further, there are two types of *shringara*: love-in-union when the partners are together, and love-in-separation when they are forced apart (see *sambhoga* and *vipralambha*). This is a poem of love-in-union. Poems of lovers separated by circumstance or quarrel can be quite anguished, but since both have attraction as their enduring emotion, the two types of *shringara* are two different conditions of savoring this attraction. *Shringara* includes relishing both the joy of union and the tortures of frustrated love.

Thus far, this description represents the views of most of the aesthetic theorists. But it would be a shame not to mention the distinctive views of King Bhoja, a subtle theorist of *rasa*, who wrote a text called *Illuminating the Erotic* in the eleventh century. Bhoja argues that *shringara* is *rasa* par excellence, so fundamental to human experience that it in fact underlies *all* emotion and aesthetic feeling. For Bhoja, *shringara* is a "special capacity of a person's ego; it is the very essence of love." It is what allows us to taste all kinds of *rasas*. *Shringara* is

> an indescribable transformation of primal matter consisting of one's sense of self that awakens in the heart of those in whom sensitivity predominates; a transformation born of a special untainted property, arising by way of predispositions formed by experiences in past lives, and functioning as the single source of the appearance and intensification of the entire range of the self's attributes.

This is to say that *shringara* is "a sense of self" (which he elsewhere refers to as *abhimana*) that is awareness itself. It is the capacity of the self to be aware and thus immerse one in all experience. In those who are sensitive and have the deep karmic predispositions to become engrossed in the pleasure in all experience—to taste and savor it all—*shringara* is the source of all intensity of feeling. Bhoja's extraordinary theory puts the savoring of attraction at the very heart of the human engagement with the world.

See also **abhimana; lajja; prema; rasa; rati; romaharsha; sambhoga; sattvikabhava; sthayibhava; vasana; vipralambha**

REFERENCES

"Seeing that the attendant" . . . From the *Amaruśataka* trans. and discussed by D. Ingalls, "Introduction," DL: 17.

"achieved the ultimate bliss" . . . *Locana* of Abhinavagupta 4.2. DL: 684.

"special capacity of a person's ego" . . . See *kārikās* 3 and 4 at the beginning of the *Śṛṅgāraprakāśa* and Bhoja's interpretation of these immediately following. This is Pollock's translation (RR: 119–123); see also S. Pollock, "Bhoja's *Śṛṅgāraprakāśa* and the Problem of Rasa: A Historical Introduction and Annotated Translation," *Asiatische Studien / Études Asiatiques* 70, no. 1 (1998): 117–192, and V. Raghuvan Bhoja's *Śṛṅgāraprakāśa*, Madras: Punarvasu, 3rd edition, 1978.

smita

Smile (Sanskrit)

While *hasa* is smiling and laughing in amusement, *smita* is smiling or gentle laughter that can be a response to funniness, but need not be. We smile in greeting one another, or in thinking fondly of those we love, and neither need be a matter of mirth. More darkly, we also grin in flattery, arrogance, derision, or contempt. Smiles can be perfunctory, performative, and ritualized. Still, if we consider that the underlying phenomenology of *smita* is blossoming and blooming, there would seem to be an expansive radiance in the face, whatever the cause, in a proper *smita* (see *hasa*, where a similar blooming occurs).

Buddhist scripture censures as "childish" excessive laughter where one bares one's teeth, but it doesn't prohibit a gentle smile: "if you must smile, taking delight in something, just smile." Sublime beings like the Buddha are known to give enigmatic smiles that are not matters of amusement but rather wonder or compassion. Smiles of great beings often indicate higher knowledge, seeing things where others don't.

Consider one of the Buddha's closest disciples, Moggallana, a monk especially renowned for his supernatural and psychic powers. He once smiled while walking with a friend. His friend queried him—why are you smiling? Moggallana explained that as they were walking, he saw a skeleton flying through the air being pecked at by vultures and birds of prey as it screamed in pain. This unfortunate skeleton had been a butcher during a previous lifetime, who lived by stripping meat from the bones of cattle. Moggallana smiled not out of pleasure or schadenfreude, of course, but out of amazement. He notes that people don't believe him when he mentions seeing such things, so he permits himself only a smile that registers his acknowledgment of such an extraordinary sight.

See also **hasa; hasya; vira**

REFERENCES

blossoming and blooming . . . Monier-Williams, *Sanskrit-English Dictionary*, for the verb *smi*.

Buddhist scripture censures . . . *Aṅguttara Nikāya* i.261, NDB: 342; "taking delight in something" could also mean "taking delight in the Dhamma." The Pali for *smita* is *sita*, used here and in the Moggallana story.

Moggallana . . . *Saṃyutta Nikāya* ii.254–255, see CDB: 700–701.

sneha

Tender Love and Affection (Sanskrit)

That state when two become one
in joy as in sorrow,

where you find rest together
and feelings never age
but deepen and ripen as you move
through the layers of time,
that rare state of human fullness
is real. You *may* find it, once,
in life.

Sneha is this bottomless love evoked so beautifully here by the extraordinary playwright Bhavabhuti. Stroking his beloved Sita affectionately, Rama utters this verse about the melding and ripening of pure love.

Sneha—a word whose first meaning is viscosity—is a liquification of the self, as one melts into the other. It is not limited to the romantic sphere, but can occur toward anyone whom we love the most. Elsewhere in this play, Rama melts into the grasp of his long-lost son.

As if my body's very essence, poured out
limb from limb because of my *sneha*;
as if my consciousness, prime element,
were standing there, manifest outside me—
should be drenched by the flow from my own heart
shaken by these deep feelings of bliss, and then
drench me in return when I embrace his limbs
with a true flood of nectar-like *rasa*.

Something ushers forth of his inner stuff as he hugs his child, and the bliss from the embrace drenches him back. It might even be, Bhavabhuti suggests, that the highest degree of *sneha* is the love for one's children, for it is the source of further bonding of their parents. It adds more layers to time's palimpsest of a couple's love.

See also **anuraga; kama; prema; priti; rati; udana; vatsalya**

REFERENCES

"The state when two become one" . . . Bhavabhūti's *Uttararāmacarita* 1.170–173. Trans. D. Shulman in "The Arrow and the Poem," *New Republic*, August 13, 2008. *Sneha* is used in Rāma's affectionate stroking and is present in the verse itself.

"As if my body's very essence" . . . Bhavabhūti's *Uttararāmacarita* 6.95–96. RLA: 342–343.

highest degree of sneha . . . Bhavabhūti's *Uttararāmacarita* 3.105. RLA: 192–193.

somanassa

Delight (Pali)

Our capacities to feel pleasure and pain are considered "faculties" in Buddhist psychology, and in this sense *somanassa* is something the mind *does*. Delight is both something we feel and something we make happen—the mind *takes* delight in things. It is a cheerfulness that we bring to experience. Buddhaghosa says that it functions "in one way or another" to enjoy the agreeable aspect of something; it finds the joy in things. Its opposite is *domanassa*, the mind-born distress we generate and impose on ourselves.

States of joy (*piti*), happiness (*sukha*), and delight pervade the meditation practices known as the *jhanas* that were widely practiced in ancient India. In the Buddhist interpretation, the fourfold *jhanas* involve increasingly rarified states of *piti* and *sukha*, culminating, however, in the final stage in which one leaves them behind, along with faculties of delight and distress, to experience the bliss (*sukha*) of equanimity. Meditation is highly pleasurable, but its final pleasure is when one stops being yanked around by the propensities of the mind to seek pleasure.

The Sanskrit equivalent of *somanassa* is *saumanasya*, with much the same sense in Sanskrit sources. The *Yoga Sutras* see it as connected to the *sattvic* qualities of the mind, which involve brightness, kindness, and all sorts of good cheer.

See also **domanassa; piti; priti; sattva; sukha**

REFERENCES

Buddhaghosa says . . . Visuddhimagga XIV.128, PP: 463.
the jhanas . . . Majjhima Nikāya i.247. See MLD: 340–341.
The Yoga Sutras *see it . . . Yoga Sūtra* 2.41, YSU: 55.

sthayibhava

Stable Emotions (Sanskrit)

In Bharata's *rasa* theory, there are eight stable emotions (*sthāyibhāva*), and it is these eight emotions that come to be aestheticized and savored in *rasa* experience. These are attraction (*rati*), amusement (*hasa*), grief (*shoka*), anger (*krodha*), determination (*utsaha*), fear (*bhaya*), disgust (*jugupsa*), amazement (*vismaya*). One possibility is that the stable emotions are more enduring and basic in human experience than the other categories of *bhavas*. They are like a king, while the others attend as retinue and support. It is these enduring emotional ways of being human, even if some are painful, that art can allow us to savor. Another possibility is that these eight are the stable emotions that performance theory and practice are most interested in portraying and savoring, and that is why these eight are listed (but that there might be other "basic" emotions that Bharata is not particularly interested in for his purposes).

As the centuries went on, an additional *bhava/rasa* pair was added. Writing in the eleventh century and following Anandavardhana, Abhinavagupta takes it for granted that *shama*, tranquility or absence of passion, is a ninth *sthayibhava* with *shanta*, peacefulness, as its corresponding *rasa*.

This addition accommodates religious feelings in what prior to this had been a largely aesthetic body of reflection (although, to be sure, not all religious texts deliver peace).

Abhinavagupta suggests that the stable emotions are basic to human experience because they are "the forms of consciousness that encompass a creature from the moment of his birth." For

> every being is pervaded with desire for sex; laughs at others out of a misplaced sense of his own superiority; burns at separation from a loved one; becomes speechless with anger at those responsible, and then because of his own powerlessness, becomes fearful; is keen for some acquisition but then is overcome with repugnance if the object is unsuitable, thinking it undesirable; feels amazement well up in him at beholding the various things he is about to do; and, last, is prepared to give up something or other.

For Abhinavagupta at least, *rasa* theory offers a philosophical anthropology of emotions that gives an account of what humans are actually like. He goes on to distinguish between these basic experiences inherent to what it is to be human with the "transitory emotions" (*vyabhicaribhava*) that may or may not come into a given person's experience, and when they do appear, are more unstable and fleeting.

See also **bhava; rasa; shama; shanta; vyabhicaribhava**

REFERENCES

like a king . . . Nāṭyaśāstra 7.4. The eight are listed at 6.17, RR: 50.
"the forms of consciousness" . . . Abhinavabhāratī 1.276. RR: 199.

sukha

Pleasure; Happiness; Bliss (Sanskrit and Pali)

Every bit as much as the awareness of suffering (*duhkha*), the study of pleasure and the achievement of happiness constituted the central project of early Indian religion. The Pali Buddhist sources carried forward many of the concerns the Upanishads voice about the fleeting and unreliable nature of pleasure (*sukha*), and like them, also sought a permanent bliss that transcends the vicissitudes of pleasure and pain. But Buddhists did not call this bliss *ananda*, as the Upanishads did, and instead, sometimes confusingly and often very playfully, called it *sukha*. So *sukha* can be both the problematic and transient pleasures driving our desires and attachments, *and*, often in the same textual passage, it can be the highest bliss that transcends all such pleasures, a synonym for nirvana! It is my contention that the Buddha took great pleasure in confounding the expectations that people had about his teachings by skillfully reworking *sukha*.

Sukha often means the bare hedonic tone of pleasant feeling, contrasted with painful and neutral feeling; one or the other is felt in every moment of experience. But *sukha* can also mean all sorts of happiness that the Buddha was eager to describe at length: "Friends, the Blessed One describes pleasure not only with reference to pleasant feeling; rather, the Tathagatha describes as pleasure any kind of pleasure wherever and in whatever way it is found." Such happinesses include worldly sorts, like the pleasures of ownership, enjoying wealth, freedom from debt, and blamelessness. The pleasures of the moral life are time-honored and important, and the pleasures of the bedroom are duly acknowledged. Certainly, kings enjoy great pleasures when they achieve beauty, long life, health, and the adoration of their people.

But these pale compared to the delights of the heavens, where the deities "are overflowing with *sukha*, drenched with it, full of it, immersed in it, so that they occasionally exclaim, 'Oh, what *sukha*!'"

With such descriptions, the Buddha made it clear that, whatever his teachings on *dukkha* and the dissatisfaction of life in samsara, he was not unaware of the pleasures that life can offer. Indeed, he argued against other ascetics that he knew both the pleasures of the senses and the pleasures of highest bliss—and charged his rivals with ignorance of both.

But a ranking of pleasures emerged, and sensual pleasures (the *sukha* of *kama*) are cast as low, vulgar, and worldly. Far more sublime are the higher happinesses achieved by meditation practice, which include *sukha*, *piti* (joy), and *somanassa* (delight). To practice meditation to achieve such pleasures one needs freedom from the endless compromises of householder life, and so renunciation is a prerequisite for these advanced explorations of happiness. Aware that the larger society around him saw the life of monastics (who lived on alms, practiced celibacy, disavowed attachments, and so on) as a life of deprivation, the Buddha was said to offer this delightful inversion:

> What others speak of as happiness (*sukha*),
> That the noble ones say is suffering (*dukkha*);
> What others speak of as suffering,
> That the noble ones know as bliss (*sukha*).

This formulation turns worldly values of happiness on their head—far from suffering, the monastic life is happiness, and far from happiness, life lived chasing sensory pleasures is suffering.

While on one flank, hedonists criticized him for renunciation, on the other, more strident ascetics attacked him for being too lax. The Buddha warned his disciples that they'd be accused of "being addicted to a life of pleasure," and so he urged his followers to own up to this allegation: yes, in fact, we are addicted to a life of pleasure! But one must consider the many forms of base sensual pleasure (*sukha*), ranging from the "low, vulgar, worldly, ignoble, and not conducive to welfare, not leading to disenchantment, to dispassion, to cessation, to tranquility, to realization, to enlightenment, to nirvana." In contrast, there are ways of living a "life devoted to *sukha*" that are "entirely conducive to disenchantment, to dispassion, to cessation, to tranquility, to realisation, to enlightenment, to nirvana," and he goes on to describe the pleasures of the higher stages of meditation.

The highest bliss of all is nirvana, and the Buddha and his rivals both claimed that nirvana is *sukha*. Even before he was awakened, Siddhartha intuited this in a beautiful story where as a young man he had a brief taste of the pleasures of meditation. Upon coming out of this experience, he was momentarily frightened, but then asked himself, "Why am I afraid of that *sukha* that has nothing to do with sensual pleasures and unwholesome states?" In his next thought, however, everything shifts. "I thought: 'I am *not* afraid of that *sukha* since it has nothing to do with sensual pleasures and unwholesome states.'"

But what sort of happiness or bliss is nirvana, since it transcends all of our notions of happiness and pleasure? The disciples asked this same question: "What happiness could there be when nothing is felt there?" If happiness is beyond feeling anything, how can we still call it happiness? If nirvana is the blowing out of all conditioned phenomenal experience, how can it be pleasure? The answer is simple, but sublime: "Just this, friend, is the happiness here, that nothing is felt here." There is bliss in stepping off the hedonic treadmill altogether.

These ideas become ubiquitous in Indian religion. But the Buddha inaugurated a more practical and worldly insistence on *sukha* as well. In the hands of the great emperor Ashoka, *sukha* becomes a state project. Preempting the American Declaration of Independence by two millennia, Ashoka proclaims the happiness of the people as a fundamental aim of his governance. Lifting language from the Buddhist sources, Ashoka wishes to promote everywhere the "welfare and happiness of all beings," an aspiration prominently reiterated by kings and emperors thereafter.

See also **ananda; duhkha/dukkha/duha; kama; moksha; nirvana/nibbana; piti; somanassa; vedana**

REFERENCES

"Friends, the Blessed One" . . . *Majjhima Nikāya* i.400 in MLD: 505. The Buddha often refers to himself in the third person and with these epithets, the "Blessed One" and the "Tathāgata" (Sublime One).

Such happinesses include worldly sorts . . . the moral life . . . the bedroom . . . *Aṅguttara Nikāya* ii.69, iv.58–69, in NDB: 452, 1039–1049; and *Majjhima Nikāya* iii.170–72, MLD: 1022.

kings enjoy great pleasures . . . delights of the heavens . . . *Majjhima* iii.172–177 in MLD: 1023–27; *Dīgha Nikāya* iii.218–19 in LD: 485.

he knew both the pleasures of the senses . . . *Majjhima* ii.44, MLD: 664.

"What others speak of as happiness" . . . *Saṃyutta Nikāya* iv.127, BW: 1209.

"being addicted to a life of pleasure" . . . *Dīgha* iii.130–132, LD: 433–434. The pleasures of higher meditation are the distinctive happinesses and raptures of the four *jhānas*.

The highest bliss of all is nirvana . . . *Majjhima* i.509–10, MLD: 613–615. The Buddha claims that his rivals say this without knowing what it means. We see similar ideas in Jain texts, as in YŚ: 195, verses 50–51, using both *ānanda* and *sukha*.

"Why am I afraid" . . . *Majjhima* i.246–247, MLD: 340.

"what happiness could there be" . . . *Aṅguttara* iv.414–418, NDB: 1292–1294.

"welfare and happiness of all beings" . . . Ashoka's edicts on happiness are translated and discussed by U. Singh in PV: 55, 107, 195.

T

tamas

Dark; Dull; Lethargic (Sanskrit)

When the quality *tamas* prevails, the mood is dark, inactive, negligent, and deluded. Light gets pulled out of the world. *Tamas* is one of the three *gunas* or modes of reality (the others being *rajas* and *sattva*), and when it pervades a disposition or a mood, one is "despondent (*vishada*), unbelieving, inclining to the lack of Dharma, devoid of intelligence and knowledge, weak in wisdom, inclined to inaction, and given to sleepiness." It bears affinities to the humor *kapha,* also heavy and stolid. In the *Mahabharata, tamas* takes the forms of "contempt, delusion, carelessness, sleep and lassitude."

See also **guna; kapha; rajas; sattva**

References

dark, inactive, negligent, and deluded . . . Bhagavad Gītā 14.13.

"despondent, unbelieving" . . . Suśruta Saṃhitā III.1.18.

In the Mahabharata . . . *Mahābhārata* 12.194.35; also 219.27. Trans. A. Wynne, *Mahābhārata Book Twelve Volume Three, "The Book of Liberation,"* New York: CSL, 2009: 178–179, 402–403.

trasa

Fright (Sanskrit)

Trasa (*trāsa*) is not the fear one gets upon reflection, but rather the shock or startle of sudden terror. A flash of lightning, thunder, earthquake, the amassing of ominous clouds, or the roar of a wild animal can provoke it. *Trasa* is performed on the stage variously: paralysis, perspiration, trembling, horripilation, choking words, and babbling. Considered one of the thirty-three "transitory emotions" in aesthetic theory, it adds its distinctive phenomenology of startled panic to shades of the macabre and the fearful *rasas*.

We find instances of *trasa* when Hanuman, the "foremost among leaping monkeys" and a warrior on Rama's side against the *rakshasa* Ravana, goes to Lanka to meet Sita and warn Ravana of Rama's impending war against him. His mission accomplished, this mighty monkey (who can expand his size to be that of a mountain), first destroys the pleasure garden of the female *rakshasas,* and then, when he is captured and his tail is set on fire, escapes his bonds to set ablaze the entire great city. The inhabitants are terrified, frantic with *trasa,* not just because of Hanuman's violence but also because of the element of surprise. Who would have thought that one small monkey could bring to its knees the splendid capital of these nearly invincible monsters?

See also **avajna; avega; bhaya; bhayanaka; bibhatsa; vyabhicaribhava**

References

not the fear one gets . . . Nāṭyaśāstra 7.90 and *Rasataraṅgiṇī* 5.79. BRRR: 236–237.

Hanuman . . . Rāmāyaṇa V.40.1, 52.15; we find both *trāsa,* fright, and *trasta,* terrified.

trishna

Craving; Desire; Thirst (Sanskrit)

A certain parable widely circulated in the religious texts describes a poor and wretched man who leaves home for a better life only to find himself lost in a forest, thick with trees and infested with ferocious animals. He is charged by an elephant and then chased by a sword-wielding demoness. They pursue him through the woods as he runs, tripping over roots, crashing about until he spots a huge banyan tree. Upon reaching it, he can't find a way to climb it to safety, and so in his panic he hurls himself down an old well, covered with grass. On his way down the pit, he snags on a clump of reeds and clings there, terrified, at the edge. Below him, the hot breath of hissing snakes, above him the leering red-eyed tusker. He clings to the reeds. But then he notices two mice gnawing above at the reeds to which he clings. The furious tusker, unable to reach him, rams into the banyan until down falls a honeycomb along with its furious bees who sting the poor man all over his body.

By chance, a drop of honey falls on the man's face and drips down to his mouth. A moment's sweetness. He longs for more. Thinking nothing of the snakes, elephant, mice, or bees, he craves another drop of honey.

In the Jain account, the drops of honey represent the trivial pleasures that we crave even in the midst of the perils of samsara. In our folly, we thirst for the meager drops of honey we chance to get, and this craving, this unquenchable *trishna* (*tṛṣṇā*), blinds us to the reality of our condition and the true urgency to be liberated from it.

Trishna in these traditions is the bottomless desire that cannot find lasting satisfaction in its objects; acquiring its object only amplifies the craving. It is not just desire, but an existential thirst that creates the people we are as it drags us about. "Craving is the one thing that has everything under its control." Spiritual release involves extirpating it at the root.

See also **eshana; iccha; kama; lobha**

REFERENCES

A certain parable . . . The Jain version is in Haribhadra's Prakrit *Samarādityakathā* 2.55–80. Trans. A. Embree, *Sources of Indian Tradition*, volume 1, New York: Columbia University Press, 1988: 59–61. The

Buddhist Candrakīrti uses the story as well (K. Lang, *Four Illusions*, New York: Oxford University Press, 2003: 22), and it is, of course, found in the *Mahābhārata* (11.5.2–9, trans. K. Crosby, *Book XI, The Women*, New York: CSL, 2009: 200–205).

"Craving is the one thing". . . *Saṃyutta Nikāya* i.38–39 on craving (Pali *tanhā*). CDB: 128–131.

tushti

Satisfaction (Sanskrit)

Satisfaction in the sense of contentment is usually a good thing (see *samtosha*), but when it becomes complacency, it can hinder progress and development. The *Samkhya Karikas* enumerate nine types of *tushti* (*tuṣṭi*), seeing some as varieties of satisfied complacency that stall liberation, and others as contentments that create the conditions for it. Four *tushtis* inhibit liberation: when one leaves spiritual development to the exertions of nature; when one is satisfied that renouncing the world is enough (and so does not meditate); when one thinks liberation will happen in the fullness of time and so brings no urgency to the project; and when one leaves the matter to the vagaries of fate.

But five *tushtis* are conducive to renunciation and liberation because they involve being satisfied with little when one sees the trouble involved with having stuff. Acquiring, preserving, wasting, being disappointed by, and finding stuff harmful each ideally leads to distinctive varieties of a contentment gained from steering clear of stuff altogether.

See also **dhriti; samtosha**

REFERENCE

The Samkhya Karikas. . . *Sāṃkhya Kārikā* 50, with Gauḍapāda's commentary (H. T. Colebrooke and H. H. Wilson, *The Sankhya Karikas*, Bombay: Theosophical Society's Publication, 1887: 205–207).

U

ucchvasita

Sighing with Relief (Sanskrit)

When the Indian Cupid, Kama, infuriates Lord Shiva by trying to shoot him with an arrow of love, his body is incinerated by a dart of fire shot from Shiva's third eye. To lose his body is surely the worst of all fates for the god of sensual pleasure (and his wife, Rati, the Goddess of Sexual Love, feels the loss acutely as well). Lord Brahma softens this horrible fate by making it possible that Kama will regain his body once Shiva unites with Parvati, his future wife. As Kalidasa portrays him, bodiless Kama, watching the nuptial events slowly come to pass, heaves a mental sigh of relief: his mind is *ucchvasita*.

See also **rati; udana**

REFERENCE

his mind is ucchvasita . . . Kālidāsa's *Kumārasaṃbhava* 6.14. BK: 212–213.

udana

A Joyous Exclamation (Pali)

Just as a flood is described as water that cannot be contained in a lake that rushes out, spilling over it, so too a joyous exclamation is described as the heart unable to contain a joyful word, and it becomes too much, it cannot be held back, and it bursts out.

In Sanskrit, an *udana* (*udāna*) is a sharp breath upward. In Pali, it becomes an irrepressible exclamation of joy. Emotions don't exist in our heads or hearts alone, of course, but are also often in our tears, sighs, words, eyes, and limbs. Perhaps the most poignant *udana* in Pali literature is that of the wretched king Ajatasattu. He emits just such an *udana* hailing a glorious moonlit night when, sleepless and anguished, he is suddenly overcome with the beauty of the night.

The circumstances are tragic. Ajatasattu is a wicked king who has just killed his father, the good king Bimbasara. Shortly after this, he learns that his queen has given birth to a son; "at that very instant affectionate love for his son arose in the king and shook his entire body and cut to the very marrow of his bones." This man had never remembered love and joy such as this. But it is a bittersweet moment because with this rush of love, he only now realizes that his own father must have felt this same rush of love for him when he was born. He confirms with his mother that Bimbasara had in fact felt the same thing for him. Ajatasattu's immense joy of parental love is matched only by the simultaneous realization of his guilt and horror at having killed his father. Unable to sleep, wretched and lamenting, he wanders out on his balcony this night and is overcome with beauty. Having become a father and feeling such love, he now feels the beauty of the world for the first time, and despite his despair, he cannot repress a breathless exclamation on the beauty of the night.

See also **dohada; preyas; sneha; ucchvasita; vatsalya**

REFERENCE

"Just as a flood" . . . *Sumaṅgalavilāsinī* i.140–141, on the Sāmaññaphala Sutta in the *Dīgha Nikāya*. See M. Heim, "Careful Attention and the

Voice of Another," *In Dialogue with Classical Indian Traditions*, ed. B. Black and C. Ram-Prasad, New York: Routledge, 2019: 188–193, for this story and my translations of the pertinent passages. Affectionate love is *sineha* (Sanskrit, *sneha*). *Udānas* become a genre in Pali literature of inspired verse, another example of emotion inventing poetry (see *shoka*) and poetry being the manifestation of emotion (see *preyas*).

uddhacca

Flurry; Agitation (Pali)

Uddhacca is the flurry of agitation when the mind is overwrought, overheated, and overstimulated. It is usually paired with *kukkucca* ("worry") to make the onomatopoetic pair "flurry and worry," or, less melodiously but in keeping with the harder sounds of the Pali, "agitation and confabulation." *Uddhacca* is "disquiet, like water stirred up by the wind." Or, it "flutters about a flag whipped by the wind" and is "turmoil like ashes flung up when pelted with stones." Just as in a bowl of water agitated by the wind, rippling, swirling, and churned, one cannot see the reflection of one's own face, so too when the mind is beset with flurry and worry, one cannot see how things really are. *Uddhacca* is the epitome of distraction and thus an important word for our times.

Uddhacca and *kukkucca* are the workings of an unsettled mind, and they reinforce one another. They occur together in the Pali Buddhist sources as one of the five "hindrances" of the moral and religious life. There are five hindrances that block contemplative progress and must be dismantled if one is to advance. These are sensual desire (*kama*); malice (*byapada*); sloth-and-torpor; flurry-and-worry; and doubt. Each of them "causes blindness, obscures vision, distorts knowledge, blocks wisdom, delivers vexation, and leads away from awakening." In their frantic movement, flurry-and-worry may be the opposite of sloth-and-torpor, the sluggish and apathetic obstructions equally thwarting calm and awakened experience.

See also **byapada/vyapada; kama; kukkucca**

REFERENCES

"agitation . . . pelted with stones" . . . *Visuddhimagga* XIV.165, PP: 472–473. Buddhaghosa is echoing and developing *Dhammasaṅgaṇi* 429.

bowl of water . . . *Saṁyutta Nikāya* v.124. CDB: 1612.

"causes blindness" . . . *Saṁyutta Nikāya* v.97. CDB: 1593.

udvega

Edgy Distress (Sanskrit)

In *rasa* theory, *udvega* is one of the acute stages of love-in-separation as the lover pines for the absent beloved. Bharata says that this experience is represented on the stage in showing anxiety, sighs, lassitude, and burning of the heart. The lover awaits impatiently the beloved's return and can't get comfortable in bed or chair. One wretched lover cries out:

Full moon—root of the poison tree.
Springtime—elephant on the lotus of pity.
Evening—dagger of the king of love.
Dear god, what am I supposed to do now?

The charming conditions for lovemaking—a full moon evening in spring—now only mock him waiting with edgy nerves for his darling to return. But will she?

See also **abhilasha/ahilasa; autsukya; vihara; vipralambha**

REFERENCES

Bharata says . . . *Nāṭyaśāstra* 24.180–181.

"Full moon" . . . Bhānudatta's *Rasamañjarī* 275. BRRR: 116–117.

ugrata

Mercilessness (Sanskrit)

My bow is made of strong arm bones
of kings slain in battle.
Its string is woven of strands of hair
of the wives of enemy princes.
And my arrow is made of broken tusks
of wild elephants killed
by the sharp blows of my cruel axe—
and it's been seeking a target.

These words, spoken by Parashurama, boast the mercilessness that is *ugrata* (*ugratā*). Parashurama is the warrior brahman who slayed the *kshatriyas* when they had grown unrighteous and abused their power. As an avatar of Lord Vishnu, Parashurama came to earth to accomplish this task, and his ferocity is the stuff of legends.

Ugrata is the wrathfulness of highborn men against evildoers that aims to make them suffer. It is exemplified when a robber is arrested and brought before the king, who subjects him to violent retribution, be it capital punishment, imprisonment, beating, or rebuking. It can also be the ferocity of vengeance when someone has harmed one's children, wife, or friends.

See also **daya; krodha; raudra**

REFERENCES

"My bow is made" . . . *Rasataraṅgiṇī* 5.28. BRRR: 230–231. Bhānudatta defines *ugratā* as "mercilessness" (*nirdayatā*). *Ugratā* is a transitory emotion in *rasa* theory. *Nāṭyaśāstra* 7.81 gives the example of the king's cruelty that follows.

ferocity of vengeance . . . *Bhāvaprakāśana of Śāradātanaya*, as cited in IP: 244–245.

upayasa

Despair (Pali)

As we have seen in the mourning that is *parideva* and other words for suffering, the Buddha's First Noble Truth refuses to sugarcoat our basic condition as it sums up life in samsara: "birth is suffering; aging is suffering; death is suffering; sorrow, mourning, pain, depression, despair are suffering; association with what is disliked is suffering; separation from what is liked is suffering; not getting what one wants is suffering." (Of course, the other three Truths offer a plan out of this veil of tears.) As suggested by this listing, Buddhists are quite interested in a granular description of the shades of pain, and the commentaries carefully parse them.

What is meant by *upayasa* (*upāyāsa*)—despair—is a turbulent state. Buddhaghosa defines it as a "humor" produced by "excessive mental suffering" when one loses loved ones. Its "characteristic is burning the mind, its function is to bemoan, and it manifests as dejection," a "dejection that is found in the body." It is prompted by the subliminal conditions. Buddhaghosa uses this formal style of definition not to name the essence of an experience but to give a functional definition of its operations, how it manifests, and what causes it.

To further distinguish between sorrow, mourning, and despair, he gives this analogy: sorrow is like oil heating up in a pot on a slow flame; mourning is when the pot boils over; and *upayasa* is what remains in the pot after it has boiled over, as the flame dessicates and burns up the residue.

See also **domanassa; duhkha/dukkha/duha; parideva; shoka; vishada**

REFERENCES

"birth is suffering" . . . This is the classic statement of the First Noble Truth, found everywhere in the Pali canonical sources, but said to have been announced first at the Buddha's first sermon. For a translation, see BW: 75–78.

Buddhaghosa defines it . . . *Visuddhimagga* XVI.52–53. PP: 510–511.

upeksha/upekkha

Equanimity (Sanskrit/Pali)

For Buddhists, equanimity—often glossed as neutrality, indifference, equilibrium—is in fact a feeling, and a highly valued one at that. Sthiramati says that *upeksha* (*upekṣā*) is "equilibrium, tranquil flow, and effortlessness of the mind." It is a mind rid of both the slumps of depression and the elevations of excitement, remaining instead fully focused and effortless, come what may. Positive psychology might call it the "flow" or being "in the zone" that artists and athletes achieve when they are "lost" in their practice.

Buddhists do not conceptualize *upeksha* in relation to practices other than meditation, but meditation will ideally reconfigure one's experience to make equanimity readily available all the time. *Upeksha* is, after all, the nature of the Buddha's enlightened state of perfect composure. Equanimity is a feeling (*vedana*)—specifically, the feeling of neither pleasure nor pain. The Pali sources describe *upekkha* (*upekkhā*) as a kind of awareness basic to our psychology, but it needs to be cultivated in a kind of meditative absorption called *jhana* that abandons, in stages, thinking, happiness, and pleasure, to achieve a pure state of equanimity and mindfulness. Equanimity is also a "divine abiding" (*brahmavihara*), an expansive feeling that looks on the doings of the world in an even, balanced, and impartial way. It should be practiced only when lovingkindness, compassion, and sympathetic joy are well developed. And it is not to be confused with apathy or indifference to the world based on ignorance.

The Nyaya texts reject the notion that *upeksha* is a feeling, seeing it rather as a cognition devoid of feeling tone. To be sure, Hindu systems highly value the achievement of equanimity or equipoise, though they tended to use different language for it. The *Bhagavad Gita* extols "sameness" and the person of "steady wisdom" who is free of all passion, fear, anger, and longing for pleasures, unperturbed even when beset with sorrows. It advises that we "hold pleasure and pain, gain and loss, victory and defeat to be the same" and then adds this important addendum: "and then brace for the fight!"

See also **brahmaviharas; vedana**

REFERENCES

Sthiramati . . . As quoted in G. Nagao, *Madhyamaka and Yogacara: A Study of Mahayana Philosophies*, Albany: State University of New York Press, 1991: 92. "Equilibrium" is *samatā*, "tranquil flow" is *praśaṭhatā*, "effortlessness" is *anābhogatā*, "depression" is *laya*, and excitement ("mental exaltation" in Nagao) is *auddhatya* (see *uddhacca*).

awareness basic to our psychology . . . That is to say, it is a *cetasika*, a *dhamma* or phenomenon that occurs in moments of awareness as they are deconstructed in the Abhidhamma texts.

called jhana . . . The four *jhāna* meditation attainments culminate in the fourth, characterized chiefly by equanimity (*Dīgha Nikāya* i.75–76; LD: 102–103).

a "divine abiding" . . . The remainder of this paragraph is based on *Visuddhimagga* IX.88, 96, 101, PP: 309–312.

The Nyaya texts . . . *Nyāyasūtra Bhāṣya Vārṭika* on *Nyāyasūtra* 1.1.3, trans. G. Jha, volume I, Delhi: Motilal Banarsidass, 1999: 100. J. Sinha is helpful on this (IP: 78).

"sameness" . . . *"steady wisdom"* . . . *Samatvā* and *sthitaprajñā*, in the *Bhagavad Gītā* 2.48, 2.52, 2.56, and 2.38.

urjasvi

A Haughty Declaration (Sanskrit)

With *preyas*, we've seen emotion inhabiting poetic language. The literary theorists who developed this idea also discussed "haughty declarations," where an expression can manifest haughtiness. Such is *urjasvi* (*ūrjasvi*), poetic expression dripping, we might say, with arrogance, bravado, and power. When Ravana boasts the following verse, the words themselves embody this haughtiness:

> I would sacrifice my life in the fire of battle should some powerful enemy appear before me.
> But were I ever to be so cowardly—I, Ravana!—as to give back Sita, I would cease to draw breath.

The utterance itself is the intensification of his feeling of boldness.

See also **avajna; avamana; darpa; garva; mana; preyas**

REFERENCE

"I would sacrifice" . . . This example of an *ūrjasvi* is given by Ratnaśrījñāna, commentator on Daṇḍin's *Kāvyādarśa* 2.290, RR: 65. (See *preyas* for a fuller discussion of utterances saturated with emotion.)

ushma

Fiery Rage (Sanskrit)

Though not nearly as common as some of our other words for anger—*kopa, krodha, manyu*, and *rosha*—*ushma* (*uṣma*) shares their heat. Indeed, *ushma* can also mean heat or the hot season. We find an example of it in Vedanta Desika's contrast between the fiery heat of God's rage and the cooling compassion of Daya, God's gentler feminine half.

Time and again we break the rules
And the God of Bull Hill boils with rage.
But then you marshal the reasons
for having patience, Compassion,
and make him mindful, once more,
of you.

The verse depicts the eternal struggle between God's justice, which rails against our persistent failings, and the mercy that cools the rage. See also the role of patience (*kshama*) as the counter to anger through careful attention.

See also **daya; kopa; krodha; kshama/kshanti; manyu; rosha**

REFERENCE
"Time and again" . . . *Dayā,* verse 27. SPCM: 94–95.

ussuka

Zealousness (Pali)

Ussuka is the zeal of the convert and is generally regarded with suspicion in the Buddhist sources as a greediness for spiritual accomplishment and recognition. A nun recalls how when she first became an ascetic, she ranged about, "zealous for gain and recognition," before eventually rejecting the "dominance of craving," and achieving true insight. Many may renounce the world as ascetics, but, zealous though they may be, who among them has really vanquished craving? Isn't craving for spiritual attainment and its rewards just another kind of craving, no different from a king coveting his neighbors' riches? Perhaps it is for this reason that the Buddha is described as being "of little zeal" upon first attaining enlightenment. His eventual teaching career is portrayed as a matter of yielding to the god Brahma's imploring him to teach, rather than driven by a self-promoting eagerness to missionize.

See also **dambha; trishna**

REFERENCES

"zealous for gain and recognition"... *Therīgāthā* v.92, my translation. But also see C. Hallisey, trans., *Therigatha: Poems of the First Buddhist Women*, Cambridge, MA: MCLI, 2015: 58–59.

Many may renounce the world... This sentiment is expressed at *Saṃyutta Nikāya* i.15 (see CDB: 103 and 361 n. 54).

"of little zeal"... *appossukka. Saṃyutta* i.137; see CDB: 232.

utsaha

Courageous Determination (Sanskrit)

Utsaha (*utsāha*), the valorous strength, energy, and determination of the warrior, is the emotion savored in the *rasa* of heroism (see *vira*). *Rasa* authorities insist that, while the battlefield may be its chief arena, *utsaha* is exercised in two other domains as well—namely, in munificence and mercy (*daya*). Munificence displayed by great persons is celebrated everywhere in Indian literature, and it is hard to conceive of a virtue more admired than generosity. Unless it is merciful compassion, also a heroic virtue. *Utsaha* is the energy driving them both.

In *utsaha*, various factors come together: lack of despair, power, composure, and boldness. At its best, *utsaha* is not the blind or frenetic exercise of power, but the focused and unruffled strength of purpose that we admire in saviors and heroes. We see it in the male heroes whose wars structure life in the great epics. While his companions fret all around him as they prepare to face the villain Ravana, Rama performs his twilight devotions with calm composure, and doesn't miss a step of his yogic breathing, evincing a quiet coolness that speaks volumes about his restrained energy.

Giving to brahmans, beggars, and religious mendicants is the generosity required of all great men (and women, too, but this is somehow less praised in the literature). The great king Raghu gives away all his wealth after his royal sacrifice; asked for more by a great sage he promises to raid the treasury of the God of Wealth himself, to give even more lavishly.

For an example of the courageous determinism that is the *utsaha* of mercy or compassion, we turn to the heroism of the bodhisattva, that great Buddhist hero perfecting the energy required for attaining the highest compassion and spiritual prowess of the Mahayana goal. The sheer strength of this being's endurance and energy is the "skillful determination" to rid oneself of the defilements and develop the highest compassion to save all beings; one should seek to cultivate this powerful determination and then, in turn, be mastered by it.

See also **daya; dhairya; vira**

References

two other domains . . . *Rasataraṅgiṇī* 1.22–29. BRRR: 140–143. The example of Rāma's calm breathing that follows is from this text (3.27; pp. 180–181); and the verse celebrating the king's munificence is at 3.30–31, pp. 182–183.

lack of despair . . . *Nāṭyaśāstra* 7.21. A. Chakrabarti takes *utsāha* in an intriguing direction when he suggests that it is the patriotic feeling one has when hearing one's national anthem (*The Bloomsbury Research Handbook of Indian Aesthetics and the Philosophy of Art*, ed. A. Chakrabarti, London: Bloomsbury Academic, 2018: 7).

heroism of the bodhisattva . . . Śāntideva's *Bodhicaryāvatāra* 7.2, 7.18, 7.75; see also translation by BCA: 67, 68, 74. The perfection being cultivated here is called *vīrya*, spiritual exertion, and "skillful determination" is *kusala-utsāha*.

V

vaira

Enmity (Sanskrit)

> I feel rage surging uncontrollably within me, such rage as I have never felt before. Rama has aroused in me deep, ferocious enmity.

Ravana, the monstrous man-eating nightstalker, a shape-shifting *rakshasa* who is the main villain in the *Ramayana*, steals Rama's lovely wife, Sita. *Rakshasas* are by nature angry, cruel, lustful, and arrogant, and Ravana is even more so. A particularly mighty *rakshasa*, having won great power from his austerities, he rules all of Lanka, and his minions increasingly harass even ascetics in their ashrams in India. Here, as he recounts Rama's destruction of his *rakshasa* forces long before they will do final battle, Ravana looks inward to note a dreadful (*daruna*) hatred and ferocity—*vaira*—stirring within him, such as even he has never known.

Vaira is an enmity or hostility between two adversaries full of grudge and vengeance that must be eventually played out with the destruction of one side. Rama is of course a man-god: Lord Vishnu has taken human form for the particular purpose of slaying this tyrannical Ravana. And so the *vaira* between them is of a cosmic nature in the impending battle between the demonic and the divine.

See also **avajna; daruna; dvesha; matsara; vilapa; vira**

REFERENCE

"I feel rage surging" . . . *Rāmāyaṇa* III.52.22. Trans. S. Pollock, *Rāmāyaṇa, Book Three, The Forest*, New York: CSL, 2006: 312–313.

vairagya

Dispassion and Disenchantment with the World (Sanskrit)

If *raga* is the pull of attraction, *vairagya* (*vairāgya*) is a condition free of it. Sometimes identified with *nirveda*, despair and world-weariness, *vairagya* is at other times seen as a further development of it, to indicate complete cessation of all desires. *Vairagya* is said to be prompted by considerations like this:

> Truly fair women are objects of delight
> and truly wealth is fair;
> but life is unsteady and as quickly gone
> as the glance of a tipsy girl.

While this verse is a tad glib, religious thinkers take *vairagya* very seriously. They sometimes identify *vairagya* with the highest peace that comes from equanimity and the quieting of the pulls and pushes of desire and aversion. King Janaka boasts of his achieving highest spiritual emancipation in terms of *vairagya*, defined as freedom from reacting to pairs of opposites, claiming that "he who smears sandal paste on my right arm and he who hacks off my left with an ax are both the same to me." (It cannot fail to be noted, however, that Janaka proceeds to demonstrate that he has not achieved such freedom because he hasn't gone beyond attachment to the duality of gender—as his loss in a debate with a brilliant woman yogi makes abundantly clear).

In some formulations, *vairagya* is an initial dispassion that may be more fully developed into perfect peace (*shama, vishranti, upashama*) through spiritual development. In its opening chapter on *vairagya*, the *Yoga Vasishta* describes the great hero Rama as a young man in despair and depression at realizing the cruelties of samsara and the hollowness of desires. He is tutored by a wise sage, and through philosophical instruction leading to higher discernment, his *vairagya*, initially conveyed as a type of despair, develops into peace and composure.

See also **nirveda; raga; shama**

REFERENCES

Sometimes identified with nirveda . . . Abhinavagupta does so at *Locana* 3.19 (DL: 479). Others see *vairāgya* as a higher form of *nirveda*, as Abhinava points out in the *Abhinavabhāratī* (ŚR: 127).

"Truly fair women" . . . Abhinavagupta gives this verse as an example of one disenchanted with the passions (DL: 384).

King Janaka boasts . . . Mahābhārata 12.308.31–37. See HB, ch. 2, on this story of the debate between Janaka and Sulabhā.

The Yoga Vasishta *. . .* The first chapter of the *Laghu Yogavāsiṣṭha* is "Vairagya," and the last is "Nirvana." This text is an Advaita Vedānta text instructing Rāma as a young man.

vancha

Desire (Sanskrit)

Desire my body, love my feet, love my eyes, and love my legs.
Let both your eyes and hair, fond girl! be dried and parched through love of me.
I make you hang upon my arm, I make you lie upon my heart.
You yield to my wish, that you may be submissive to my will.

May they whose kisses are a bond, a love-charm laid within the heart,
Mothers of butter, may the cows incline this maid to love of me!

The *Atharva Veda*'s magical spells and ritual power can accomplish all aims. One can ward off jaundice and snake bites, hair loss and dysentery, worms and hostile rivals. Magic words can deliver whatever one wants—a successful pregnancy, the birth of a son, victory in battle, long life. With this charm, you can make a woman fall in love with you. *Vancha* (*vāñcā*), this somewhat rare word for desire and lust, becomes a command here, a directive ordering a woman's desire.

Love charms reveal that instigating others' desire for us is the key to our power over them. This charm prompts the desire that makes her submissive. Charms can make her follow him as smoke does the wind or entwine her arms around him like a creeper clasps a tree. For her part, a woman can use a charm to make a man crazy and burning for her, while she remains coolly aloof. Or she can deploy a spell to let him think he can flee even while he remains tethered to her: *Let him run away, three leagues, five, a horse's full tilt, but then come back and father a son with me*. Or, if love has faltered, she may need a charm to "restore the fracture of our severed love" to "drive us together, him and me, and give us both one heart and mind."

See also **kama**

REFERENCE

"Desire my body" . . . *Atharvaveda* 6.9. This is R.T.H. Griffiths's translation (*The Hymns of the Atharva Veda*, Varanasi: Chowkhamba Sanskrit Series, 1968, originally published 1895), which I have updated slightly from the Victorian English. The other charms mentioned here are 6.8, 89, 130, 131, 139. *Vāñca* here is an injunctive form of the verb, but *vāñcā* is also a noun. Other words for desire and love in these spells are *kāma* and *smara*. For more charms, see *irshya* and *bhaya*.

vasana

Memory Traces and Unconscious Impressions; Predilections (Sanskrit)

If Indian thought has a counterpart to the Freudian unconscious, the *vasanas* (*vāsanā*) are it. These are the deeply rooted traces and conditions from past lives that "color" or "infuse" present experience. They are so deeply rooted as to be inaccessible to all but the highly spiritually realized adepts who practice demanding disciplinary techniques to root them out. For religious thinkers across the spectrum, *vasanas* are the latent tendencies that generate our confusion and problematic emotions, obscuring a clear grasp of reality. Advaita thinkers describe the cutting off of the predilections as the central religious task. They list three broad categories of them—those obsessed with the body, those concerned with social life, and those fixated on scriptural study. Only a rigorous discipline of discernment can rid one of the pervasive conditioning of thought and emotion that is *vasana.*

While *vasanas* were deplored by religious thinkers as the latent desires that ensnare us in samsara, they were celebrated by poets and literary critics as the distant memory traces that underlie our deepest emotions and aesthetic responses. Kalidasa's famous verse about this doesn't mention *vasanas,* but later theorists saw it as suggesting the memory traces that stir the human heart in ways the conscious mind does not always understand. When Kalidasa's romantic hero Dushyanta has forgotten his beloved, he one day happens to hear beautiful music and is filled with disquiet. In his bewilderment at this response he says,

> Looking at well-crafted objects
> hearing sweet music

even the contented person
grows edgy
pierced by unknown desires.
Could it be deep
in the heart one uncovers
the trace of a lover
from lifetimes ago?

This most romantic conceit suggests that tugging on us when we encounter beautiful art is a deeply buried love cherished long ago. Abhinavagupta cites this verse when he tries to account for the experience of *rasa*. Since people watching a play have their own distant *vasanas*—"everyone's mind being studded with an infinite array of such predispositions"—they can savor emotions deep in the recesses of their being they may not even be aware that they have.

See also **cakshuraga; kleshas/kilesas; samskara/sankhara; sauharda**

REFERENCES

Advaita thinkers . . . Vivekacūḍāmaṇi, traditionally attributed to Śankara, verses 270–272. Trans. Swami Madhavananda as *The Crest-Jewel of Wisdom,* Champawat: Advaita Ashrama, 1921. The three types are *dehavāsanā, lokavāsanā,* and *śāstravāsanā.*

"Looking at well-crafted objects" . . . Kalidasa's *Abhijñānaśākuntala* 5.24. BAM: 42–43.

Abhinavagupta cites this verse . . . Abhinavabhāratī 1.273. RR: 195.

vata/vayu

Gustiness (Sanskrit)

In the Ayurveda theory of the three humors, *vata* (*vāta,* also called *vāyu*) is the wind and gustiness that pervades us all with "dry, cool, light, subtle, moving, bright, and sharp" qualities. In excess, this humor causes many illnesses, and can make the patient sluggish, dull, and discontented. Although

Indian thought relied less on a humoral psychology to describe emotions than did the long-standing Western belief in Galen's humors, terms like *vata* sometimes get at emotional experience. While invoked in the medical literature primarily to describe the biological human, the humors are larger than the human organism and can characterize types of temperaments, the foods we eat, the seasons of the year, geographical regions, and even times of the day—all of which not only influence but also help to constitute the changing person. What we might analyze as the "biological human" can really be understood properly only as part of a much larger ecosystem.

See also **kapha; pitta**

REFERENCES

"dry, cool, light" . . . *Caraka Saṃhitā* I.59, CS: 43.

sluggish, dull, and discontented . . . See chapter 1 of the *Suśruta Saṃhitā* for the many diseases *vāta/vāyu* can cause.

vatsalya

Parental Love and Affection (Sanskrit)

Love gets carved up into many varieties in the Indian tradition, with *vatsalya* (*vātsalya*) referring to the particular love parents have for their children. Mothers have it when they look upon their little ones and the milk in their breasts lets down, moistening their blouses. Smelling the sweetness of an infant's head, one is suffused with *vatsalya*, feeling an irresistible urge to cuddle the little thing. Fathers feel intense *vatsalya* too. One close observer saw a father, having led his tot around the courtyard with his finger and then seeing the little fellow toddle off on his own, become so overwhelmed with *vatsalya* that a "cascade of tears flowed down onto his chest." Even when their lad grows to be a man, parents can still see the boy in him, and their *vatsalya* flows.

For Rupa Goswami, the experience of *vatsalya* is of such an astonishing and rapturous nature (*camatkara*) that it should be considered a *rasa*, an aesthetic experience. To be sure, *vatsalya* is not just the sweet stuff: parents know well the anguished fear for one's children and the prospects of losing them. When her son left home as a young man to renounce the world, Siddhartha's mother cried piteously in her *vatsalya* for him.

By its nature, *vatsalya* is a pure kind of love that a mother cow, for example, feels toward her calf. There is no motive in it or recompense expected. This spontaneous and very natural form of love lends itself to religious texts that urge its cultivation and expansion. Jainism, emotionally austere in other respects, promotes *vatsalya* as a kind of disinterested affection toward its community, in particular, Jain renouncers. Other traditions urge its expansion toward all sentient beings—as we come to see that all creatures were their parents' children once, innocent and tender babes, universal love can grow. Hindu *bhakti* traditions celebrate the *vatsalya* we have for God (when imaged as baby Krishna) and as a love that God, parent to us all, has for us. Great figures like bodhisattvas are said to feel this protective affection toward all beings. The *Mahabharata* asserts that all proper religious paths teach us to feel *vatsalya* for all creatures.

See also **bhakti; camatkara; prema; rasa**

REFERENCES

milk in their breasts lets down . . . This image is said of Yaśodā, baby Krishna's mother, toward him in BR: 510–511. All of the images and claims in this paragraph are in Rūpa Goswāmi's chapter on *vatsala* in the context of Krishna *bhakti*, 508–533. We find both *vatsala* and *vatsalya* in the texts, with the same meaning.

of such an astonishing and rapturous nature . . . Rūpa Gosvāmin, BR: 530–531.

Siddhartha's mother cried piteously . . . Buddhacarita 9.26. Trans. P. Olivelle, *Life of the Buddha by Aśvaghoṣa*, New York: CSL, 2008: 254–255. This was the Buddha's foster mother.

Jainism . . . Jains see *vātsalya* as the eighth limb of spiritual development and as a *bhāvanā*, a meditative cultivation (Cāmuṇḍarāya as cited in R. Williams, *Jaina Yoga*, Delhi: Motilal Banarsidass, 1991: 245; and *Pañcādhyāyī* II.806 as cited in P. S. Jaini, *The Jaina Path to Purification*, Delhi: Motilal Banarsidass, 1990: 155 n. 36).

like bodhisattvas . . . Asaṅga attributes it to *bodhisattvas*, and suggests that it is a love that is unprompted by motive (*Bodhisattvabhūmi* I.18.1. BP: 465; also p. 11).

all proper religious paths . . . Mahābhārata 12.191.14–15.

vedana

Feeling; Hedonic Tone; Valence (Sanskrit and Pali)

In the philosophical sources, feeling is a hedonic tone present in every moment of experience. Humans are sensitive beings who *feel* something every instant (even if that feeling feels neutral). In Buddhist thinking, *vedana* (*vedanā*), together with certain other phenomena—sensation, perception, intention, awareness—is one of the fundamental building blocks present in all consciousness. In that body of meticulous and highly generative phenomenological analysis called the Abhidhamma, feeling is meticulously studied as the meditator learns to notice and thereby reconfigure even the most basic and fine-grained processes in her awareness.

The Buddha was once asked how many different kinds of *vedana* there are, and his answer reveals his overall approach to emotions and how we make lists of them. In the discussion in question, he is asked to settle a dispute between two disciples. The first argues that, at bottom, there are *two* kinds of feeling, pleasant and painful, while the second insists that there are *three*: pleasant, painful, and indeterminate. The Buddha rejects their whole way of thinking by pointing out that he sometimes teaches that there are two kinds of feeling, sometimes three, sometimes five, or six, or eighteen, or thirty-six, or one hundred and eight, and so on. Depending on context or purpose when investigating and teaching about experience, one can offer coarser or more granular distinctions. Feelings are not ontological essences where there is a final, basic list of them, but a matter of slicing up the endless and fine details of experience and grouping them variously, inflected by the purposes of the analysis itself. There is simply no need to argue about basic lists.

See also **duhkha/dukkha/duha; sukha; upeksha/upekkha**

REFERENCE

how many different kinds of vedana . . . The Bahuvedanīya Sutta (*Majjhima Nikāya* i.396–400), MLD: 502–505. See also M. Heim, "Some Analyses of Feeling," BRH: ch. 4.

vihara

Separated (Sanskrit)

Vihara isn't an emotion; it's a condition. But it is a condition so saturated with feeling that it must be included among our treasures. *Vihara* is the state of being separated from the one you love, and in Sanskrit letters it is ground-zero of the deepest longing, anguish, and despair of the human heart as it pines for the distant lover. *Vihara* is the condition that makes possible the agonizing relish that is *vipralambha*, love-in-separation.

One of *vihara*'s most celebrated genres is the "courier poem," where an exiled lover sends a message to his or her sweetheart conveying the deepest longing for the distant beloved. Inaugurated by Kalidasa in his *Cloud Messenger*, tidings of anguished love sent by an aerial messenger became a favorite poetic conceit in the centuries following.

Cloud Messenger depicts a certain unfortunate resident of a Himalayan city punished by the king to spend a year exiled far away in middle India. One day, in his despair, he sees a drifting cloud—normally a harbinger of the monsoon season's reunification of lovers—and enlists it as a courier to carry a love letter to his beloved wife pining for him at home. The poem gives us a gorgeous cloud's-eye view of the landscape of the cloud's journey across India, a landscape that comes itself to be etched with images of the anguish of loss, erotic anticipation, and the hopes for reunion.

As the centuries go by, the skies over India are crisscrossed with lovers' messengers. Not just clouds, but now ganders, parrots, peacocks, bees, and even the wind take wing across the subcontinent to deliver messages from lovesick lovers. Vedanta Deshika conveys Rama's anguished missive to the distant Sita via a gander, explaining that "people shaken by separation are reduced to begging help from clouds, mountains, trees, and so on—to say nothing of living creatures," and ganders become the favored emissary. But a bold young woman in the Western Ghats, having fallen in love-at-first-sight with Lakshmana Sena, King of Bengal, sends her declaration of love via the wind.

These messengers give us word-pictures of the grieving lovers, none more vividly than Vedanta Deshika as Rama gently warns his gander about how he will find Sita languishing in separation from him.

A vacant stare, unbounded sighing, too much grief,
lotus face shut tight as a bud,
yet tears flow from closed eyes in fierce rushing torrents
of rivers,

lament without end:
  by what inexorable law or fate has she,
so deeply bound to me,
  been drawn into such inconceivable misery—
her slender sweet body—
  o my heart now burns within me.

Rama's imagining of Sita's misery (and how it burns him too), is all the more poignant when we remember that this is not just the anguish of separation at a human and erotic level, but has divine meaning too as Rama is conceived to be God, and Sita, his divine consort. Sita suggests, much as Radha does in the *vihara-bhakti* of Krishna in Vrindavan Forest, the ideal longing for God in times of anguished separation—along with, of course, anticipation of eventual reunion.

See also **bhakti; vilapa; vipralambha**

REFERENCES

Cloud Messenger . . . *Meghadūta*. Trans. J. Mallinson in *Messenger Poems*, New York: CSL, 2008. This collection includes three courier poems: *Meghadūta*, Dhoyi's "Wind Messenger," and Rupa Goswāmi's "Swan Messenger."

"people shaken by separation" . . . *Haṃsasandeśa* 1.5. SPCM: 6–7. For more on these extraordinary courier poems, see Y. Bronner, "Birds of a Feather: Vāmana Bhaṭṭa Bāṇa's *Haṃsasandeśa* and Its Intertexts," *Journal of the American Oriental Society* 133, no. 3 (2013): 495–526.

"A vacant stare, unbounded sighing" . . . *Haṃsasandeśa* 2.23. Trans. S. Hopkins, *The Flight of Love: A Messenger Poem of Medieval South India by Veṅkaṭanātha*, New York: Oxford University Press, 2016: 85; see Hopkins's discussion of this "word-picture" in his commentary on the poem, especially pp. 192–195.

vilapa

Lamentation (Sanskrit)

Tradition records the laments of women whose children and husbands have been torn from them by the ravages of war or, not infrequently, by the (largely male) hero's quest for religious renunciation (see *parideva*). Women get abandoned but also stolen, raped, taken from their families, humiliated.

But they speak back. Women's laments are artful and disruptive cries of pain and resistance against the spectacular cruelties that shape their lives. Sita, the heroine goddess of the *Ramayana*, is kidnapped from her husband by the monster Ravana, and now lives in his palace where his harem women mock her and Ravana threatens to eat her for breakfast. Dwelling in "the pinch and dip of raw emotion," she waits, and she waits, and she waits to be rescued by her husband Rama and his faithful brother Lakshmana. Her lamentations pour out both wrath and sorrow:

Sita stung by sorrow,
lovely passionate Sita, filled
with wrath. "What the wise say
is all too true, it's hard for a man or woman to die
before their time—just look at me, still alive,
even for a moment here,
without Rama,
tortured by these cruel
monsters. A miserable, grieving woman,
with so little merit and no one
to protect me, I am like a little boat, full laden,
struck hard by a storm wind
in the middle

of a great ocean. In the clutches of these ghouls,
out of sight of my husband, I crumble
in my sorrow like sandbanks
in a torrent
flood.

She threatens to kill herself, so "wretched and shameful" is this captivity that puts her in another's power. That she should be made to feel such shame and self-blame itself stands as a reproach against the harm done to this faultless woman.

To be sure, men lament too. They lament when they lose those they love the most. Rama's tearful lamentations for Sita are legendary, as many entries in our treasure chest show (see *ashru, daruna, dhairya,* and *hridayamarman,* for example). Rama's father Dasaratha laments the loss of Rama to exile in long and sorrowful lamentations. The Buddha's father laments Siddhartha's abandoning of the family with an onomatopoietic *vilalapa.* And in formal analyses of the *rasa* of love-in-separation, *vilapa* (*vilāpa*) is an advanced stage of lovesick separation, where thwarted lovers gaze vacantly at places their lovers once occupied and murmur to themselves: "he sat here, he stood there, he approached me there."

See also **ashru; dina; hridayamarman; manyu; parideva; shoka; vihara; vipralambha**

REFERENCES

"Sita stung by sorrow" . . . This passage from the *Rāmāyaṇa* is translated and discussed S. Hopkins, "Lament and the Work of Tears: Andromache, Sītā, Yaśodharā," (BRH: 116). "The pinch and dip of raw emotion" are Hopkins's words, and this entry is heavily indebted to his work.

Rama's father Dasaratha . . . As at *Rāmāyaṇa* II.11.7–10, in just one example; see *dina.*

The Buddha's father . . . *Buddhacarita* 8.80. Trans. P. Olivelle as *The Life of the Buddha by Aśvaghoṣa*, New York: CSL, 2008: 240–241.

advanced stage of lovesick separation . . . *Nātyaśāstra* 24.183; see also *autsukya* and *vipralambha.*

vippatisara

Remorse (Pali)

> Now a poor destitute wretch lacking faith, shame, apprehension, energy, and insight into wholesome things commits evil with body, speech, and mind. I call that his "getting into debt." Then, in an effort to cover up his wicked bodily deeds, he generates a wicked hope: he wishes "may none know me," he resolves "may none know me," he says aloud "may none know me," and he exerts himself physically so that "none may know me." I call that the "interest on his debt." Then well-behaved monks say, "this venerable one has done such and such deeds, has practiced such and such conduct." I call that his "being reproved." So he runs to a forest, the root of a tree, or a lonely spot, but *vippatisara* (*vippaṭisāra*) accompanies him, and wicked, unwholesome thoughts assail him. I call that his "prosecution."

The Buddha gives this stark depiction of the poverty and debt entailed in wrongdoing and the remorse it generates in a vicious cycle of impoverishment, indebtedness, and prosecution.

The account has elements of shame and its concomitant desire at every turn for concealment. The repeated refrain "may none know me" is itself a wicked idea. But even as he flees from human society, the wretch is dogged by his own remorse that continues to follow and prosecute him. He cannot turn back and yet there is no place to hide.

See also **anutapa; hiri/hri; kukkucca; ottappa; pashcattapa; vrida/vridita**

REFERENCE

"Now a poor destitute wretch" . . . *Aṅguttara Nikāya* iii.352–353, my translation, but see also NDB: 915. Faith is *saddhā* (Sanskrit, *śraddhā*), shame is *hiri*, and apprehension is *ottappa*.

vipralambha

Love-in-Separation (Sanskrit)

Of the two kinds of erotic *rasa*, or aesthetic savor, the love felt when lovers are separated may be the most acute. *Sambhoga*, love-in-union, may be charming, but the frustrated *shringara* that is *vipralambha* is exquisite. Kalidasa's *Cloud Messenger* asserts that "they say absence makes the heart grow less fond—but in fact the *rasa* for the beloved grows from enjoyment's lack, and it turns into a mass of love."

Here is a young man parted from his beloved—

She's in my house
she's west and east
she trails behind me she goes
out ahead
she's in my bed on path
after path
what a fever—I can't
even see Nature now that she's left me—
just she she she she she she
across the whole wheeling planet.
And Nondualism
they say is for yogins.

The poem plays with the very distinction between love-in-union and love-in-separation. It starts off with what sounds like love-in-union, but we soon realize that she's left him.

Yet in his fever, he can still see her everywhere and all he can see is her. In a delightful way, he refers to the philosophical and religious doctrine on "Nondualism" that posits a lack of distinction between the self and the Absolute, but here the poem claims that the ultimate Nondualism is not that of the religious but rather that of the lover submersed in union with his beloved, even when she is gone.

Love-in-separation is the result of lovers parted by all the usual cruelties—parents, kings, exile, plot devices. Most often, though, they are separated by a quarrel, with jealousy, pride, and anger driving them apart. There are said to be ten stages of such erotic wretchedness, especially as they are felt and represented on the stage by women separated from their beloveds: longing (*abhilasha*); anxiety (*cinta*); recollection; enumerating the beloved's merits; edgy distress (*udvega*); lamentation (*vilapa*); madness; illness; stupor; and finally and most tragically, death. To be sure, love-in-separation differs from the tragic *rasa* (*karuna*) in that the dominant emotion savored is attraction, not grief, and there is an expectation that the lovers will be reunited at some future point. But because the separated lovers don't know this, anguish tears their hearts.

See also **karuna; rasa; sambhoga; shringara; vihara**

REFERENCES

"they say absence makes" . . . Abhinavagupta cites this verse by Kalidasa's *Meghadūta* as an example of savoring this kind of *rasa*. RR: 218.

"She's in my house" . . . From the *Amaruśataka*, BAM: 22–23.

ten stages . . . *Nāṭyaśāstra* 24.169–190.

vira

The Heroic (Sanskrit)

> "Lanka's lord is formidable in battle,
> strong enough to dispel Indra's pretensions."
> As Hanuman gave his anxious report,
> the only reply Rama gave was a smile.

Hanuman is frightened as he informs Rama of the strength of his foe, Ravana. In this highly suggestive and beautiful evocation of the manly heroism of Rama, we see his courage and composure emerge not in boasting and swagger but in a cool and confident smile. We are immediately reassured of Rama's victory, and we relish the valorous strength that is heroism.

Vira (*vīra*) is the *rasa* of heroism that great tales of war—that is, the epic traditions of the *Mahabharata* and *Ramayana*—invite us to relish in male warriors. (The *rasa* theorists do not provide examples of its occurrence in women or persons of lower stock.) As suggested in Rama's smile, *vira* arises "from intentness on unleashing one's energy without distress, surprise, or confusion." *Vira* savors the heroic determination that is *utsaha*. And it can also be the masculinist heroism of religious masters, such as the Jain Tirthankara, "Great Hero" (Mahavira).

Rama's cool smile before battle notwithstanding, heroism trades in violence. The following poem does not seem at first to be a poem aimed at the savor of heroism. It flirts with two other alternating *rasas*, deeply opposed to one another and to the heroic sensibility that emerges only at the end of the poem, when we realize that the heroes who perished in this gruesome scene at the battlefield are now being spirited away by the heavenly nymphs who greet valiant warriors who die in battle.

On bodies soiled with dust they looked,
they whose breasts were scented with the pollen
of garlands from the trees of paradise;
bodies seized greedily by jackals,
they whose bodies were now embraced by nymphs;
bodies fanned by the flapping, bloody wings of vultures,
they who were fanned with silken garments,
dipped in sandal ointment, from the wishing trees of
heaven:
thus did the heroes then, reclining upon couches
in their flying chariots, look down with curious gaze
on their late bodies, pointed out by their companion
damsels,
on the battlefield.

The literary critics note the jangle of potential *rasas* here, but insist that the erotic and macabre are only transient elements into which intervenes heroism, made explicit when the heroes look with detached curiosity down on their slain bodies. I think the poem is deeply insightful about this relish—martial valor looks best from a distant vantage point, ideally looked down upon from the very heavens to which warriors celebrating battle aspire to ascend by their deaths. It is also psychologically astute, weaving in the erotic and grisly elements that sometimes combine in the aesthetics of violence.

See also **dhairya; rasa; smita; utsaha; vaira**

References

"Lanka's lord is" . . . Bhānudatta gives this example of *vīra* at *Rasataraṅgiṇī* 2.21. BRRR: 158–159. "From intentness on unleashing" is his definition at 2.20, 156–157, with my slight change in the translation.

"On bodies soiled" . . . This poem and Anandavardhana's and Abhinavagupta's discussions of it are in DL: 527–530. The poem is Mammaṭa's

(7.334–335), who discusses it in similar terms. See *Kāvyaprakāsha of Mammaṭa*, trans. G. Jha, Varanasi: Bharatiya Vidya Prakashan, 1966: 293–294.

vishada

Depression; Despondency; Despair (Sanskrit)

To take her ritual bath, a woman once left her newborn baby in the care of her husband. But just then he is summoned by the king, and cannot delay. In desperation, he leaves the infant with a mongoose, their pet raised with care and love. While the mongoose is babysitting, a black cobra slithers up to the baby and the mongoose kills it and tears it to pieces. When the man returns, he sees the paws and mouth of the mongoose smeared in blood, and fearing the worst, kills it. Moments later, he sees the baby healthy and fine lying next to the slain snake. The horror of what he has just done in his rage and haste sinks in. This is *vishada* (*viṣāda*).

At its most acute, there is a darkness and gloom in *vishada* that is not easily lifted, it being the valence of the "tamasic" mode of reality (see *guna* and *tamas*). It is the despair that sinks the hero Arjuna to his knees when he refuses to fight on the battlefield of the great war. Here, *vishada* is existential as he realizes the sheer horror of the war and violence his family is facing. It takes the extraordinary words and visions of divine wisdom of the rest of the *Bhagavad Gita* to lift his despair.

See also **dainya; guna; shoka; tamas**

REFERENCES

To take her ritual bath . . . *Hitopadeśa* 4.266–273. FA: 512–515.

sinks the hero Arjuna . . . At, for example, *Bhagavad Gītā* 1.28, 2.1, 2.10. The word used is *viṣīda*, describing Arjuna as having *viṣāda*.

vismaya

Surprise; Astonishment; Awe (Sanskrit)

In the most hair-raising tale in all of Buddhist literature, the Bodhisattva performs the final act of generosity and renunciation that allows him to achieve the perfection of character enabling him eventually to become the Buddha: he gives away his adored children as slaves to a wicked man. This story compares with Abraham's (near) sacrifice of his beloved only son Isaac, a story that continues to confound all three of the Abrahamic faiths to this day. It resonates with Tamil stories of the extraordinary sacrifices demanded of the devotees of Lord Shiva, a deity who also claims one's children as offerings.

What is it about religion that requires the terrifying gift—the sacrifice—of the most cherished and innocent of our attachments?

In Arya Sura's telling, the grief and anguish caused by the Bodhisattva's extreme and heedless generosity is palpable. He courts the knife's edge between eliciting intolerable anguish at the innocent young children cruelly given away by their parent on the one hand, and promoting sublime wonder at the Bodhisattva's highest religious aspiration on the other. He subtly channels the initial horror of the characters and readers into *vismaya*, astonishment.

The Bodhisattva's gift prompts the natural world to register its astonishment too: "the roll of celestial drums reverberates in every direction. The Earth heaves her breasts, the great mountains, as though shivering in ecstasy. Flowers of gold fall from the heavens so that the sky seems ablaze with lightning." Such ambiguous celestial and terrestrial reactions—frightening events of thunder, mountains quaking, and lightning—are rendered marvels that cue the reader to respond with astonishment rather than grief, and instruct us to "not give way to sorrow." *Vismaya* is the apprehension of the sublime that lies far beyond the reaches of human comprehension, and for Arya Suya in this story, it is the only proper response to the Bodhisattva. The Bodhisattva is operating on a transcendent plane of reality that subverts our ethical and worldly understanding and is best apprehended through amazement and awe.

While *vismaya* is often surprise or awe, at its highest and most refined level such amazement becomes wonder. Roughly contemporaneous with Arya Sura was the great theorist of drama and aesthetics, Bharata, who understood the aesthetic taste (*rasa*) of wonder (*adbhuta*) to develop from this emotion (*bhava*) of astonishment. In Arya Sura's work, we find an early poetic mastery of the sublime *rasa*, akin perhaps to what German theologian Rudolph Otto termed the *mysterium tremendum* that apprehends the "numinous," or "wholly other" he saw at the heart of all religion.

See also **adbhuta/abbhuta; bhava; camatkara; rasa; samvega**

References

Abraham's (near) sacrifice . . . Genesis 22.

with Tamil stories . . . See D. Shulman, *The Hungry God: Hindu Tales of Filicide and Devotion*, Chicago: University of Chicago Press, 1993.

astonishment . . . See S. Mrozik, "Astonishment: A Study of an Ethically Valorized Emotion in Buddhist Narrative Literature," in *Embedded Languages: Studies of Sri Lankan and Buddhist Cultures*, ed. C. Anderson, S. Mrozik, R.M.W. Rajapakse, and W. M. Wijeratne, Colombo: Godage International Publishers, 2012: ch. 10.

"the roll of celestial drums" . . . *Once the Buddha Was a Monkey: Ārya Śūra's Jātakamālā*, trans. P. Khoroche, Chicago: University of Chicago Press, 1989: 71–72.

Rudolph Otto . . . *The Idea of the Holy*, trans. J. Harvey, London: Oxford University Press, 1923.

vrida/vridita

Shame/Ashamed (Sanskrit)

If *hiri* (*hri*) is the valuable sense of shame that can prevent us from disgracing ourselves to begin with, *vrida* (*vrīḍa*) is the uncomfortable shame that sets in after-the-fact, when it is too late and the mortifying transgression has occurred. For all its pain, *vrida* has the virtue of repentance prompting it, for otherwise one is shamelessly insolent in the face of one's wrongdoing. Bharata notes that such shame involves the "afterburning" (*pashcattapa*) of remorse prompted by the eyes of the respectable upon the transgressor. Phenomenologically, *vrida* involves squirming and wishing to hide: "the ashamed person will cover his face, scratch the ground, break his nails, finger his clothing and rings." A commentator describes it as a "lack of boldness evidenced by keeping the body averted, trying to hide, changing color, lowering the head, etc." Later commentators find that *vrida* involves a "contraction in the mind" as one shrinks inward.

Vrida can, like *lajja* and *hri*, also involve modesty, bashfulness, embarrassment, and shyness, and in women it is a desirable quality. The literary theorists note its dual and gendered nature: *vrida* is the "sense of shame or moral disapprobation of an immoral action, and the shyness which is a cause of a young lady's excellence." In this second sense, it is "a constraint on one's ability to act freely": modesty inhibits the free run of desire (see *lajja*).

We find a fascinating instance of great warriors feeling *vridita* (*vrīḍita*), which we might also translate as "humbled," in the *Mahabharata*. In the disturbing story of the Pandavas' encounter with the extraordinary archer Ekalavya, they are humbled, abashed, embarrassed—*vridita*—when they see his feats with the bow. Ekalavya, it turns out, is very low caste, the son of a forest tribal, which only further discomfits these highborn princes. Ekalavya purports to be Drona's pupil, leading Drona to ask him for his teacher's fee. Because Drona has promised that none shall ever best Arjuna at archery, he asks that Ekalavya chop off his own right thumb, thus crippling him and making sure that Arjuna will be unsurpassed. Ekalavya does so, Arjuna is satisfied, and the *Mahabharata* moves briskly on.

In another scene from the *Mahabharata*, the horrific episode of Princess Draupadi's near disrobing in the assembly hall, the odious Dushasana, who has been assaulting the princess and attempts to strip off her sari, is thwarted in his assault by Lord Krishna's intervention, ensuring that her sari becomes endless and intact. Dushasana sinks down, "ashamed," and the shame of the assault is, the text insists, his to bear.

See also **hiri/hri; lajja; pashcattapa**

REFERENCES

Bharata notes . . . Nāṭyaśāstra 7.58.

"the ashamed person" . . . Nāṭyaśāstra 7.59.

"lack of boldness" . . . The Daśarūpa: A Treatise on Hindu Dramaturgy, ed. G. Haas, New York: AMS Press, 1965: 118 (ch. 4, verse 30). My translation.

"contraction of the mind" . . . (*Cetaḥsaṁkoca*), as specified by Śāradātanaya and Hemacandra, as cited in IP: 229.

"sense of shame" . . . J. Sinha paraphrasing Sarveśvarācārya (IP: 229).

"a constraint on one's ability to act freely" . . . Rasataraṅgiṇī 5.34. BRRR: 216–217.

extraordinary archer Ekalavya . . . Mahābhārata 1.123.21.

Dushasana sinks down, "ashamed," . . . Mahābhārata 2.61.48.

vyabhicaribhava

Transitory Emotions or States (Sanskrit)

This category of experience must be understood within the context of *rasa* theory, as first laid out in Bharata's *shastra*, the *Treatise on Drama* (see *bhava* and *rasa* for the basic picture). *Vyabhicaribhavas* (*vyabhicāribhāva*) are thirty-three less stable and enduring experiences than the stable emotions (*sthayivbhavas*), and not all of them can be stretched to be included among "emotions" as English speakers currently use the term. The thirty-three transitory states are despair (*nirveda*), fatigue, disquiet (*shanka*), indignation (*asuya*), intoxication (*mada*), exhaustion, torpor, desperation (*dainya*), anxiety (*cinta*), confusion, remembrance, fortitude (*dhriti*), shame (*vrida*), fickleness (*capalata*), elation (*harsha*), panic (*avega*), numbness, haughtiness (*garva*), depression (*vishada*), impatient yearning (*autsukya*), sleepiness, being possessed, dreaming, waking, envy (*amarsha*), dissimulation, mercilessness (*ugrata*), sagacity, sickness, madness, dying, fright (*trasa*), and perplexity. Those that most English speakers would recognize as emotions are given in the Sanskrit and have entries elsewhere in the *Treasury*.

Transitory emotions supplement and cause variation in the stable emotions in the production of the *rasas*. For example, in producing the erotic *rasa*, the underlying stable emotion is of course attraction, which remains steady throughout. But any particular presentation of the experience on the stage will be modulated by different transient and psychophysical states, sometimes longing or despair, other times joy, bashfulness, or haughtiness. (In fact, Bharata suggests that the erotic can have more transient emotions supporting it than any other *rasa*.) Such transient supplements to the basic experience inflect the experience in a myriad of ways. In this way, aesthetic analysis can begin to get at the rich and varied forms that the erotic can take.

Unlike the stable emotions that are "constitutive of living creatures," the transitory emotions may not appear with any regularity or at all in a person's life, according to Abhinavagupta. And the transitory states have different facets, stages, degrees, and ways of presenting depending upon how they occur together with the stable emotions and other *bhavas*. They are modal in this important sense. Abhinava gives a beautiful illustration of this feature:

> Therefore, the transitory emotions, their existence marked by a myriad of varied stages of coming into being and going out of being, are strung on the thread of those mental states that are the stable emotions. They are like precious stones threaded on a red or blue string—stones of crystal, glass, mica, ruby, emerald, sapphire, and the like, with their thousands of different properties—which can be individually perceived thanks to their interstices. Although these transitory emotions leave no latent impression of their own on the string of the stable emotion, they derive embellishment from the string itself; moreover, themselves dappled, they dapple the string of the stable emotion; and they bring the string, pure though it remains on the very inside of the stones, to the point of manifestation and even while doing so, show themselves to be producing a variegation from the luster of the stones—the transitory emotions—that precede and follow.

In this complex simile, we see that while much human emotional and physical phenomena can be identifiable as discrete beads, these will also have properties and aspects, and will pick up and reflect light and catch our notice depending upon the thread onto which they are strung, the other beads on the string, and their own particular qualities of shape, color, cut, and so forth. Abhinava is attempting to get at both the infinitely complex and myriad ways emotions are felt even while they can be identified as operating with some regular elements and patterns for the sake of analysis.

See also **bhava; rasa; sattvikabhava; sthayibhava**

References

The thirty-three transitory states are . . . Nāṭyaśāstra 6.18–21. For the most part, I follow S. Pollock's translation of these (RR: 50, 328–329).
than any other rasa . . . As pointed out in DL: 486.
"constitutive of living creatures" . . . Abhinavabhāratī 277. RR: 200.
"Therefore, the transitory emotions" . . . Abhinavabhāratī 277. RR: 200.

vyatha

Devastation (Sanskrit)

"Are you not devastated?"

For as much as the epics celebrate the martial heroism of war, they never flinch from describing the devastation it wreaks. At the end of the great *Mahabharata* war, King Dhritarashtra's wise counselor, Sanjaya, berates him for his folly in supporting his own sons' unrighteous instigation of the war. Because Dhritarashtra is blind, it is Sanjaya who recounts to him what happens. As he describes how each of the great heroes fell in battle, he mixes in memories of Dhritarashtra's own failings in preventing the war. As he does so, he repeatedly asks, "Are you not devastated?"

Indeed, as he hears each episode, Dhritarashtra again and again cries out: "I am devastated." Each death and each horror devastate him anew. Sanjaya later tries to suggest that in the hands of fate, being devastated is unwise. Still, the damage is done, and devastation—and anguish, misery, and desolation—shape the dominant mood of the war's aftermath.

See also **dina; parideva; shoka; vishada**

Reference

"Are you not devastated?" . . . Mahābhārata 8.2.5–25, using *vyathā*, devastation, and *vyathita*, devastated.

Y

Yoga

The Discipline of Calm (Sanskrit and Pali)

"Yoga is ceasing the fluctuations of awareness." So says Patanjali, author of the *Yoga Sutras*. Ordinary awareness is quite flappable, incessantly changing, buffeted about, swinging from highs to lows, and subject to all manner of incursions from within and without. Yoga is the therapy that smooths out the fluctuations of emotion and thought, bringing them to stillness, and allowing one to reside in perfect calm awareness. Such pure contemplation is like a polished crystal where color and light can shine through but the crystal itself remains clear and unperturbed. According to the Samkhya metaphysics shared with the *Yoga Sutras*, this peaceful awareness aloof from the shifting flow of experience (*prakriti*) is the *purusha*, or spirit of the human being.

Through ascetic and contemplative exercises, the yogi stops identifying with the changing vicissitudes of thought, desire, and emotion, and instead becomes "yoked" (the literal meaning of yoga)—that is, disciplined. By this detachment, the yogi is released from all suffering. Yoga is the discipline that makes one free.

This disciplinary quest to quell the emotions runs deep in Indian ascetic religions. In addition to the Yoga system of Patanjali, we find various formulations of yoga (in its broader sense) in the Upanishads and the later philosophical systems such as Advaita Vedanta that they inspire; we find it in Buddhism and Jainism, too. The closest Western equivalent to the ideal yogi would be the Stoic sage, who also sought to extirpate the emotions. The ideal Stoic remains indifferent to torture, slavery, and even the death of a child. (As Anaxagoras was reported to have matter-of-factly stated on receiving news of his child's death: "I was already aware that I had begotten a mortal.") But the Stoics differ from the Yoga philosophers in that they held rationality and moral character as highest values, and this view shapes their therapies. One quells emotion by changing one's view of the matter by reasoning differently about it. As Richard Sorabji puts it, tackling painful emotion is "not a matter of gritting your teeth. It is about seeing things differently, so that you do not need to grit your teeth."

The Yoga tradition is more radical in the sense that even the rational judgments of the evaluating mind are considered to be as problematic and unstable as emotions. Thought and emotion are to be disciplined and eradicated for total freedom. Pure, clear awareness is free of the ruffles of even rational thought and moral conviction.

See also **brahmaviharas; dvesha; guna; kleshas/kilesas; samskara/sankhara; samtosha; shama; shanti; upeksha/upekkha**

REFERENCES

"Yoga is ceasing" . . . *Yoga Sūtra* 1.2, YSU: 29.

like a polished crystal . . . *Yoga Sūtra* i.41, YSU: 39–40.

"I was already aware" . . . Cicero reports approvingly Anaxagoras's words as an ideal Stoic response as cited in M. Nussbaum, *The Therapy of Desire*, Princeton, NJ: Princeton University Press, 1994: 363.

As Richard Sorabji . . . *Emotion and Peace of Mind: From Stoic Agitation to Christian Temptation*. Oxford: Oxford University Press, 2000: 1.

even the rational judgments . . . "The fluctuations [of awareness] whether corrupted or uncorrupted, are five: valid judgment, error, conceptualization, sleep, and memory." *Yoga Sūtra* 1.5–6, YSU: 31.

In Lieu of a Conclusion, Further Reading

Entries are entry points, never the last word. And treasuries don't really "conclude." To be sure, one can reach the end of the stockroom and count the last coin. But in a prosperous kingdom, there will always be more riches to amass, jewels to appraise, baubles to collect, and bonds to call in. And surely there can be found no more prosperous a kingdom for word gems than the textual worlds of India. Those who love Indian words—and those who have come to love Indian words for how they can convey and prompt the subtle nuances of experience—will find that many more treasures await them. I offer here a few suggestions about where they may be found and where to go for further thinking about emotions.

Above all, the reader must go to the sources. There has never been a better time for English speakers to explore Indian classical literature, thanks to the fifty-six volumes published by the Clay Sanskrit Library (New York University Press) and the translations steadily emerging in the Murty Classical Library of India (Harvard University Press), committed to publishing translations of hundreds of classics from South Asia in all literary languages and making them available in perpetuity. In these libraries, and the many other marvelous translations that I have explored throughout these pages, we see brilliant and learned humanistic scholarship bringing to the modern world priceless literary and philosophical achievements from India's long and extraordinary history.

Readers may also turn to scholarship on emotions in Indian textual history, starting with J. Sinha's erudite study, "Emotion and Will," in volume II of his *Indian Psychology* (Motilal Banarsidass, 2008 [1961]), from which I have learned a great deal. For two edited volumes with multiple authors sharing the task of thinking about emotions, see *The Bloomsbury Research Handbook of Emotions in Classical Indian Philosophy* (edited by M. Heim, C. Ram-Prasad, and R. Tzohar, Bloomsbury, 2021) and *Emotions in Indian Thought-Systems* (edited by P. Bilimoria and A. Wenta, Routledge, 2015). For anthropological considerations of emotion in South Asia, see M. Trawick's *Notes on Love in a Tamil Family* (University of California Press, 1990); O. Lynch's edited volume *Divine Passions* (University of California Press, 1990); and Tulsi Srinivas's *The Cow in the Elevator: An Anthropology of Wonder* (Duke University Press, 2018). For the colonial period, see M. Pernau, *Emotions and Modernity in Colonial India* (Oxford University Press, 2019).

On the history of emotions outside India and focused on European history, see J. Plamper, *The History of Emotions* (trans. K. Tribe, Oxford University Press, 2012); U. Frevert, ed., *Emotional Lexicons: Continuity and Change in the Vocabulary of Feeling 1700–2000* (Oxford University Press, 2014); and T. Dixon, *From Passions to Emotions: The Creation of a Secular Psychological Category* (Cambridge University Press, 2003). Work on emotions in Western antiquity advances a method for studying emotion terms within the "scripts," or literary contexts, in which they are written, as suggested by R. Kaster in *Emotion, Restraint, and Community in Ancient Rome* (Oxford University Press, 2005); see also D. Konstan, *The Emotions of the Ancient Greeks: Studies in Aristotle and Classical Literature* (University of Toronto Press, 2006), and

D. Cairns (ed.), *A Cultural History of the Emotions in Antiquity* (Bloomsbury, 2019). For ancient China, see C. Virág, *The Emotions in Early Chinese Philosophy* (Oxford University Press, 2017). For a charming wordbook on emotion terms from many languages, see T. Watt Smith, *The Book of Human Emotions: An Encyclopedia of Feeling from Anger to Wanderlust* (Profile/Little, Brown, 2014).

Interested readers should consult the *Routledge Handbook of Emotion Theory*, edited by A. Scarantino (Routledge, 2022), for a comprehensive, interdisciplinary, and multi-authored volume on theoretical approaches to emotions. For some of the accessible current neuroscience of emotion, see L. Feldman Barrett's *How Emotions Are Made* (Mariner Books, 2018); she counters the notion of biological "basic emotions," such as we see proposed by P. Ekman ("Basic Emotions," in T. Dalgleish and M. Power [eds.], *Handbook of Cognition and Emotion*, John Wiley & Sons, 1999: 45–60), and of course, Darwin's *The Expression of Emotions in Man and Animals* (New York: Oxford University Press, 1998, originally published 1872). For emotions in the philosophy of mind, see A. Noë, *Out of Our Heads: Why You Are Not Your Brain and Other Lessons from the Biology of Consciousness* (Farrar, Straus and Giroux, 2009), and R. Solomon, *Thinking about Feeling* (Oxford University Press, 2004).

I hope the *Treasury*'s entries have stimulated readers' curiosity about the systematic treatments of human experience that we have only been able to glimpse reflected in the facets of the gemstones of the particular words we find in their lists. S. Pollock's splendid *A Rasa Reader: Classical Indian Aesthetics* (Columbia University Press, 2016) is required reading on *rasa* theory. Readers will also benefit from P. V. Kane's *History of Sanskrit Poetics*. A beautiful collection of Sanskrit, Prakrit, and Tamil love poetry with an accessible discussion of *rasa* theory can be found in M. Selby's *Grow*

Long, Blessed Night (Oxford University Press, 2000). Intrepid scholars interested in literary theory will benefit from plunging into *The* Dhvanyāloka *of Ānandavardhana with the* Locana *of Abhinavagupta* by D.H.H. Ingalls, J. Masson, and M. V. Patwardhan (Harvard University Press, 1990). Also for the intrepid are the Abhidhamma/Abhidharma traditions of Buddhist psychology. The best work on the Pali Abhidhamma is Nyanaponika Thera's *Abhidhamma Studies* (Wisdom Publications, 1998 [1949]), and for the Sanskrit tradition of Abhidharma, see Vasubandhu's *Abhidharmakośabhāṣya* (translated by de La Vallée Poussin, University of California Press, 1988–1991; English translation by L. Pruden).

Last, for sophisticated studies of Indian thought in areas adjacent to, but overlapping with, emotions, see C. Ram-Prasad, *Human Being, Bodily Being* (Oxford University Press, 2018); D. Shulman, *More Than Real: A History of the Imagination in South India* (Harvard University Press, 2012); and the work of Gurcharan Das.

Index

abhaya, 33–34. *See also* anrishamsya; anukampa; bhaya
abhayadana, 34
Abhidhamma Buddhist psychology, 23–24, 44, 93, 221, 308 9
abhijjha, 35, 113. *See also* byapada/vyapada; iccha; kama; lobha; raga
abhilasha/ahilasa, 36–37, 271. *See also* autsukya; madana; udvega; vipralambha
abhimana, 37–38. *See also* ahamkara; atimana; mana; shringara
Abhinavagupta, 243, 266, 272–73, 305; on bashfulness, 180–81; on bliss, 97–98; on the softening of the heart, 163; on the stable emotions, 278–79; on the transitory emotions, 324–25
Abraham, 320
adbhuta/abbhuta, 39–40. *See also* camatkara; rasas; vismaya
Advaita Vedanta, 191, 202–3, 263, 304
aesthetic savoring of emotions. *See* rasas
affect, 145–46. *See also* kama
affect and expression. *See* ingita and akara
affection, 53, 75, 91. *See also* anuraga; cakshuraga; kama; prema; preyas; priti; rati; sauharda; sneha; udana; vatsalya
afflictions, 167–68. *See also* anushaya/anusaya; asava/ashrava; vasana; yoga
agitation, 57, 86, 114, 178, 220, 238. *See also* uddhacca
ahamkara, 41–43. *See also* abhimana; mana; moksha; omana
ahimsa, 34, 52, 177
akara, 145–46. *See also* kama
akkhanti/akshanti, 43–45. *See also* amarsha; appaccaya; asuya; dvesha; irshya; kshama/kshanti
Amarasimha, 1–2, 29, 44, 74, 93
amarsha, 45. *See also* akkhanti/akshanti; asuya; irshya; matsara
amazement, 22, 242, 261, 275, 278–79. *See also* adbhuta/abbhuta; vismaya
amhas, 47
amusement, 21–22, 242, 274, 275, 278. *See also* hasa
ananda, 47–49. *See also* bhakti; moksha; sukha
Anandavardhana: on bashfulness, 181; on developing happiness, 265; eroticism of newlyweds, 272; on poets' use of material, 13–14, 268–9; on sorrow, 162–63
anannatannassamitindriya, 50

anger, 2, 9–12, 22 (*see also* kopa; krodha; manyu; raudra; rosha; ushma); Buddha's disavowal of, 200; corrosive nature of, 177; the counter to, 176–77, 297; of Draupadi, 11–12, 177, 195; and hate, 114–15; as one of the four passions in Jain psychology, 166; relationship to rajas, 239; as a root of suffering, 93; as unstoppable rage, 169–70; use of to counter systematic oppression, 176–77; women's, 195
angst, 47. *See also* amhas; samvega
anrishamsya, 51–52. *See also* anukampa; anukrosha; daya; karuna; nrishamsa
anukampa, 53–54. *See also* anrishamsya; anukrosha; daya; karuna; kripa
anukrosha, 54–55. *See also* anrishamsya; anukampa; daya; karuna
anumodana, 55–56. *See also* kritajna/katannu; mudita
anuraga, 56–58. *See also* kama; raga; ranj/rajjati; rati; shringara
anushaya/anusaya, 59–60. *See also* anutapa; asava/ashrava; hridayakrosha; kleshas/kilesas; pashcattapa; vippatisara
anutapa, 60–61. *See also* anushaya/anusaya; hridayakrosha; pashcattapa; vippatisara
anxiety, 21, 47, 73, 85, 139, 149, 214, 291. *See also* cinta; kukkucca; shanka
Apastamba, 105
appaccaya, 61. *See also* akkhanti/akshanti
Appayya Dikshita, 80
apprehension, 217–18, 257–58. *See also* hiri/hri; ottappa; samvega
arhat, 62
Aristotle, 5, 67, 88, 164, 175
Arjuna, 78–79, 139, 170–71, 251, 319, 323
arrogance, 54, 70, 184, 224, 274, 296. *See also* darpa; garva
Arthashastra, 18–19, 145
Arya Sura, 320–21
Asanga, 176
asava/ashrava, 62–63. *See also* anushaya/anusaya; kleshas/kilesas; samskara/sankhara; vasana
ascetic traditions, 17–18, 49, 120–21, 152
asha, 63–64. *See also* cinta
Ashoka, King, 53, 59–60, 186–87, 283
ashru, 65–67. *See also* karuna; rasas; sattvikabhavas; vipralambha
Ashvaghosa, 207–8, 210
astonishment, 40. *See* vismaya
asuya, 67–68. *See also* akkhanti/akshanti; amarsha; irshya; vyabhicaribhava
Atharva Veda, 147, 303
atihasa, 69–70, 133–34. *See also* hasa; hasya
atimana, 70–71. *See also* darpa; garva; mada; mana
atman, 43, 48–49, 121, 144
attraction, 20, 22, 96, 121, 141, 166–67, 188, 242, 301, 316, 324 (*see also* anuraga; raga); and disgust, 89; and love, 231; pull of, 144, 301; sexual, 234–35, 272–74 (*see also* rati)
audarya, 71–72. *See also* asuya; bhakti; kritajna/katannu
Augustine, Saint, 5
autsukya, 72–73. *See also* abhilasha/ahilasa; anuraga; madana; udvega; vihara; vipralambha
Avadanashataka, 198–99
avajna, 73–74. *See also* amarsha; atimana; avamana; darpa; garva
avamana, 75. *See also* avajna; mana

on envy blocking, 206; and hope, 63–64, 131; and love marriages, 154; and lovingkindness, 200; and nirvana/nibbana, 208–10; in others' doing well, 56, 91, 115, 205; and patience, 176; and an underlying unease, 119
harsha, 131–32. *See also* ananda; piti; priti; romaharsha
Harsha, King, 211–12
Harsha, Shri, 193, 246
hasa, 132–34, 242, 274, 278. *See also* atihasa; hasya; smita
hasya, 135–36, 167, 242. *See also* atihasa; hasa; rasas; smita
hate, 100, 114–15, 120–21, 145, 168, 225, 227 (*see also* dosa; dvesha); freedom from our, 163, 176; and greed, 182; and love, 263
haughtiness, 185, 191, 324. *See also* garva; urjasvi
heart (*see* hridaya); cry of the (*see* hridayakrosha); soft core of the (*see* hridayamarman); vital spot in the (*see* marman)
hedonic tone. *See* vedana
Hemacandra, 166–67, 220
heroic rasa, the, 22–23, 104, 109, 242, 298, 317–18. *See also* vira
Hinduism, 203, 232, 235, 307. *See also* Advaita Vedanta
hiri/hri, 137–38. *See also* lajja; ottappa; vrida/vridita
hope, 115, 135, 165, 199–200, 314. *See also* asha
horripilation. *See* romaharsha
horror rasa, the, 22, 33, 86, 139, 289, 319–20, 326. *See also* bhayanaka
hostility, 44, 60, 114, 168, 173, 176, 201, 300. *See also* patigha
hridaya, 138–40. *See also* hridayakrosha; hridayamarman; sauharda; shoka
hridayakrosha, 140–41. *See also* anutapa; hiri/hri; pashcattapa
hridayamarman, 142–43. *See also* ashru; avamana; hridaya; shoka; vilapa
humility, 187. *See also* dainya

I-making. *See* ahamkara
I-will-come-to-know-what-is-unkown faculty. *See* anannatannassamitindriya
iccha, 144–45. *See also* dohada; dvesha; eshana; kama; lobha; raga; rati; trishna; vancha
impatience, 43–44, 68, 73, 239. *See also* akkhanti/akshanti
indignation, 44, 67–68, 114, 324. *See also* asuya
Indra, Lord, 54–55
indriya, 50
indulgence, 269. *See also* marsha
ingita and akara, 145–46. *See also* kama
instinctual drives. *See* eshana
insult, to. *See* avamana
intoxication, 21, 324. *See also* mada
irshya, 44, 146–48. *See also* akkhanti; akshanti; amarsha; asuya; matsara; vancha

Jainism, 17, 23, 25, 49, 62–63, 203, 264–65, 286, 317; on the cause of suffering, 256–57; on freedom, 201–2; on friendliness toward all beings, 92; on human destruction, 33; on passions, 166–67; on renouncing all desire, 265–66, 307
James, William, 3
Janaka, King, 301
jealousy, 44, 146–48, 196, 316. *See also* irshya
jeguccha/jugupsa, 149–51. *See also* bhavas; bibhatsa